VOWS

A ROMAN CATHOLIC NUN'S JOURNEY OF LOVE

VOWS

A ROMAN CATHOLIC NUN'S JOURNEY OF LOVE

By Mercy Anselm

Vows

Tellwell Talent
www.tellwell.ca

ISBN
978-1-77370-726-6 (Paperback)

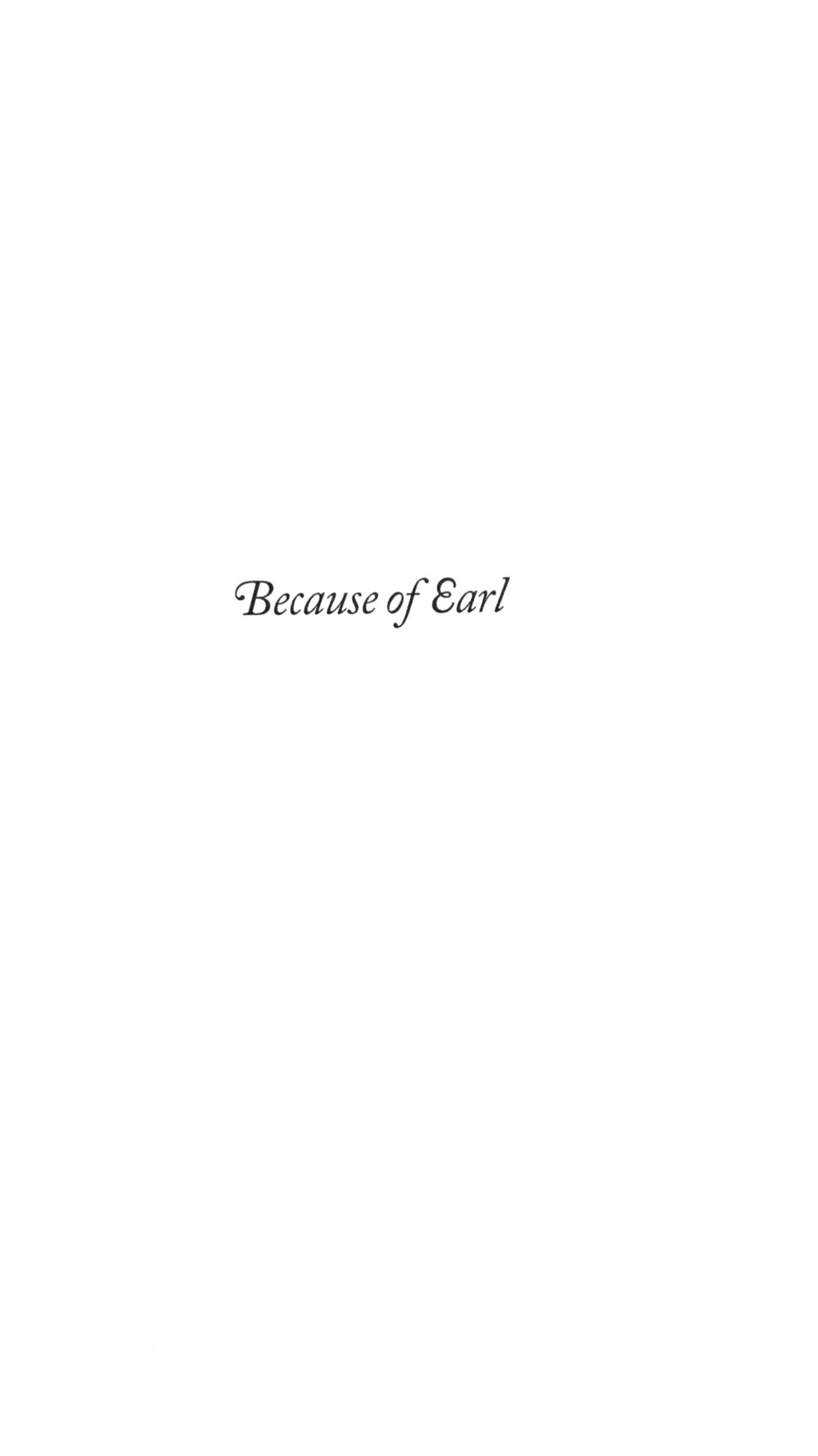
Because of Earl

Foreword

"MERCY, YOU SHOULD WRITE YOUR STORY!" I took my cue from her – Sister Angela Hurley, my Sister Superior in Stella Maris College, Chennai (Madras,) India. She had just returned to Ireland, her country of origin, after having spent almost sixty years toiling tirelessly in the missions of India and Africa. The topic surfaced as we caught up and recollected the incidents leading up to April 2, 1972. That's when Earl, now my husband of forty-five years, had flown down from Mumbai to ask me to marry him. At the time, I was a fully committed nun in the Order of the Franciscan Missionaries of Mary.

This is our story – the story of Earl and Mercy Anselm. It is set in the Anglo-Indian community of India – a community of a proud people with mixed identities. A community of hyphenated designation signifying persons of Indo-Briton descent – "mixed blood." The term "Anglo-Indian" was included in the Government of India Act of 1935, which was framed by the British Parliament to describe the community in the census of that year. Under this definition, the term comprised "all persons of European descent in the male line whose parents were habitually residents in India." Generally, the term was taken to signify "persons who were of European descent in the male line but of mixed European and Indian blood." (Anthony, Frank: *Britain's Betrayal in India*; 1969 Allied Publishers Private Limited)

After India's independence from British rule, the community was left confused – did they belong in India? Some stayed on in India, while many left in droves to the English-speaking world of

Britain, the U.S.A., Australia, Canada and New Zealand. This diaspora of the community, which started in the late 1950s, heralded a new beginning. With English as their mother tongue, they were able to skillfully forge new beginnings. As a people we realized it was our destiny to move beyond the narrow and confined dreams of our small community back home.

It is in this dynamic that Earl and I were brought together. Although early in our lives, fate had chosen divergent paths which we followed in good faith, through divine intervention we were brought together, to marry and raise a family.

This memoir is also a testament to my husband Earl, a man of simple virtue and integrity – a man of warmth and feeling and, above all, a man of rock-solid values. As a former Roman Catholic nun whose religious training took place during the tumultuous Sixties, I have come full circle to realize that ultimately what counts in life are the simple values we learn at the knees of our mothers – these are the intractable values of human decency and integrity.

These values are at the core of my husband's magnanimity. Ultimately, it was these simple values of honesty, integrity and family values that prompted him to walk away from India and what was truly his, at a tremendous financial loss, to build a new life in Canada. Except for the names of our parents, our siblings, our children, some relatives, and my very close friends in the convent, the names of others have been changed to respect their privacy.

This memoir would not have been possible without the help and support of my beloved husband Earl – the source and inspiration of this work. With patient understanding, he encouraged me along the untrodden path of a literary undertaking.

My gratitude also goes to my four precious children and their spouses, who offered me useful suggestions, constructive criticisms and, above all, technical support in the completion of this work. To Beth Kaplan, my instructor in Memoir Writing, I owe a debt of gratitude. My grateful thanks go to Margaret Davidson and Terry Poulton, my editors, who painstakingly guided me with their professional expertise. To Steve Glassman, who coordinated all our efforts, and to graphics designer Alicia Brown for her exquisite work on the cover. To my daughter-in-law Jennifer Anselm and to Erika Mulder of York University for their painstaking effort in the finishing touches of the revised edition, my grateful appreciation.

This book is dedicated to Sister Angela Hurley, my Sister Superior at Stella Maris College in India. A woman of deep faith and prayer, it was she who, with wisdom and grace, guided me along the tumultuous path of my decision-making process – to redirect my vows to a religious vocation and embrace my vows of marriage. To her I will remain eternally grateful.

Sister Angela Hurley,
Franciscan Missionary
of Mary (2007)

PART ONE

One

MY FIRST "HEARTTHROB"

I STARED AT HIM, this young man with a muscular build, thick mop of dark curly hair and a captivating smile crowning a set of white sparkling teeth. He was swimming in the Alwaye River with friends. I was twelve, and I instantly realized that I liked him. Did he notice me? Probably not. He was nineteen and there were girls of his own age around that he preferred to spend time with. He was the younger brother of Claude Anselm, who was about to be married to my sister Doris.

Alwaye was a small rural town in the southern state of Kerala, India. My family had gathered there to celebrate Claude and Doris's wedding. The reception was to be held in the holiday home of a well-established Jewish family from Fort Cochin, about forty miles away and home to a community of Jewish people who traced its origins to ancestors who had migrated to the area about two thousand years ago. Miriam Koder, whose family owned the home in Alwaye, had been a classmate of my mother, and was kind enough to offer its use for the wedding reception.

In the evening, I remember peeping out of my window in awe of the ladies in their flowing gowns and the men in their well-tailored suits on the spacious verandah. Claude's brother was there, looking stunningly handsome, dancing the night away with Teresa, my much older cousin.

Four years later, in 1955, I saw the young man once again. I was now a studious teenager in high school. He, together with his sister, visited our little bungalow in a town called Eloor, to drop off a book.

GROWING UP IN ELOOR

Eloor in the 1950s was a small industrial town in which the local government had built a fertilizer factory. My father was the foreman in the workshop and therefore entitled to company quarters. The house was large by Indian standards – about one thousand square feet – with a verandah, living room, two bedrooms, dining room, kitchen, pantry and two bathrooms. The bungalow surrounded a courtyard, which boasted a cistern with tap, clothesline and washing stone.

The washing stone, a cement block with a sloping surface, was an important fixture in all Indian homes. We scrubbed our clothes on its surface with soap, then rinsed them and spread them in the sun. A few hours later, they were crisp and clean. My mother had a sizeable kitchen garden where she grew bananas, cassava, vegetables and mangoes. Like most Christian homes in south India, we maintained a hen coop in our backyard. Mummy took great pride in her prize poultry, which included white Leghorns, brown Rhode Islands and black Minorcas. They provided fresh eggs for our breakfast and chicken curry for Sunday lunches.

‡ Our old home in 2018

Our household at this time included my father, mother, brother Eric, sister Phyllis, me and our servant Gopalan, whom we all lovingly called "Boy." Our five older siblings had already left home. My father, the fourth of eight children – seven boys and a girl – was twenty years old when he married. Daddy had only five years of formal education when he began work as a young teenager in the factory on the tea plantations. By his late twenties, he had risen to a senior supervisory position. In 1939, at the start of World War II, he was enlisted in the British army and sent to Iraq to work in the Ammunitions Department.

I was seven years old when I saw my father for the first time in 1946 after the end of the war. My relationship with him was therefore a little distant. I did not enjoy the camaraderie that my older siblings had shared with him.

My mother had more years of formal education than my father. She was in her final year of high school when she married. While my father stood about six feet, my mother was a foot shorter. Nonetheless, she wielded enormous power in the household. While she was endowed with wisdom, she was at the same time prone to overblown claims. She loved enacting past events whose significance was often lost in the drama of her performance. However, when it came to the day-to-day decisions of our lives, common sense always prevailed.

Mummy's relationship with my father was one of absolute love and adoration. They shared true marital bliss for forty-two years, when my father passed away from a heart attack. My mother outlived my father for another forty-two years, surviving to the age of 101. Every day of these latter years would start and end with her kissing my father's picture. She loved letter writing and spent hours keeping in touch with her children, grandchildren, great-grandchildren and friends scattered around the globe. Mummy's last letter to me was written when she was ninety-nine, just before she was put in a nursing home, where she spiraled into dementia. She was a pious lady and quietly prayed in her room three to four times a day. I loved and admired her; for her part, she referred to me, her youngest child, as her "pride and joy."

‡ MY MOTHER'S LAST LETTER TO ME (2001)

I had seven older siblings to look up to: Lillian, Victor, Doris, Alf, Eric, Lovey and Phyllis. Lillian was a brilliant student. She was always first in class, and at the end of high school was awarded a scholarship to go away to university. But at the start of World War II, the Women's Auxiliary Corps of India (W.A.C.I.) was more alluring than university studies. Lillian quickly rose to the position of Platoon Commander. Victor and Alf, like so many other Anglo-Indian boys, left home immediately after high school and joined the Indian Railways in the north of India.

Doris was a nurse and a caring individual. She too was gifted and had received a scholarship to attend university. However, she chose to stay at home and be a companion to my mother while my father was away during the war. It was only after Daddy returned that she was able to pursue nursing studies. At the end of the four-year program, she was awarded The Lady Hope Medal for ranking first in the state in her Nursing Board exams. Lovey was the pretty sister, and was married at a young age to her high school sweetheart.

✣ FRONT: LOVEY; CENTRE: ALF, DORIS, LILLIAN, ERIC; REAR: VICTOR (1937)

Of all my siblings, I was closest to Eric and Phyllis while growing up. Eric was a sweet-natured young man, at school in the day and deep in study in the evening, occasionally socializing with Phyllis and me. He had few friends and was always at the beck and call of my parents whenever there were errands. Eric never said no to a request – this was the hallmark of his entire life. Phyllis was closest to me in age, and we attended the same boarding school. Despite our differences – I was focused on school and academic performance, while Phyllis enjoyed the social life of boarding school – we shared many confidences in those early years.

My earliest recollection of home was a place which provided an idyllic childhood. This was an environment that nurtured a hardworking spirit, conformity to our Roman Catholic faith, and the constant awareness that as Anglo Indians we were a privileged lot.

✣ Phyllis, Eric, Mummy, Daddy, Mercy (1954)

Boy had come to us as a young lad of twelve. After running away from an abusive father, he had found a home with my parents. When I was a child, he had already lived with us for well over 25 years. Boy was the master of the kitchen and worked on his own terms. Every morning he was up at about 4:00 a.m. The crowing of our cock woke him – no need for an alarm clock. He made himself a hot cup of black coffee and then started getting breakfast ready. Our standard breakfast was "hoppers" and soft-boiled eggs. Hoppers were like pancakes but with a raised centre, made with rice flour, toddy (sap from the coconut palm, which acted as yeast,) coconut milk and sugar.

There were no mills to grind the rice into flour; this was the chore of the servants in each household. Every afternoon, Boy would soak a few cups of rice in water and a few hours later pound the rice into flour. In the courtyard was a granite stone with an indentation in its centre. The rice was placed in this cavity and pounded with a wooden pole of about six feet in height and four inches in diameter with a metal socket at the end of the pole. Boy pounded the rice by raising the pole into the air a few feet and then aiming it right into the cavity of rice. He repeated this motion several times, alternating between his right and left hands. He then sifted the rice through a sieve, allowing the rice powder to fall on a sheet of newspaper. The unmilled grain was put back into the cavity and the motions repeated until all the rice was converted into flour. The flour was then mixed with toddy in an earthenware container, which we called a "chatty" and used exclusively for the hopper batter.

Boy baked the hoppers from 4:30 a.m. until 6:30 a.m. in the morning. He served breakfast for the family at 7:00 a.m. because the factory van came to pick up my father half an hour later. Soon after breakfast, Boy launched into cooking the lunch, preparing enough for two meals. It was usually rice, a meat or fish curry, some vegetable from our copious garden, and a lentil. Boy then showered and took my father's lunch to the factory. He always donned a clean set of clothes, which consisted of a "mundu" (a checked piece of cloth six feet long and three feet wide, tied around his waist) and a crisp shirt. He walked barefoot. I had never known Boy to own a pair of slippers.

He had three interests in life: politics, the kitchen garden and family gossip, in that order of importance. He was illiterate, but politics was a passion. He would leave home with my father's lunch at 11:00 a.m. and return four hours later. While my father lunched between 12:00 p.m. and 1:00 p.m., Boy socialized with the workers, discussing union negotiations and the most recent benefits they had secured.

After my father's lunch, Boy washed his plate, glass, spoon and fork and placed them in a small cupboard in my father's office. Only the tiffin carrier was brought home. This utensil was an indispensable item in every Indian home where a hot lunch had to be provided to a working member of the family. It consisted of about three to four circular stainless steel containers, each fitting perfectly into the other. Boy served the food piping hot into the containers, and it remained warm in the tropical sun until my father was ready to dine at noon.

From the factory, Boy made his way to the local Marxist office, where he discussed political and social issues. To him, this was a unique experience of stepping into something different, and he yearned for an understanding of it. It was a lure to his curious mind, which was filled with an insatiable desire for information. The hottest topic was the Cold War. Boy loved to spread the map of the world on the floor and explain to my father how the Soviet Union was expanding. He would point to the Atlantic Ocean and warn Daddy that all the Soviets needed were a few ships and the U.S. would be finished. Just as Boy was a committed Marxist, so was my father a committed Congress member, as he had a great respect for Mr. Nehru, the Prime Minister of India. Heated political discussions were the order of every night.

Boy usually returned home around 3:00 p.m. just in time for his afternoon nap. He refused to make the tea and tiffin, which was deemed my mother's job. Tiffin was a light snack, consisting of steamed rice flour cakes stuffed with grated coconut and molasses. Sometimes my mother made fritters from the bananas in our kitchen garden. These were slices of banana dipped in batter and deep-fried. It was now my mother's turn to serve Boy. After his nap, Mummy served him his hot cup of tea and tiffin, after which he began the ritual of pounding the rice. As the sun set, he started his work in the kitchen garden.

My father's work day ended at 4:00 p.m. Once the factory siren went off, my mother was always "looking out" for the van. The moment my father entered our home, my mother kissed him at the entrance and then rushed off to the kitchen to fetch his tea and tiffin. "Any letters?" he would ask. He then went into the living room and said a short prayer in front of the picture of the Sacred Heart of Jesus. Every Roman Catholic home in the south of India had a framed picture of Jesus Christ in their living rooms.

He changed into his home clothes which, like Boy's, consisted of a mundu and a "banyan" (an armless white cotton shirt.) He then stretched himself out on a hammock-like easy chair to read the day's mail while enjoying his tea and tiffin. Daddy then read two versions of the daily newspaper, one in English and the other in Malayalam, the official language of the state of Kerala. Meanwhile, my mother sat next to him, never leaving his side. It was their time together.

Eric, Phyllis and I, after greeting our father, would go for a walk behind our house in the cashew mango groves. Boy continued his work in the garden, and later joined my parents on the verandah and discussed family gossip and politics. As was the custom, servants did not sit on chairs, so Boy squatted on the floor. On the odd occasion when Daddy poured himself a peg of the local brew, he poured Boy one as well, and both men enjoyed a drink together. Such was the relationship between master and servant.

Boy addressed my father as "Saipay," which was the local term for "master." He addressed my mother as "Missie," which meant "madam." He called all eight of us children by our first names followed by "baby." So I was "Mercy Baby" to Boy. This practice continued even when my siblings were married, much to their embarrassment. On one occasion, my sister Doris went to a railway station to meet him. She was eight months pregnant at this time. As she was milling around the crowded station looking for him, she heard a loud voice: "Doris Baby, Doris Baby."

There were no English schools in Eloor. My parents had to place my sister and me in a Roman Catholic boarding school run by missionary nuns in a town called Coimbatore, a four-hour train run away. The academic year ran from January to December, and we were allowed two visits to our family during the year, summer and Christmas holidays. Summer holidays ran from the third week of April to the first week of June, while the Christmas break lasted for six weeks, from the third week of November to the first week of January.

At the end of our holidays, my mother packed our trunk with our clothes and some homemade goodies. My mother locked the trunk and gave the key to my sister Phyllis, with strict instructions that the key be handed over to the Sister in charge of boarders. Every afternoon after lunch, Sister would open the "tuck cupboard" and we were allowed to dig into the containers of goodies. At the end of the term, Sister would pack our trunk, lock it and return the keys to us. In my seven years at the school, not once did a piece of clothing or any of my mother's prize containers go missing.

When we left our family home to return to school after the end of the holidays, Boy carried our trunk, supported by a soft cushion, on his head. My sister and I held hands and walked close beside him. We walked to the Eloor bus stop, from where we took the bus to the railway station. At the station, while waiting for the train, Boy would advise us on the value of education and the virtues of pursuing the straight and narrow path. Then, from under his shirt, he would pull out a knotted handkerchief in which he had put a few rupees saved from his meagre earnings, saying *"Motai madiku."* ("That's to buy candy.")

As the train chugged in, Boy would jump into one of the carriages reserved for women. Holding the trunk on his head with one hand, he would hold me with the other while my sister held onto his mundu. Once he had found a place for the trunk on the luggage carrier, Boy would set about finding seats for us, preferably by the window. He would threaten the women already on board that, if they did not follow his instructions, he would summon the train guard, whom he always claimed was his friend. Since many of the women traveled without a ticket, they did as they were told.

Once we were settled in our seats and poised to start the four-hour journey, we looked out the window and waved goodbye to Boy. As the train roared out of the platform, we would strain our necks to catch a last glimpse of Boy, who continued waving to us with tears streaming down his cheeks. Six months later, Boy would be back at the platform with a big smile and arms outstretched to welcome us back and take us home for the holidays.

Very often when a new grandchild was born, Boy was sent by my parents to help the mother. As was his nature, Boy took charge of the household. During the night, on hearing the baby cry, he would go into the bedroom and gently bring the baby to the kitchen so that the parents could have a night of unbroken sleep. Boy would then prepare a bottle of formula and feed the baby and then lull it back to sleep. He would lay the baby on a mat and lie beside it until 5 a.m. when he would start making the breakfast. His standing orders were that after 5 a.m. the mother would take over. He would therefore go to the bedroom and knock on the door; if there was no response, he would open the door and shout: *"Madhi, madhi, ketti pidichu oranginnu. Eneechu, kochinu molla kodu!"* ("Enough, enough of embracing and sleeping. Get up and come nurse your baby.")

Boy was also the epitome of dramatization. On one occasion, my mother hired a house tailor. These were skilled tailors who went from house to house sewing clothes. They used the family's sewing machine and worked on a daily basis. It was customary that the family served them lunch and tea. They usually turned out an average of five items of clothing, leaving the family to do the hand sewing. It was our summer vacation and our sister Doris was visiting with her children. I thought I had swallowed a pin and screamed, "I've swallowed a pin, I've swallowed a pin."

We had no phone at home, so my brother Eric rushed to the post office, from where he phoned my father. Daddy sent the factory van to pick me up. I was taken to the factory clinic accompanied by my brother Eric. Boy was out and so was not aware of what had happened. The doctor gave me a roll of cotton with instructions to swallow chunks of it. This way, he advised us, the pin would get entangled in the cotton and be passed out.

On my return, I found Boy seated on the front steps beating his chest and crying. As I entered the yard, he carried me and placed me on his lap screaming: *"Ni panningalu kutti erenu samsarikum. Kochinay nokathilla. Ethu endoru nalla kochanu. Naala ee samayathu ellam theerinum. Devam ningalay nokatay."* ("You women just sit and gossip and don't look after the children. What a nice child! It's over! Tomorrow by this time we will be burying her. God help these women!") This reaction of Boy's was no comfort to me, till my mother appeared on the scene and silenced Boy, assuring me that all would be well.

In the mid-fifties, my brother Victor, who was now a Permanent Way Inspector on the Indian railways, asked my parents whether he could take Boy with him to the north of India to a town called Moghulsarai. Victor was married, had a couple of children and wanted a servant to run his household. Boy could be put on the Indian railway payroll, since this was one of the perks of my brother's job. This meant that Boy's salary would now be about eight times what my parents paid him. My parents agreed. Our home was never the same again. I remember the vacuum created by his absence when I returned home for the holidays. But we had to let him go.

About a year later, Boy came home on a holiday. He arrived laden with gifts for us: shirt material for my father and brother and dress material for my mother, my sister and me. He also gave me a Swan fountain pen and my brother a beautifully tailored shirt. Boy knew I loved to study; hence the gift of a pen, which I treasured and carried around with great pride.

Little did we realize that the pen and shirt were stolen from my brother Alf. Boy often played the role of Robin Hood, stealing from the haves and giving to the have-nots. While at Moghulsarai, Boy occasionally visited my bachelor brother Alf, who lived in Liluah, another railway colony about a day's journey by train from Moghulsarai. When Alf visited us, he found these items in our possession. On his return, he questioned Boy, who didn't bat an eyelid. "*Thaniku orupadu kaash ondu. Eric babyim Mercy babyku kaash illa.*" ("You have a lot of money. Eric Baby and Mercy Baby have no money.")

Boy continued to visit us and on one such occasion announced that he had decided to visit his home village and reconnect with his family. He had a substantial sum of money saved and wondered whether his parents were still around. My parents were overjoyed and encouraged him to follow through. It was now about thirty-five years since he had run away from home and all that he could remember was the name of the village. Boy left our home in search of his roots. A few weeks later he returned, a much happier individual. His father had passed on, but his mother was still alive. He had met his siblings, all of whom were married, and also his nephews and nieces. Most of all, he was happy that his mother could now die in peace because she had seen the son she thought she would never see again.

Boy later made another two visits to his family before tragically passing away in a drowning accident in a swollen river in Moghulsarai. He loved water and would venture into the river every afternoon for a swim. Unfortunately, he was no great swimmer and very often cried wolf while swimming. His buddies seated on the banks would desperately wade into the water to save him, only to realize it was a hoax. Unfortunately, the day that he was indeed drowning and screamed for help, his friends assumed he was again playing a joke. A short while later, his cold and rigid body was pulled from the water.

Boy was about fifty years old and had spent almost forty of them with our family. My father and mother mourned his loss for months. When I heard the news, I went to the chapel and prayed for the soul of the man who had been a second father to me. Boy remained a Hindu all his life, although he often worshipped in the Catholic Church. In keeping with Hindu customs, his body was cremated and his ashes cast into the very river that had claimed his life.

It was in Eloor that I once again met the young man who had fascinated me years earlier while I stood on the banks of the Alwaye River. By now he was in university, studying to be an engineer. He had heard that I needed a trigonometry textbook. He had one he no longer needed, so he brought it over to me. It was a very old book, having changed hands several times. In the India where I grew up, these foreign textbooks were precious and generally passed through several generations. On the front page, he wrote a note wishing me good luck in my studies and signed it: "with love, Earl."

He enquired about the courses I was taking in high school and was intrigued that they were predominantly math subjects. I was thrilled by the attention he paid me. It may be coincidental, but in all the courses in my entire life the highest grade I ever attained was in my high school trigonometry exam. According to my high school math teacher, the grade I actually secured was one hundred percent, but since the top mark was never awarded, the board assigned me ninety-eight percent. I treasured the book for some time, but then left it behind at home when I heard a different calling.

RELIGIOUS CALLING

My life at boarding school revolved around studying very hard to pass high school with Distinction. I was also the "Head Girl" of the school, a responsibility I took very seriously. My seven years in the Missionary boarding school shaped the person I am today. It was here that I forged lasting friendships, developed a strict work ethic, and a true appreciation for my Catholic faith.

The school was small by Indian standards. We were only four hundred students, half of whom were boarders. The school was administered by a group of fifteen Sisters, most of them from Europe, known as the Franciscan Missionaries of Mary. They ran educational institutions, hospitals, orphanages, leper asylums and a university college. This particular group had a disproportionate number of very old Sisters, most of them having toiled in the missions for over fifty years, without visits to their families even once during that time.

From 5:00 a.m. until 9:00 p.m., they worked hard at the respective chores assigned to them by the Sister Superior. These duties were carried out scrupulously in conformity with the spirit and rules of the Order. The Sisters were strict disciplinarians, yet capable of great love and devotion. During my years in this school, it was commonplace to bump into former students, with their kids in tow, returning to visit the Sisters who had once taken care of them. Many of these Sisters had become surrogate mothers and grandmothers to these former students.

The Sister Superior was Sister Elsa Garreth, a vibrant, young missionary from England. She was a convert from the Anglican Church to Roman Catholicism. In my teenage years, I held her in utter awe and wonder. Tall and stately, there was an aura of majesty and sophistication about her. She took it upon herself to instill into every member of the staff and students a sense of self-worth.

Having spent these years in such close proximity with these Sisters, I was inspired with the desire to become a missionary. Sister Elsa Garreth encouraged me in my religious vocation. From time to time, she took me aside and spoke to me about the greatness of the religious life – that total giving of one's self to Christ. It was she who first uttered the words "Bride of Christ" to me. The words were mystical, magical and beautiful. The vows of poverty, chastity and obedience, which motivated these Sisters in their religious calling, resonated in me.

On completing high school, I left behind my trigonometry textbook, with Earl's notation on its front page, and made my way in to join the same Order as the Sisters who had raised me. It was March 1957, and I was seventeen.

I was sent to a convent nestled in the middle of the Blue Mountains of South India. This range of mountains was known as the Nilgiris – "*neelam*" in the local language is translated as "blue" and "giri" as mountain/hill. As I stood on the verandah of the convent, the blue mountain peaks surrounded me. Rows of towering eucalyptus trees looked like soldiers marching into every fold of the blue hills. I can still visualize the scene and be stunned by its beauty. The trembling leaves of these trees, exuding their intoxicating aroma, together with the pine forests, provided a permanent canopy of green filled with birds of every hue. This was a place that spoke to my soul of the majesty of God and the wonders of creation. Twenty-five of us young "Probationers" lived in a small bungalow adjoining the major building of the convent. The Sisters had purchased this house, called *Rosedale*, from a British family that had left India.

Our daily life of prayer and meditation, study, household chores and religious instruction was patterned according to the rule of the Franciscan Order. St Francis of Assisi, the noted Italian saint of the thirteenth century, had lived a life of abject poverty and total self-abnegation. During my three-month stay, I became more and more convinced that the religious life was what I wanted most. I considered it a privilege to be "a chosen one" and prayed daily that I would forever remain faithful to my religious vocation. At a one-week silent retreat, I thought about Earl, but decided that he was not for me, and quietly prayed that he would find happiness.

It was the custom for every probationer to meet the Sister

Provincial when she visited the convent. We were encouraged to openly discuss any issues that we encountered. It was also during these meetings that we were given our directives. When it was my turn, I was told that my superiors felt I was still too young to enter the novitiate, and that a four-year study period at the University College would help mature and better prepare me for the religious life. I was both happy and dejected. Happy because I loved to study but dejected because it meant another four years before I could realize my dream of becoming a missionary.

STELLA MARIS

At Stella Maris College in Madras, the largest city in the south of India, the same Missionary Sisters ran the University College. I decided to major in mathematics. We were twenty young women pursuing various fields of study. The Sisters encouraged us to participate in university activities as much as possible, while at the same time remembering that we were destined for a higher calling. As such, we participated in daily Mass and Communion, and spent part of each day in meditation and prayer. Encouraged by the Sisters, I immersed myself in university life and was soon elected class representative on the student council, joined the debating team and got involved in athletics.

The Sisters saw to our every need. However, they did their best to stifle the yearnings of typical university students. We were not allowed to use make-up, and our athletic skirts fell a chaste six inches below our knees. Our hair was cut in medieval fashion and our hand-me-down clothes and shoes (sent from Europe and the United States for the poor of India) were all two to three sizes too large.

My sister Doris lived in the same city and I was allowed to visit her from time to time. On one occasion, she found me so shabbily dressed, my hair so wild and unkempt, that she immediately took me off to the hairdresser, then to the shops for a skirt, matching blouse and a good pair of shoes. She was a mother of six children and these purchases were a heavy strain on her limited budget. I was overjoyed with these items. Easter Sunday dawned and I was excited to wear my new outfit and shoes to Easter Mass. A short while after Mass, we Probationers assembled in the parlour to greet Sister Dorothea, the Sister Superior who wielded tremendous power and influence. St. Thomas Convent, with its many institutions, was under her stewardship.

While offering my Easter wishes to Sister Dorothea, I had an uneasy feeling that she wasn't happy with me. But, not overly concerned, I joined the other Probationers on a visit to the nearby Basilica of St. Thomas. Tradition had it that St. Thomas was martyred close by and a majestic Basilica was built on the site of his martyrdom. We were in time for the solemn Mass celebrated by the Bishop of the Diocese. Afterwards, I bumped into one of Doris's friends, who remarked favourably on my appearance. To a teenager, these words were sweet music.

Later in the day, I was summoned to Sister Dorothea's office. She asked me who had given me the new outfit. "Remember, you have given up all these worldly things," she remonstrated. I was told to take the items to her office immediately. I accepted this event as "God's Will" but could never reconcile myself to the fact that a loving and caring God would want me to look so shabby.

It would take a decade and a Vatican Council to effectively bring about change in this regard.

When I graduated with a Bachelor of Science in mathematics in the spring of 1961, I was allowed to visit my family one last time. My parents were ecstatic to see me, not only because we hadn't been together in four years, but also because they were so proud that at least one of their large family had been university-educated. With eight children, my father did not have the means to educate us beyond high school.

Now that my father had retired with no pension, he and my mother were dependent on the largesse of their children. My father did odd mechanical jobs, when he could find them, for extra cash. However, they did have a house of their own. The house, sitting on a half-acre plot, was beautiful to me. In keeping with Anglo-Indian tradition, the house was given the name *Millowen*, derived from my parents' names, Millicent and Owen.

It had a spacious verandah, living room, three bedrooms, an airy dining room, kitchen, pantry, servants' room and three bathrooms. A picturesque wall encircled the house's four sides. A black iron gate between two concrete pillars served as the entrance to the yard. My father had inlaid a brass plate with the name of our home in one of these pillars. Two rows of multi-coloured plants, called crotons, lined the walkway from the gate to the verandah, and the bedrooms were protected from the cruel tropical sun by two huge mango trees.

To the west of the house stood fifteen majestic coconut palms. They were another source of income for my parents, because every 40 days a coconut palm bears about ten coconuts. At the back of the house, my mother had her signature hen coop, the cistern with the tap, the cement washing stone and a clothesline. As in Eloor, bananas, cassava, papaya, pepper vines and jackfruit trees provided wholesome produce, not only for my parents but also for their many friends.

My parents seemed content with their lot. Their greatest satisfaction came from visits of family and friends. They seemed to have surmounted all the ambition that comes with youth. Their dreams now consisted of saving enough money to give a good time to the married daughter or son home for Christmas. There was a quiet recognition of destined achievement, a timely store of energy to live within their means and above all a resiliency to enjoy whatever time they had left. Their horizons had shrunk and there were no more ventures to undertake.

⁜ Millowen (1961)

Eric and Phyllis were still at home with my parents. Eric now worked as a supervisor in the local DDT factory and Phyllis was a secretary. My parents doted on me during my two-month stay, as they knew it would be the last time I would ever visit them. Eric offered to accompany me to St. Thomas Convent in Madras. That morning, my parents kissed me goodbye at the bus stop just outside our home. It was a tearful scene, although not on my part. I was convinced that God was calling me to a special vocation. "Don't come back," said my father. He believed that once a child was given to God, it was irrevocable. I was never to see him again. A ten-hour train ride and we were in Madras, where we took a cab to the convent. From there, the Sisters took charge and after a hug, my brother Eric left.

NOVITIATE

A few days later, eight of us Probationers left Madras for the Novitiate (House of Training) in the north Indian city of Pune, about one hundred and twenty-five miles to the east of Bombay. Unfortunately, there was no Boy to make room for us on the train. We were huddled in a corner of the ladies' compartment with only standing room. The ride was to be twenty-two long hours. We were given no money. The heat was stifling, the air suffocating. A few hours into the journey, I suggested that we bring our trunks down from the overhead carriers and take turns using them as seats. In true missionary spirit, we tried to smile through it all. The Sisters had packed a lunch box for us, and I was given the responsibility of "leader." At specific meal times, I would announce that we could eat, and we would then help ourselves. The sandwiches and soft drinks lasted us the day's journey. We were a highly disciplined group and treated each other with understanding and sisterly love.

At Pune, the Sisters were there to welcome us. The main building of the Novitiate sat in the middle of a fifty-acre estate that had been the palace of a former Maharajah or Prince. Other buildings on the property were used by the Sisters as dining rooms, library, dormitories, kitchen and so on.

We young Probationers were greeted in the parlour by the Novice Mistress, Sister Stefan. An Irishwoman with piercing blue eyes, she possessed a strict demeanour. I would soon realize that she was an understanding and caring human being. Sub-Mistress Sister Teresa Ann, who was English, tall and dignified, had the proverbial heart of gold. She gave each of us a warm embrace as she welcomed us into the Novitiate, smiling all the while. She informed us that the Sister Guardian would soon come to assist us. Sister Damian was a young Indian nun who was still a novice. Years later, she was to play a significant role in my life.

Sister Damian would be directly responsible for our every need. She escorted us into a large room, where our robes were all neatly laid out. We were each given a grey tunic, black veil, black shoes and black stockings. This would be our attire for the next six months until we were ready for the "Habit," the official attire of the Order. We were no longer called "Probationers" but "Postulants."

We shared dormitories with cots in rows, each separated by a curtain. These were our cells. Besides the cot, there was also a mattress and clean linen. Next to the cot was a nightstand with an aluminum basin, a plastic tumbler, a cake of unscented soap, toothbrush and paste, a towel and face cloth. Such were our worldly possessions. We asked for no more.

Our day started at 5:00 a.m., when a novice entered the dormitory and in a loud voice proclaimed in Latin, *"Benedicamus Domino"* or "Let us bless the Lord." While getting out of bed we replied, *"Ecce Ancilla Domini"* or "Behold the Handmaid of the Lord." We then got down on our knees and kissed the floor. These two exhortations summarized the spirit of the Order. We were the "Handmaids of the Lord" ready to do His Will, whatever it entailed.

By 5:30 a.m., we were in the chapel. Holy Mass followed the Divine Office and meditation. Two hours later, we assembled in the refectory for breakfast. The day was divided into prayer, religious instruction, work and study. There were two sessions of recreation, a half-hour after lunch and an hour after dinner. No private conversations were permitted during recreation. We had to partake in the general topic of discussion. Individual friendships were not allowed.

My group of fifteen postulants was scheduled to take the habit on December 15, 1961. A week before the ceremony, we entered a seven-day retreat of complete silence and prayer in preparation for the event. Two days before the ceremony, the Sister Provincial met with each of us to reiterate the seriousness of the step we were about to take. We were reminded of our lofty calling and of the "specialness" of our vocation. Sister Provincial was the highest office a sister of our Order held within India.

When my turn came to meet with her, I was excited. I had no doubts about my vocation, having thought about it for almost five years. Although the young man I had admired in my teens did feature in my mind now and again, I decided that I was destined to be a "Bride of Christ." I successfully shoved all thoughts of Earl to the recesses of my heart and soul and with the unquestioning confidence of a young Postulant, I walked into her office and got down on my knees – which is how we were trained to speak to our superiors – and gave her a broad smile.

But before I said a word, she reprimanded me so severely that, for the first time, I wondered whether I had made the right decision. She accused me of being bossy, conceited because of my education, and of lording it over others. I tried to enquire about the origins of these accusations. Her lips pursed with anger as she reprimanded me severely, "You Postulant! You dare speak to me like this?"

Realizing that it was a losing battle, I bent down, kissed the floor and left her office weeping. I had obsessive thoughts about which of my peers had denounced me. I went to the chapel often and poured out my heart to the Lord, who was my only solace. That day a part of me was engulfed in misery, trampled upon, totally decimated, crushed. I felt I was now blacklisted, and the only avenue open to me was to retreat into a smaller world filled with anger. The final blow to my already waning self esteem was the realization that if I did retaliate, if I did try to lash out I would be typecast as "rebellious" and "disobedient" – comments made by my superiors that would, in a neatly packed dossier, follow me everywhere I went for the rest of my religious life.

In the silence of the chapel, kneeling before my Lord Jesus Christ, I realized that trials are meant to bring you to the toes of your feet, and religious communities are not exempt from human discord. I was determined to continue sailing in this boat no matter how stormy the seas. Nevertheless, the taking of the habit, meant to be the climax of these years, now felt horribly clouded. I felt betrayed. I felt worthless. If this is what Sister Provincial thought about me now, what did the future hold?

But it was not all over. Sister Teresa Ann knew that something had gone awry and summoned me to her office. She quietly spoke to me of the great respect and admiration that she and the Novice Mistress had for me. A little while later, Sister Stefan, the Novice Mistress, summoned me and gave me a hug. She told me not to be discouraged, but to bear up to my challenges in the spirit of Christ's suffering. She assured me that, despite what the Provincial had said, I was one of the novices the Sisters felt privileged to have. "If you are to succeed emotionally and religiously, Mercy, you have to adopt a conciliatory approach," she said, as she described the guiding principle of religious life. "Don't be discouraged, put your trust in Our Lord Jesus Christ and move on. You will find enough traction!"

I realized that she was articulating a deep understanding that the religious life was rife with vicissitudes and that the justification for pursuing my religious goals would fade if I became an angry young nun. Before I left her office, she raised me to my feet, looked deep into my eyes and said, "Mercy, there's plenty of goodwill there!" Despite these assurances, I remained unsettled that a senior leader in the Order could have treated me with such contempt.

Two days later, I would walk down the aisle of the chapel, dressed as a bride. Eric and Phyllis were the only members of my family able to make the journey to witness the ceremony. During it, the priest stood at the head of the altar and chanted three times in Latin, *"Veni Sponsa Christi"* or "Come Bride of Christ." Each time he said the phrase, I knelt down and kissed the floor of the chapel. After this, my veil was removed and a tuft of hair was symbolically cut by the Novice Mistress. Then a white habit was placed in my outstretched hands. I left the chapel, while a sister accompanied me to the dressing room, where my head was shaven of its beautiful black curls. I donned the veil and habit, white shoes and stockings, and reentered the chapel, no longer as Mercy Jacobs but as Sister Mary Agnes Romana.

‡ MERCY (1961); SISTER MARY AGNES ROMANA (1961)

Two

TANGASSERI : EARL'S EARLY YEARS

BAREFOOT IN THE SAND AND CHASING KITES, two eight-year-old cousins named Earl and Ralph raced towards the beach, literally in the back yard of Earl's house. Tangasseri, a tiny township in the state of Kerala, is about one hundred miles from my own childhood town of Eloor. Located on a peninsula of one hundred acres protruding into the Arabian Sea, Tangasseri in the 1940s and 1950s was home to an Anglo-Indian community of about sixty families who were predominantly Roman Catholic.

It was planned like a small European town, with a main street opening at right angles to smaller ones parallel to each other. Each family lived in a bungalow surrounded by walls. In keeping with the Anglo-Indian tradition of naming houses, the Anselms lived in *Loveapple Cote*. As the youngest of five children, Earl's father had inherited the ancestral home, which traditionally went to the youngest son, who then became responsible for the care of his aging parents.

⁜ TANGASSERI

Like many South Indian homes, Loveapple Cote had a large verandah, a living and dining area, six bedrooms, three bathrooms, guest room, library, kitchen and pantry. The doors, windows and ceiling were made of solid teak. The house sat on a quarter-acre plot with a signature front garden filled with colourful crotons, and a kitchen garden in the back. The branches of two majestic loveapple trees in the front spread so far and wide that they dwarfed the house itself. The story goes that after Earl's parents had sold this house and moved north to Bombay, his mother made one last trip to visit it. Imagine her tears of sorrow at seeing the teak windows, doors and main entrance painted indigo blue.

⁜ Loveapple Cote, Mercy (in hat,) family & friends (1983)

Earl's extended family included his father Simon, mother Helen – fondly called Nel – three aunts on his father's side (one a widow, the other two spinsters) and six siblings. Simon's father was Archibald. His brother was Neri. Earl was the sixth of seven children.

His university-educated father was a man of high social standing – a forest officer and thereby civil servant of the British and, later, the Indian governments. His job entailed the supervision of the large teak forests of South India. He was an avid writer and contributor to *The Indian Forester*, a journal he read from cover to cover. Every year, the journals would be collected and tied with string, and it was Earl's job to inform the local binder that Simon needed his services. A few weeks later, an exquisite leather-bound volume with the date engraved in gold letters would be delivered to the house. By the time Earl was in university, about twenty-five volumes filled the shelves in the family library. Simon was very interested in world politics. He read the daily newspaper and kept a diary of world events. This diary is now an heirloom, a testament to Simon's acute mind in tune with contemporary events.

Per capita income – India 1947 = Rs 45
1961 = 330
U.S.A. 1958 = 9,300
Canada " = 6,300
U.K. " = 3,400
Japan " = 1,000

Anglo-Indians in India 450,000
Indian Christians 8,000,000
Catholics 4,000,000
Hindus in India in 1951 = 85%
Muslims " 10
Christians 2·3

✣ Excerpts from Simon's Diary, 1963

OCTOBER 1963

FRIDAY 11

Japanese bomb Madras, 1943
Bulgaria capitulates to the Allies
and starts fighting against the
Germans, 1944.
Second Vatican Ecumenical Council
opens, 1962

SATURDAY 12

Christopher Columbus discovered
America 1492; but Leif Ericson of Norway
landed there 500 yrs before that.

OCTOBER 1963

SUNDAY 13

Italy declares war on Germany 1943.
Riga, capital of Latvia captured by
Russians 1944.
Merola Bob born 1942.

‡ Excerpts from Simon's Diary, 1963

Nel was a simple woman, several years younger than Simon. She had a perfectly chiseled face and a tantalizing pair of legs. She and her husband made an outstanding couple when they danced. Nel was a fashion icon. Her husband took great pride in her beauty and saw to it that she was always outfitted in the most recent fashions as portrayed in the European magazines to which he regularly subscribed.

⁜ FRONT: VICTORIA, ARCHIBALD, MARY ANNE, ROSE; REAR: SIMON, NERI (1910)

Indeed, Tangasseri of the 1940s and 1950s was known as the Paris of South India. Christmas and Easter saw its families rivaling each other in a riot of colour and fashion. The church was the centre of not only religious events but social gatherings as well. Every week, families donned their Sunday best and went to church. Men wore suits and top hats; ladies bright dresses with matching hats, shoes and handbags. Nel was the talk of this little town, for she was always the best dressed, much to the chagrin of others.

During his career as a forest officer, Simon was posted to the hills of Kerala, where teak provided a steady stream of income to the state government. His spacious living quarters included a fleet of servants who tended his every need. Each day, an elephant – the main source of transport through the teak forests – would wait outside his gate. Trees were selectively chosen to be hewn for their valuable timber, numbered and later transported to lumberyards by government trucks.

Reforestation programs, measurement of rainfall, the lumbering of the teak; all these were Simon's responsibilities and he took great pride in his work. He carried out these duties with qualities he taught to Earl: a sense of dedication and the highest ethical considerations. It was, however, a solitary life for Simon. Nel and the children continued to live in Tangasseri because there were no schools on the hills. The family would reunite only during the holidays.

✣ Front: Christabelle, Verna, Aureen; Middle: Simon, Nel
rear: Claude (1930)

In Earl's youth, several of his siblings had already left home, a practice typical of most Anglo-Indian homes. Earl's elder brother Claude, having completed two years of university, had found a job in the Indian Telegraph Department. His sister Aureen had married an Englishman and moved to the United Kingdom. Christabelle had married and moved to another town in the south of India. Verna was a nurse in Bombay, and Hazel an administrative assistant to the CEO of a British multi-national company.

Left at home with their parents and aunts were Earl and his younger sister Dilores. Earl was the pet of this household. Aunt Victoria was a widowed nurse whose husband had died of tuberculosis. After retiring from the local general hospital in her fifties, she continued to work as a highly skilled mid-wife. Although busy with her work, she was always ready with a hot bowl of chicken soup for Earl whenever he fell ill.

Mary Anne, a spinster, was both a teacher and a gifted artist. She passed away when Earl was about three years old.

Aunt Rose had little education, but she was street smart. She kept a close count of her income. Loveapple Cote was surrounded by scores of coconut trees, which every forty days yielded a bountiful harvest of coconuts – a source of substantial income. The money would be divided into four equal parts, one part to Simon and the remaining three to the aunts.

A large portion of Rose's share would be spent on Earl. She bought him clothes, shoes and books whenever he needed them. Even his first wristwatch was a gift from her. During his university days, she would send him pocket money from time to time. Whenever he wrote an exam, she would walk to the local church and pay the priest a few rupees to offer Masses for his success. Whatever jewelry she had would one day be given to Earl.

Simon was a strict disciplinarian and expected his children to be high achievers. Earl attended the local Catholic school for boys, where he excelled in studies and sports. The core teachings of the Catholic Church were instilled into these young pupils, who were expected to fulfill their every task in conformity with these principles. It was both in school and in his home environment that Earl developed his basic tenets of ethics and morality that in later life would form the hallmark of his personality – an outcome not from any conscious decision but rather a spontaneous, natural development from past experiences.

CHRISTMAS AND EASTER

In Tangasseri, Easter usually arrived before the monsoons and Christmas afterwards. A few months before the feast of Christmas, the ladies of the home bought turkeys and piglets from nearby farms and started the process of fattening the animals and birds for slaughter. Each lady had her secret methods, such as hard-boiled duck eggs, copra (coconut residue after the oil was extracted) or chopped papaya leaves. Easter and Christmas lunches would never be complete without duck, suckling and roast turkey. The tomato sauce and mustard were made months in advance to add extra zest to the festive meals.

Christmas was also the time to refurbish the exterior of the houses. Tiles blown away by the ferocious monsoon winds had to be replaced, woodwork painted, and the walls whitewashed. Inside, furniture was given a new coat of varnish, new curtains were sewn, and brass vases and candlesticks polished. Chinese lanterns and paper streamers adorned the verandah and living room. This was also the time when adult children working in the big cities of Madras, Bombay, Calcutta and Delhi came home for the holidays, laden with gifts of suit and dress materials, as well as catalogues of the most recent European fashions.

Months before Christmas, the tailors of Tangasseri were kept busy. Every lady wore a new dress to church, and a splendidly tailored gown for the Christmas ball. Mary Anne Gonsalves was the professional seamstress as well as a neighbour and friend to Nel. Many ladies would curiously ask Mary Anne about Nel's choices. But, faithful friend that she was, she kept them a secret. Nel always wanted to surprise the folks with what was "in fashion" in the big city of Bombay.

Before the feasts of Christmas and Easter, Nel went shopping to Quilon, a larger town nearby. She generally shopped at Spencer's, a department store dating from the days of the British Raj that now catered principally to the needs of the middle and upper classes of Indian society. It was here that Nel found dress materials and hats for the aunts – gifts from Simon and Nel to them.

The day before his mother's trips, it was Earl's task to inform Mr. Pillai that Nel needed the use of his bullock cart to go shopping. By 8:00 a.m. the following morning, an ornate cart, fully enclosed and drawn by two muscular white bulls, arrived at the entrance of Loveapple Cote. Earl enjoyed the privilege of sitting alongside Mr. Pillai and maneuvering the cart through the tiny streets that connected Tangasseri and Quilon. This experience, he would later confide, was far more exciting than the hours spent at Spencer's.

Christmas started with the midnight mass in the parish church. Every Tangasseri family participated in this religious service. Afterward, families wished each other "Merry Christmas" and all animosities were put aside on this one special day. Back home, each family stood in front of the "Crib" and – in a European tradition that had found its way into the Catholic homes of Kerala – sang *Adeste Fidelis* or *Silent Night*. Fruitcake and wine, made months ahead by the lady of the house, were served, but gift giving was not considered an essential part of the festivities.

Whatever the religious festival, the community looked forward eagerly to the delicacies of the season. Christmas breakfast was invariably hoppers and Irish stew, the latter reserved for special occasions because of the high cost of mutton. However, lunch was the big meal of the day: coconut rice (rice cooked in coconut milk,) cutlets (ground beef, mixed with spices and deep fried,) roast turkey, roast suckling, duck curry, steamed vegetables and the ever present beetroot salad (beets boiled, sliced and mixed with vinegar, oil, chopped onions and green chilies.) Plum pudding, again made months ahead of Christmas, topped off the meal.

It was customary in Tangasseri that the more affluent families hosted the Christmas dance, held on the evening of December 25. The Fernandez family had a built-in dance floor made of concrete in their front yard that attracted hundreds of couples. While the gramophone bellowed out waltzes, fox trots and cha chas, couples danced the night away.

Easter was a more sombre occasion. Confession was a must. Reluctant members of the family were encouraged or even cajoled into going to confession and starting a new life. A popular story of the time related the trials of a certain European missionary. He was hearing confessions on Good Friday in the sweltering tropical heat, and as he peered out of the confessional he saw a never-ending queue of parishioners. Exhausted from hearing hours of confession, he loudly exclaimed, "All those with mortal sins stay; others may go." Everyone vanished.

No house fires were lit between Holy Thursday afternoon at 3:00 p.m., when Christ traditionally instituted the Holy Eucharist, and the early hours of Holy Saturday. Only when the sacred fires were lit in church on Holy Saturday were kerosene torches lit and carried back to individual homes and the cooking fires started. It fell to Earl, as the young lad in the Anselm home, to make the torch and then stand in queue at the church to bring home the sacred fire.

KARUNAGAPALLI

Earl's maternal grandmother lived only twelve miles from Tangasseri, but it seemed a great distance to a little boy growing up in the Forties. With his grandmother lived his aunt Lennie, elder sister to Nel, and her only child Ralph, about the same age as Earl. Ralph's father Harry was employed in a nearby village called Chavara. Apparently, six children had preceded the birth of Ralph, but tragically all of them passed away before their first birthday. In desperation, Lennie made the professional gravedigger Ralph's godfather. The boy survived.

Earl rarely slept the night before he left for his grandmother's home. His mother had already helped him pack his suitcase, making sure that none of his good town clothes were included. A cloth bag of goodies – pathicums (thinly sliced banana deep fried) and kulkuls (little rounded pieces of dough deep fried and then dripped in syrup) – were Nel's contribution to Earl's grandmother for his stay.

On the morning of his departure, Earl would wake up well before dawn. After a quick breakfast, with hurricane lantern in hand, the servant of the house accompanied him to the bus stop. The driver would blow his whistle for the passengers to get on board. In place of flooring, planks of wood ran across from one side of the bus to the other. The passengers sat on these planks with their legs dangling below. The twelve-mile trip took almost the whole day, with stops at wayside teashops every few hours. By the time Earl arrived at Karunagapalli, it was dusk. There at the bus stop, waiting for him with a hurricane lantern, were Ralph and Uncle Stephen. The trek to the village home was another three miles. At last he would see his grandmother and Aunt Len.

For Earl, an important ritual at Karunagapalli was swimming in the pond with Ralph. It looked like an inverted pyramid hewn perhaps eight feet deep in the ground and was fed by natural springs. Every village home had two ponds, one for bathing and washing clothes and another for cooking and drinking. The ponds were drained after monsoon season and allowed to refill. The two cousins were delighted by their own private swimming hole. Afterwards, they always enjoyed a sumptuous supper prepared by their doting elders.

Earl and Ralph shared the same room, sleeping on rope cots with a thin quilt serving as their mattress. Each night, they would spend the first few hours planning the events of the next day – pigeon hunting, picking mangoes, climbing the majestic jack trees, and scampering through the large rice fields. After a quick breakfast of hoppers and soft-boiled eggs, Earl and Ralph took off for the fields armed with their catapults. They returned a few hours later, laden with their booty – often half a dozen pigeons. The servants now had to de-feather the birds and then cook them into a pungent stir-fry called "devil," which was eaten with hot rice.

From time to time, Earl and Ralph accompanied Ralph's father to Chavara. Harry lived in a rented cottage a few miles from his American employer's mansion. Mr. Hughes, as managing director of the company, was provided with lavish perks such as the American cars parked in the driveway, which fascinated the two little boys. At the rear of the house was a swimming pool. The boys spent endless hours peering at their shadows in the pool water, ensconced as if it were in a blue glass bowl. Never did they venture into the pool for a swim; they knew that dream was beyond their reach. So affluent was Mr. Hughes's way of life that when a maidservant jokingly told the boys that the lemonade was from the drinking-water well, they believed her.

It was in this strongly linked family milieu that Earl grew up. He graduated from high school with distinction at the age of sixteen. His father was so pleased with his son's success that he decided Earl would go to university. Simon was prepared to pay the expenses, despite his meagre retirement income, because Earl had identified engineering as his career goal. At that time, engineering involved two years of undergraduate studies in a science faculty, followed by four years in an engineering university college, provided you secured a seat – no small feat in a highly competitive country like India. Earl was accepted for undergraduate studies in the highly esteemed Jesuit University College in Madras, about six hundred miles from Tangasseri.

UNIVERSITY

Away from home and living in a big city for the first time, studies proved to be the last preoccupation in Earl's mind. He spent more time in the movie theatres and on the hockey and cricket fields than in the classroom. As might be expected, he failed his first year. His chemistry mark was a dismal two percent. Worse, he was expelled from the College. His devastated parents, who had pinned such high hopes on Earl, felt that he had let them down miserably by squandering his opportunities.

There was no other option for the seventeen-year-old but to join the work force. With only a high school diploma, the avenues open were limited. Earl took up an office job with a paltry salary. Humiliated and depressed, he did the best he could, but as he later reflected, he went to daily Mass and Communion to pray for a miracle. It arrived in the shape of a letter from his sister Verna, by now a nurse in Bombay and engaged to a wealthy businessman called Bihari. The prospective bridegroom had agreed to finance Earl's education.

Overjoyed at his newfound opportunity, Earl decided to pursue his studies in a quiet little town called Ernakulam not far from home. Unfortunately, all the first year science seats were filled and Earl was turned away from the college. Not one to take no for an answer, especially when his future depended on securing this seat, Earl decided to use pressure tactics. From 8:00 a.m. to 8:00 p.m., he shadowed the principal of the college, who was also a priest, even to the extent of squatting on the floor outside his office. Within two days, the college relented and created a spot for Earl with the student number 100A.

He now applied himself assiduously to his studies. His character – as those who knew him would soon realize – rested on his determination and fortitude. He was a person with an innate capacity to reinvent himself. Cricket and hockey would still be part of his college life, but not the movie theatres and the social scene. He frequently remembered his mother's advice to push ahead and pursue his dreams without faltering. She had instilled in him the determination to push against whatever power had first kept him from his studies. He now realized how hard he would have to work to secure a seat in engineering.

During final exams, Earl avoided the temptations of hostel life by renting a little cottage from a family. From morning to night, he focused on his studies. He made the grade. Entrance to the engineering program would be equally tough, as there were only one hundred seats for five hundred applicants. After a grueling written exam, followed by an interview entailing the use of hand and machine tools, Earl received notification that his application had been accepted.

Two years after a humiliating expulsion, he proudly entered the portals of the engineering college, but the same rules applied: fail the first year and you were out. Although he continued to play cricket and hockey (even captaining the hockey team,) he focused the rest of his time on his studies. During his two months of vacation, he volunteered to work without pay at several manufacturing plants. With this invaluable experience, he was poised to become an exceptional engineer.

Four years later, Earl graduated with a mechanical engineering degree, much to the pride of his family and greatly to the satisfaction of Verna and Bihari, who had helped make his dream a reality. His future path was clearly chalked out. His sister Hazel, now entrenched in the corporate sector, used her influence and arranged an interview for Earl in the British company she worked for. The new management trainee soon found his way to Calcutta in the northeast of India.

ENGINEERING CAREER

Calcutta was the cradle of the East India Company, the founding institution of the British presence in India. When Earl arrived, he soon became aware of the dichotomy of the city: part poverty and squalor; part first-rate theatres, tennis courts, ice rinks, flashy restaurants and palatial mansions.

As a young professional, Earl found himself among the remnants of the British Empire. His life revolved around working at the company and socializing in the evenings and weekends with a wide circle of friends. He lived in the Berkmire, a hostel for educated, urbane bachelors. Each resident had a spacious suite and shared a common dining room, where liveried butlers served the young men, and a lounge where choice whiskies and cigars from around the world were available. While in Calcutta, he dated several young women, among them Sarah Williams and Jane Flynn. However, marriage was still a far-off notion for a man on the threshold of his career.

⁜ CALCUTTA – EARL (RIGHT, 1957)

In 1959, while reading a newspaper in the hostel lounge, Earl came across an advertisement for a position in Ahmedabad, one thousand miles to the west of Calcutta. The job description was challenging and the salary and perks astronomical. Earl was young and unfettered. Why not apply? Within a week, he was called for an interview at Alpha Industries; an air ticket soon followed.

The C.E.O. and owner was Mr. Desai, a dynamic and inspiring entrepreneur in his early forties. At this time, Ahmedabad was the heart of the textile industry in India. A close competitor of Alpha Industries, in collaboration with a British company, had become the sole manufacturer of lappets – a loom attachment that carries thread into the body of the fabric. Mr. Desai had decided to venture into this market and needed the assistance of a young, brilliant engineer. He knew he had found his ideal candidate after interviewing Earl for the position of Works Manager. Within a few months, genius that he was, Earl had applied his engineering prowess to the production of lappets. About a year later, the competitor was off the radar, and Alpha Industries now provided the Indian market with lappets at a fraction of the former price.

Earl was now making about six times his salary at his former company. With the new job came a fully furnished bungalow, a retinue of servants, paid holidays and a car. By Indian standards of the Fifties, this was a life meant only for the rich and the famous. Earl had made it by the age of twenty-seven. Every month, he sent his parents a substantial sum to keep them in comfortable circumstances, and he provided for a nephew still in university who could not depend on his divorced parents for support. Earl also paid back with interest every penny of the loans given to him by Bihari for his university education.

Life in Ahmedabad was not as glamorous as in Calcutta, but Earl compensated by making close friendships. Dances, picnics and house parties with group singing were common social activities. Colleen and Wilfred D'Mello, both from Bombay, became especially dear friends.

‡ AHMEDABAD – EARL (CENTRE, 1960)

Earl made frequent visits to Bombay, which had become home to his family. His parents had sold the ancestral home in Tangasseri and moved to Bombay to be close to Verna and Bihari and their family, Hazel (also married) and Christabelle. Sadly, Earl's father Simon was in the last stages of cancer.

Earl was by now one of the most eligible bachelors in the Anglo-Indian communities of Ahmedabad and Bombay. Anglo-Indian parents were anxious that their girls marry into Christian families, a challenge in a country predominantly Hindu and Muslim. Earl quickly had a string of beautiful young women after him. Gifted with charm, sophistication and personality, he was nonetheless the perfect gentleman, making him all the more desirable. Families in Ahmedabad and Bombay doted on him and frequently invited him to their homes. He lived by his Roman Catholic principles and went to church for Holy Mass and Communion as often as possible and prayed for "the right spouse." His father, whose cancer had now become aggressive, prayed that his son might soon be married.

Despite his new circle of friends in Ahmedabad and Bombay, Earl still thought of his Calcutta days. He sometimes wondered whether he was still part of Sarah Williams's life. One day while shopping at Spencer's in Ahmedabad, he came across a Toblerone chocolate bar. He bought it and quickly drove to the airport, where he had it sent by freight to Sarah in Calcutta with a note: "A yard of chocolate especially for you, with love, Earl." She thanked him with a terse note that made it clear – she had moved on.

Jane Flynn, the other girl he had occasionally dated while in Calcutta, had moved to England with her parents and siblings. She had myriad opportunities for dating other men, but she secretly treasured thoughts of Earl, whom she had left behind in India. She knew him to be "a fine guy" and preferred to wait and dream.

It was 1962. Earl was thirty years old, an age when it dawned on him that he was not obliged to follow in the footsteps of his father or uncles or brother. It was also a time when young Indians increasingly realized that the hangovers of the long-gone British Raj no longer dictated one's sense of self. This identity, he realized, was not to be found in imported cigars or scotch or on the racks of imported suits. He was to find it within himself. It would be an identity forged through acts of self-discipline and self-creation.

With this in mind, Earl continued his everyday practice of Mass and Holy Communion, his search for a suitable wife, and his aspiration of one day building his own factory. He would wait for the dream to unfurl.

Three

EARL BIHARI: THE QUEST FOR SUCCESS

SEATED AT THE HEAD OF THE TEAK TABLE, Earl's brother-in-law, Bihari, cut his knife through a piece of tandoori chicken. His china plate was heaped with basmati rice, spoonfuls of yoghurt mixed with cucumber and cilantro, curried okra – dishes that lent their spicy aroma to the dining room. To his right sat his wife Verna; to his left was Earl, who had flown in from Ahmedabad to spend the weekend with them. A servant in uniform – called a "liveried bearer" in that epoch – stood at the doorway, attentive to the beck and call of the three diners.

The conversation, as it often did, turned to future prospects. "Earl, for a very long time now, I've been thinking about us starting a business together," said Bihari. "You are a brilliant engineer and in the past three years you have made Mr. Desai rich. Why not use your talents and make yourself rich?"

Earl looked up. Never one to be swayed easily, he said nothing. In moments like these, moments that screamed for some tangible reaction, Earl was noncommittal. The two men rose from their seats and made their way towards the sprawling living area while Verna oversaw the clearing of the dining table by the *chokra*. Soon a bearer approached the two men with a silver tray laden with a bottle of cognac and two crystal glasses. Earl and Bihari sipped their drinks as Verna joined them. The discussion soon meandered into the topic of forming a company.

Earl was to catch a flight back to Ahmedabad the next morning. "Let me think about it, Bihari." Characteristically, he refrained from overwrought dreams of the future and exaggerated sentiments. Honesty and common sense were the qualities that mattered to him.

The following morning, Bihari drove down to the family's woolen mills business in his DeSoto convertible while Earl made his way to the airport to catch his flight. Once back in Ahmedabad, Earl continued with his daily schedule: Holy Mass and Communion, breakfast on the lawns of his spacious bungalow and a ten-hour day at Alpha Industries.

Just turned thirty, Earl was a tremendous asset to his employer. His success at the company was phenomenal. As Mr. Desai's equity soared, thanks to Earl's ingenuity and hard work, his generosity to the young engineer also increased.

Despite the considerable advantages offered by his work at Alpha Industries, Earl continued to mull Bihari's suggestion at the dinner table in Silver Oaks. Like a Ferris wheel, his mind turned and turned, relentlessly pondering the appeal of Bihari's suggestion, "Why make another man rich with your talents – why not make yourself rich?"

Despite enjoying a salary and perks beyond the reach of the average executive working in a multi-national corporation, Earl had begun to feel restless. Life, he was starting to realize, was an open road with no tollgates; yet once embarked upon, a wrong turn could exact a hefty price. This road that Bihari had opened for him was alluring with its promise, yet threatening with its dangers. Earl decided to wait and pray.

With prayer and waiting came light. After three years at Alpha Industries, he had set in place processes for the manufacture of parts for the textile industry. He decided that it was not yet time to tell his employer of his ambitions. In a week's time, he would be flying back to Bombay to spend Christmas with his parents, his sisters and their families. He knew Bihari would be waiting for an answer.

When Earl arrived, Bihari and Verna were having their customary tea on the lawns. "Guess what," said Earl. "I was the only passenger on the flight. The weather was so bad that I guess everyone changed their minds about flying." The bearer now was pouring tea into Earl's cup. Verna offered a plate of samosas. "So, Bihari," Earl continued, "I have decided to offer my resignation to Mr. Desai. I'll wind up my affairs in the next few months and then move permanently to Bombay."

"No, Earl, don't do that," Bihari responded. "Hold on to your job for some time. Let me first look out for a place not too far from Bandra; then with your help we can purchase some basic machinery, and perhaps initially we can hire some professional engineers to get the place running. Once these steps are taken, and once you have decided on the product line, you can hand in your resignation."

"Fine," replied Earl, "I think that is the better strategy." "Once you resign, you can move in with us," continued Bihari. "The room downstairs with the attached bathroom will be all yours."

The bearer cleared the table. Verna stood up to see to dinner while the two men continued to sit at the table. As the crows cawed and the sun's rays grew dimmer, there was a soft breeze carved by the swaying row of Ashoka trees. The gardener entered the grounds and began the watering of the tropical plants and beds of flowers. Anthuriums, roses, African daisies, gladioli and chrysanthemums competed with coral vine, morning glory, jasmine, Rangoon creeper and bougainvillea. Verna was an avid gardener and Silver Oaks boasted of one of the most extensive gardens in the suburb of Bandra. It was a riot of colour.

Indoors, Earl lit his pipe while Bihari took a cigarette from his pack and fixed it to a gold-gilt holder. The conversation now focused on planning for the new company. About an hour later, Bihari summoned the bearer to bring in the scotch and ice. In a few minutes, the bearer first placed a cube of ice in each glass and then poured a peg of Scotch. "What about the finances?" Earl enquired. "How do we work around it?" "Well," Bihari said, "I can put in about one hundred thousand rupees. And you?" "About fifty thousand rupees," was the reply. "With this initial amount, we can qualify for a loan from the state government. In the next few days, I will look into this matter and keep you informed," Bihari reassured Earl.

The next day, a Saturday, Verna and Bihari were having a few friends over for a party. Earl inquired with interest about the invitees. Other than his sister Hazel and her husband Herbert, several young Anglo-Indian women whom Verna and Bihari had befriended over the years would be in attendance. Earl, who had been dating Patricia Smith in Ahmedabad, realized their relationship would end once he moved to Bombay. The demands of his current job were far too challenging to allow for pursuing anything very serious. It was time to move on.

As Saturday dawned, Earl made his way to the parish church. Even on vacation, he nearly always started his day with Holy Mass and Communion. After the service, as was customary, he was greeted by old friends, one of whom was Mrs. Miriam Vaz. She ran a boarding house for young professional Anglo-Indian women working in Bombay's multi-national corporations. A close friend of Earl's mother, Mrs. Vaz had promised Nel she would be on the lookout for a suitable partner for Earl, and was pleased to learn that he would be returning to Bombay permanently. "Your mother is so anxious to see you married," she said. "There are many nice girls out there who could bring you happiness." "Fine," Earl replied laughingly, "find me one." His broad, bright smile illuminated his tanned face.

At Silver Oaks, Earl began to relish the prospect of the party that afternoon. He shaved, showered and dressed for the evening. A pair of beige dress pants, dark brown dress shoes and a short-sleeved, pinstriped English linen shirt completed his outfit. He looked at himself in the mirror and was not displeased at what he saw. He was still evolving an identity of his own. His mind leaped through time, thinking of experiences with previous relationships, which had somehow led nowhere.

At 4:00 p.m., as the party got underway, Earl eyed the main entrance and soon spotted three young women – Vanessa, Cheryl and Joyce. They had heard that an eligible bachelor was going to be present and looked forward to an exciting evening. Earl introduced himself. The music started. The dancing began. Within the first hour, Earl had danced with all three young women. But he was disappointed, for they were, in his view, far too young and immature for a man of his age and stage.

His sister Verna then introduced another young woman to Earl. To his surprise, Sally turned out to be the sister of his dear friend Colleen D'Mello in Ahmedabad. Colleen had spoken to Earl about this younger sister, hinting that perhaps she could be a suitable match. Earl soon hit the dance floor with her. She seemed interesting and of the right age. He was also aware of her traditional Roman Catholic background, which boded well. Before the evening had ended, he told Sally that he would be returning to Bombay permanently and asked her out. She accepted.

Back in Ahmedabad, Earl followed Bihari's advice to continue in his job until such time as the basic infrastructure of the new business was established. He had begun to see new horizons open with few boundaries in sight. This was both frightening and exciting.

As planned, Bihari rented a building of about five thousand square feet in an industrial area outside Bombay. Soon an application for a loan of one hundred and seventy-five thousand rupees was made to the State Financial Corporation. Earl took a week off from his duties in Ahmedabad and spent the time in Bombay. The first step was to get the paper work done to establish the company. It would be called *Earl Bihari* after the two founding partners. As a small business, it fell into a sector that received preferential treatment from both the central and state governments. Purchasing and installing machinery was to be the next step.

The day the business was established was a busy one, but Earl and Bihari took the time to visit Simon and Nel. Generally, no major venture in India is undertaken without the blessings of parents. Simon, ill as ever, was reclining on his bed. Hearing the good news, he congratulated the two young men. Then, turning to his son, he said, "Earl boy, you take only forty-nine percent and let Barry have fifty-one percent." "Yes, Daddy," was Earl's spontaneous reply. Simon wanted it this way out of gratitude to Bihari, who had helped Earl become an engineer. Little did Earl realize that fulfilling his father's wish would one day be his nemesis. With the blessings of Simon and Nel now showered on their new venture, the two men returned to Silver Oaks.

It had been decided that initially the company would hire a team of four professional engineers to develop the basic processes indispensable to the setting up of a tool room. For the next while, Earl shunted between Ahmedabad and Bombay. Unfortunately, the engineering team at the new company did not meet Earl's high standards. He now realized that giving up his job at Alpha Industries was imminent.

Earl sat facing Mr. Desai, the mahogany table between them reflecting the shadows of the two men. The twenty-year age difference between them had instilled in both a mutual respect. Mr. Desai had given Earl an opportunity to showcase his engineering skills. In return, Earl had made his employer a very rich man.

"I'm planning to resign from this job shortly, Mr. Desai," Earl began. "I knew it would happen some time, but I didn't think it would be so soon," said Mr. Desai. "Why do you want to resign now? Are you not happy here?"

"I'm going to start my own business with my brother-in-law in Bombay." "Bombay!" Mr. Desai exclaimed. "Then you will soon be my competitor." "No, Mr. Desai, I will never be in competition with you. You have my word." Mr. Desai felt reassured. This young man, he knew, was an exceptional one.

"How long will it be before you leave?" Mr. Desai enquired. "Two weeks," Earl replied. "Starting tomorrow, then, introduce Brian to your responsibilities," replied Mr. Desai. "I will meet with him later in the evening." A promising young engineer, Brian D'Sousa, had been hired to assist Earl, who had known that someday he would have to resign but didn't want to leave Mr. Desai in the lurch.

‡ STERLING SILVER SHIELD - GIFT OF APPRECIATION FROM MR. DESAI TO EARL

Two weeks would soon pass. Earl would leave his bungalow, his servants and his close-knit friends, with whom he would continue to keep in touch for many years. He would also leave Patricia Smith behind. He knew they were not meant to be together. His precious German Shepherd Honey was the only reminder of this phase of his life to accompany him to Bombay. He booked a first class coupe on the train and undertook the nine-hour ride.

Earl was gambling away a lucrative future with Mr. Desai. But in its place was the dream of making a difference. By creating a company, he could be instrumental in changing the plight of many poor people. India was plagued with socialism. Despite having gained independence from Britain almost fifteen years earlier, India was still struggling with a stifling bureaucracy, corruption at all levels of government, and the total absence of a middle class – the backbone of any modern civilization. The country could boast of only two economic groups – the rich and the poor. Centralised Planning the hall mark of all socialist economies seemed to have failed miserably, leaving millions of Indians on the fringes of dire poverty.

These were the thoughts that pervaded the young man's mind as the train chugged along the wide-open spaces of western India. As he rested in his comfortable coupe, the thought of the desperate lives of the poor in India kept resurfacing. He realized their lot was to walk within the narrow passage that fate had hewn out for them – a path of dire want with no hope of a better tomorrow. Earl awoke in the early morning with renewed energy and hope for the future.

BOMBAY IN 1963 – EARL'S NEW HOME

On a January morning, the taxi pulled into Silver Oaks. Earl's sister Verna had prepared the bedroom downstairs. This room would become Earl's living quarters for the next few years. After a shower and breakfast, it was bedtime. Even Honey was too tired to explore her new surroundings. After a meal, she was content to curl up in bed with her master. Earl had gone into a deep sleep when he heard the laughter of two children. At his bedside were his niece and nephew. They had just returned from school, wearing their navy blue and white uniforms. "Uncle Earl, Uncle Earl, wake up, we want to talk to you."

Both Earl and Honey sprang from the bed. Earl hugged the children and the three of them started a pillow fight. Soon he opened one of his suitcases and gave Jennifer a beautiful celluloid doll and Geoffrey a football, gifts each wanted. Then came a box of candy, purchased from Spencer's, the exclusive British store. They were thrilled and ran to their mother Verna to show her the gifts. The children had their tiffin and then went upstairs to do homework. Life at Silver Oaks was structured. Verna ran a tight ship, insisting that homework precede playtime.

Tea for the three adults was set on the lawn. Soon Bihari was home from the family mills. Earl confessed that it had been difficult to leave Ahmedabad. "After all, you build friendships and it is always difficult to break them. Anyway, Bombay is my home now and there is no looking back. I am determined to make a success of Earl Bihari."

‡ Verna and Bihari (1963)

Earl's father Simon, now in the last stages of cancer, was resting. He had accepted his illness with graciousness and serenity. "What cannot be helped must be endured" was his philosophy. His ever-beloved wife Nel was at his side, seeing to his every need. They said the rosary together.

On a visit to his father, Earl took care to keep him abreast of the new venture that Bihari and he had undertaken. Before Earl left the house, he handed his mother a wad of cash. As a dutiful son in a country where there was no universal health care, he knew his responsibilities.

Another early visit was to Hazel and Herbert's home. They lived in a two-storied mansion, befitting an executive in the Indian Railways. Earl brought gifts for their two children, Gillian and Mark, identical to those he had given Verna's kids. Earl willingly accepted a dinner invitation. The cook in charge of the family kitchen, Yusuf, was an alcoholic but when sober could turn out the most exotic dishes that were a feast to the eye and palate. In a few hours, typical Anglo-Indian fare was served: rice pilaf, mutton korma, beef cutlets, cabbage fugath and raita, followed by leechees and ice cream. The adults avidly discussed the new business and Earl's move to Bombay.

⁜ VERNA, BIHARI, HAZEL (1965)

Returning home along Carter Road, parallel to the shores of the Arabian Sea, Earl pondered his childhood and the intervening years. Fate had now brought him to Bombay, as it had brought his sisters Verna and Hazel, and their parents Simon and Nel. As Earl turned his gaze to the West, he heard the majestic waves beat against the rocks. The tide had just come in. A beautiful half moon was waxing, the tropical sky brilliant with a canopy of stars. Bombay was now home, and it was a homecoming beyond any other.

Earl made a brief stop at the Church of St. Anne's. It didn't matter that its doors were shut. As a little boy, his mother and the priests in school had time and time again reminded him of the real presence of Jesus Christ in the Blessed Sacrament. He leaned his head against the pillar and said a short prayer. "Thy will be done, O Lord. May this new venture that I am about to embark upon be in accordance with your holy will." He had spoken to the Lord. "All will be well," he told himself. Earl always carried this almost frightening confidence.

Back in Silver Oaks, the lights were out. Honey was in the porch waiting for her master. Early next morning, Earl made his way to the Church of St. Peter's. This would now become his new parish church. After breakfast, Earl left for his new place of work, about twenty-five kilometres from Silver Oaks. The chokra had placed a tiffin carrier with lunch in the car.

EARL BIHARI – EARLY SUCCESS

Driving along the four-lane highway, Earl witnessed the squalor and poverty of the thousands who had made the streets of Bombay their home. Slums had sprung up on every available plot of land. As he drove to the factory, he wondered where the solution to this appalling poverty lay. Could he reach his goal of making a difference by creating jobs? He carefully made his way to the factory that for the next twenty-one years he would lovingly identify as his "brain child." For the moment, the office would be housed at Silver Oaks. Bihari would be handling much of the administrative work, thus leaving Earl free for product development.

With the unsatisfactory performance of the professional engineers terminated, Earl now got down single-handedly to the task of making the company a viable proposition. He realized that sometimes it takes a new person, fresh ideals, and renewed motivation to see promise and potential in a future. After his years at Alpha Industries, Earl knew he had the hallmarks of an innovator: an innate capacity to make decisions and implement them. Above all, he knew that he had the confidence to identify and solve problems.

The first prospective client he approached was I.B.M., which had started operations in India a few years earlier. Cyril D'Costa, a designer, had promised to introduce Earl to Mr. Manoj Kumar, Director of Product Development. Earl asked for the opportunity to quote for tools and components and was handed a sheaf of drawings. Back at Silver Oaks, he pored over the drawings and then prepared a quote. Very soon, Earl was handed a handsome contract.

His next venture was Siemens. Long established as one of the main suppliers of switch gears, with a well-established supplier base for switch gear components, this would be a tough account to land. However, here too he had a personal contact: Jerry D'Sousa, a Product Manager. Not only were Earl's quotes competitive, the finished product was also excellent.

Spread by word of mouth, Earl's reputation as a brilliant engineer reached the boardrooms of several other corporations. Soon a similar contract followed with Phillips for carbon resistor caps, transistor cans and bases for semi conductors. Hindustan Brown Boveri, which had a division for the manufacture of electrical motors, was next to sign up.

With these product lines in tow, Earl and Bihari now approached the State Financial Corporation, which helped budding entrepreneurs with their start-up costs. The partners requested a loan of Rupees ten lakhs. Reading the financial statements of the previous year, the bureaucrats were impressed with the potential for growth of this nascent company. The full amount was granted, which at the exchange rate that prevailed in 1964, would translate into $300,000 U.S. dollars. Earl Bihari paid it all back within the specified time period, never defaulting on a single payment and earning the company a "Certificate of Appreciation" from the Financial Corporation. By the end of the first year of operations, Earl had created an atmosphere not only of cooperation but excitement as well among the senior engineers he had recruited. He greeted their ideas with enthusiasm, natural grace and the critical eye of a seasoned engineer, which they appreciated.

CARTRIDGE LINKS

Earl received a call from a government official in 1964 requesting that he attend a meeting of businessmen to be held at 3:00 p.m. that same day. No further details were provided. Intrigued, Earl drove through the heavy smog and traffic characteristic of Bombay and reached the office, only to be told the meeting was over.

But Mr. Mukherjee, the Director of the State Financial Corporation, invited Earl to his office. There on the table was a 7.62 mm cartridge link for a machine gun. India at that time depended on imports of this component. Mr. Mukherjee showed Earl the drawings and specifications and asked if he would be interested in manufacturing the product. As Earl drove back to the factory, his head teemed with ideas. The rest of the day, he grappled with the technical issues surrounding the component.

At Silver Oaks, Earl showed the link to Bihari. Together they realized the potential it represented for the growth of their company. Bihari encouraged Earl to go ahead, stressing that opportunities like this one were rare, and Earl Bihari would have to be quick to beat the competition. That night as Earl tossed and turned in bed, he recognized that the link had become the defining challenge of his future as an industrialist.

The following day, Earl analyzed the drawings and specifications. He realized the type of steel required for its manufacture was not available in India and would have to be imported from Japan. In itself, this was not a formidable task, since the Indian government was liberal in granting licenses when it came to the import of raw material for the manufacture of essential products.

Earl then studied the engineering processes required to manufacture the link. It was evident to him that the link's manufacturers in the West used automated systems to produce it – something that was not available in India. Even if it were, the price would be too steep for a small company like his to bear. So Earl realized that if he were to offer the product at a competitive price, he would have to install processes that were predominantly labour-intensive. He knew that the successful manufacture of cartridge links would put Earl Bihari on a new trajectory.

LIFE IN BOMBAY

Away from his work, Earl remained deeply immersed in his

family's life. He was a devoted son, brother and uncle. His parents, particularly the ailing Simon, were concerned about their youngest child, Dilores. Employed in Bahrain, she was still unmarried. They prayed that she would soon find her mate. Not long afterwards – and not too surprisingly, given that she was a great dancer with shapely legs and a captivating smile – Dilores caught the eye of a young R.A.F. cadet, Colin D'Avilar.

Soon the young couple was formally engaged. Dilores, knowing that her father had only a short time to live, decided the ceremony would be held in Bombay. She had always dreamed of having a storybook wedding. With enough petro-dollars in her wallet, she could well afford ten metres of expensive Swiss lace and the services of the top gown maker in Bombay. A lavish reception at Silver Oaks, with the best band that Bombay boasted, followed the Church service. Earl was best man and a young woman named Peggy Faulkner acted as bridesmaid.

‡ Wedding of Colin and Dilores (1963)

Two months after Dilores' wedding, Simon passed away peacefully at the age of seventy-four, in the presence of his family. Nel, eleven years younger, was now left helpless. She had leaned on Simon's decision-making for forty-one years of married life. Now she was left alone to look after Simon's elderly sister Rose. Earl's sister Hazel and her husband Herbert stepped forward and asked the two seniors to move into their spacious home with them and their young children.

Family and work life continued to intertwine. A year after Simon's death, Doris's husband Claude, at the request of Bihari, resigned his job in Madras with the Indian Telegraphs and joined Earl Bihari as Manager. The company was now running on two shifts and had about two hundred employees. Claude was in charge of human resources, personnel management and general administration.

Doris and their six children moved to Bombay soon after Claude's appointment. In the Sixties, the city was home to a large group of Christians, most of whom adhered to western customs. House parties and formal dances – the latter held in various gymkhanas around town – were the order of the day.

Earl was now in his early thirties and the family was starting to apply pressure on him to settle down. He thought seriously about Dilores' bridesmaid, Peggy Faulkner, an attractive young woman who was not afraid to use her keen intellect. However, there was one major problem for Earl: she was a Protestant. He nevertheless thought he would give the relationship a chance. With this in mind, he invited Peggy to a picnic at a botanical garden on the outskirts of Bombay. But by the end of the day, it was clear to Earl that they had basic ideological differences.

Whenever in doubt, fear or pain, he always found solace in the quiet atmosphere of his church. Later that evening, he made his way to the statue of the Virgin Mary. Kneeling before her, he prayed, knowing that in her maternal graciousness She would listen attentively to his expression of faith. Through his prayer Earl felt empowered. He left in peace, content in the knowledge that Peggy was not for him. Some time later, he received an invitation to her wedding. His heart sank, but at the same time he found acceptance in the fact that she had found love.

Meanwhile, Earl remembered the young woman named Sally, whom he had met at one of Verna's many house parties. Her parents were most welcoming to Earl. He could walk in at any time of day and was sure to be welcomed with a drink and a hot meal. After a year, however, they wondered why this successful young man, who was financially secure and evidently interested in their daughter, was dragging his feet. They decided to put him to the test.

It was 1965 and December 31 was fast approaching. The family booked a table at the gymkhana for the New Year's Eve dance and invited Earl to join them. This was traditionally the night when young men proposed marriage. Earl seemed to be having a great time, dancing every dance with Sally, including the midnight waltz.

When 12 :00 a.m. struck, he stood facing Sally with a broad smile but no proposal. He knew how to express his deepest and subtlest emotions without a gesture – just his eyes. A crestfallen Sally understood all too well. Some time later, Earl would receive an invitation to her wedding.

CARTRIDGE LINKS – GREAT SUCCESS

At the company, Earl continued in the development of the processes that would make the cartridge link competitive. He realized that "Austempering" was crucial to the development of the link. It is an isothermal heat treatment process, which, when applied to ferrous materials, produces a structure stronger and tougher than comparable structures produced with conventional heat treatment processes. Austempering was something Earl had studied in his engineering courses but had no practical experience implementing. Yet he knew instinctively that this was the process he would have to adopt to produce links of exceptional quality.

But there were hurdles. The equipment required for the Austempering process was non-existent in India and would have to be imported, which the company couldn't afford to do. Never one to be discouraged, Earl once again did his research. Using books provided by the American Society of Metals, he studied the process in detail. Then he designed and built the necessary equipment. Trial runs withstood the high temperatures. Soon he would be submitting the samples to the Defence Department together with his price quotes.

The time came for the first samples of the cartridge links to be manufactured and submitted to the Defence Department for the firing test. Other competitors' samples would also be subjected to the same test. Earl now traveled to Verangoan to witness the results. Earl Bihari's links surpassed all expectations. The Austempering process, unknown to his competitors, won the day and he returned home with a hefty contract in his pocket.

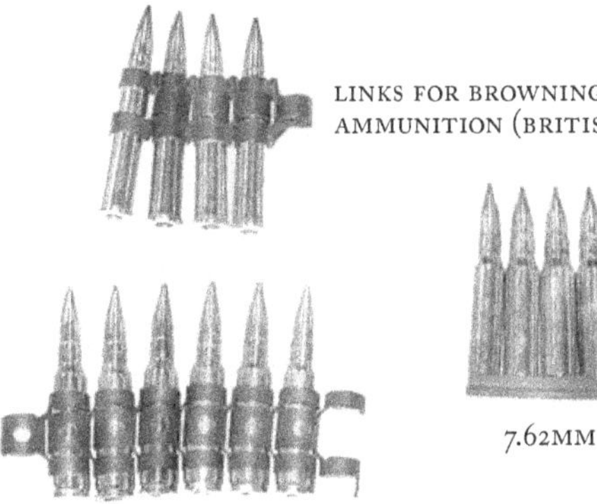

LINKS FOR BROWNING AMMUNITION (BRITISH)

7.62MM CHARGER CLIP

7.62MM LINK CARTRIDGE FOR MACHINE GUNS (NATO)

With the cartridge links now a successful item in his portfolio of products, Earl was asked by the Defence Department to develop other products. These included the Browning link for British ammunition and the larger Russian link for ammunition used on M.I.G. fighter aircraft. Later, the company won the bid for charger clips, required for semi-automatic weapons.

These successes were followed by international requests. Earl Bihari was now poised to meet both domestic and foreign demands. The company was awarded privileged treatment, especially when it came to import licenses. India was in desperate need of foreign exchange. Earl Bihari was a route to earning these coveted resources with the export potential of its products.

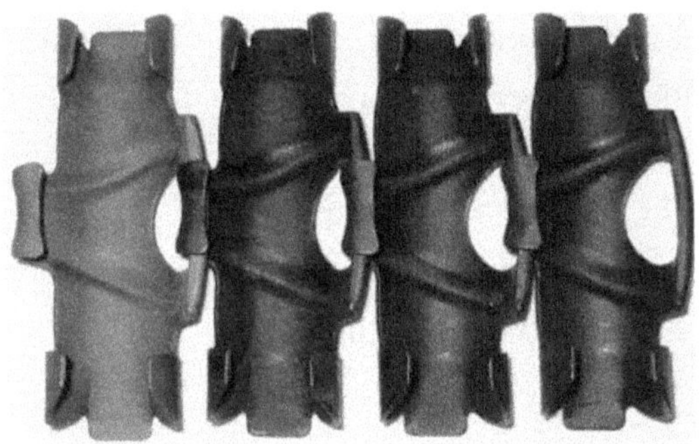

‡ Cartridge Clips for MIG Aircraft

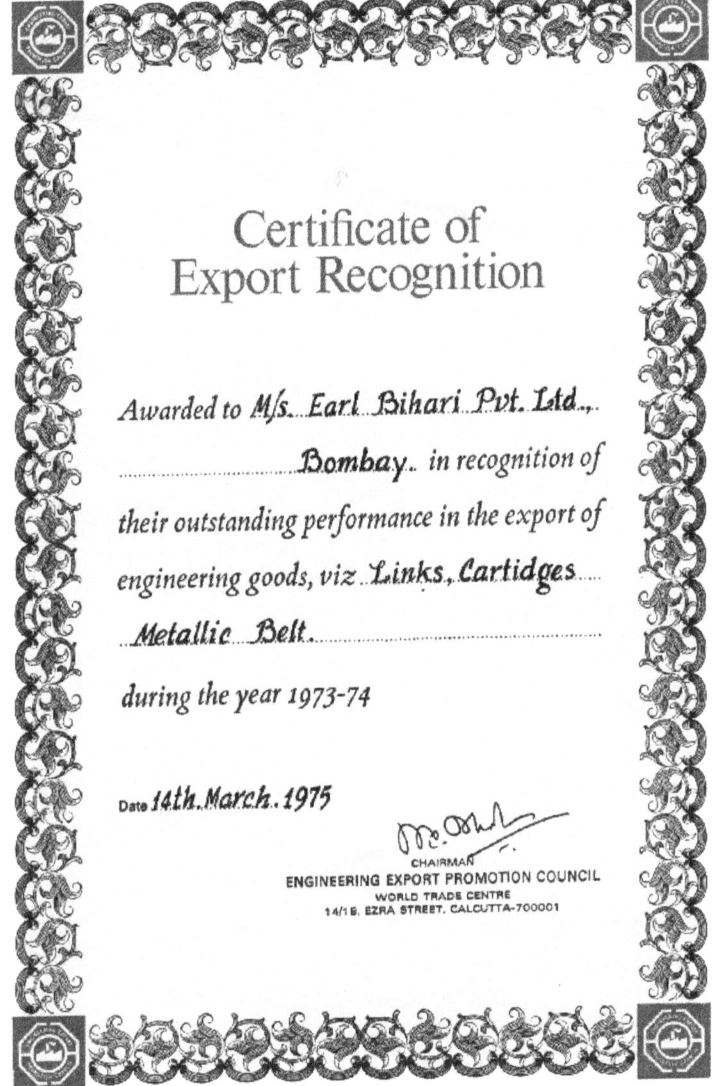
Certificate of
Export Recognition

Awarded to M/s. Earl Bihari Pvt. Ltd.,
Bombay.. in recognition of
their outstanding performance in the export of
engineering goods, viz Links, Cartidges
Metallic Belt.
during the year 1973-74

Date 14th. March. 1975

CHAIRMAN
ENGINEERING EXPORT PROMOTION COUNCIL
WORLD TRADE CENTRE
14/1 B, EZRA STREET, CALCUTTA-700001

✣ Export Certificate (1975)

✣ Products of Earl Bihari (1973)

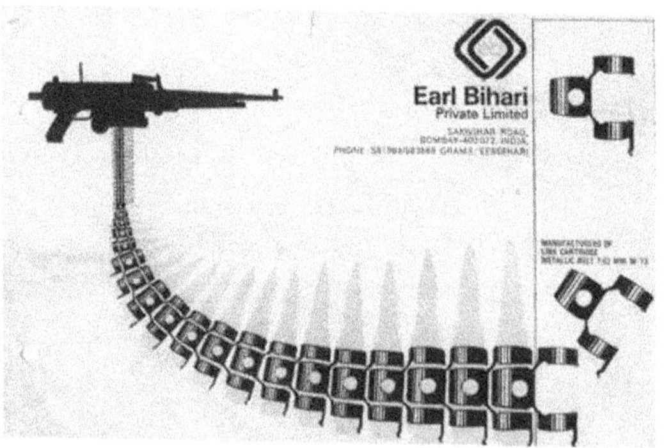

✣ Exhibit of Cartridge Links (1971)

Earl was at the helm of Earl Bihari – still a small company, but one that in a span of four years had grown into a powerhouse of high-precision tools, coveted products, a team of highly skilled professional engineers, and a work force of about three hundred employees who were devoted to Earl, their Managing Director.

Decades later, because of shifting loyalties and selfish motives, some witnesses to this brilliant success – including those who had profited from Earl's expertise – would trivialize these achievements. Earl and I were married by then, and in my frustration, I would utter words of anger. Earl's response was always calm and measured. "Pet Girl, my father often used to say: 'What if a dog barked at the moon?' This is what these folks are up to – barking at the moon. They are a sorry lot. Forget about them!" Always capable of surmounting his own feelings, he couldn't seem to fathom my own private struggle to deal with the blows to my husband's good name. Earl, however, handled the situation magnanimously and exhorted me to take the high road as well.

ANOTHER MARRIAGE PROSPECT

With the cartridge links and other products on their successful route to manufacture by 1966, Earl, at age thirty-four, once again turned his mind to marriage. His widowed mother constantly reminded him that she was looking forward to moving in with him once he had found a suitable mate. Her sister-in-law Rose had by now passed away. Her beloved daughter Hazel and family were to soon emigrate to Canada, and Nel now feared having to live alone in a flat. She yearned to move in with her son and, hopefully, his family.

Earl's mind and heart turned to Jane Flynn, whom he had dated almost ten years earlier while he had worked in Calcutta. In the meantime, Jane had emigrated to England with her parents and siblings. However, she and Earl had kept in touch with letters as well as birthday and Christmas cards. Earl realized he was developing strong feelings for her, which she reciprocated.

He decided to invite Jane on a holiday in India and even sent her a gift of five hundred pounds. She was ecstatic. Towards Christmas, she arrived with the intention of spending five weeks. It was a busy time for Earl at his business, but he managed to spend every evening with Jane – going out for dinner, walking along the beach or sitting on a park bench. More and more, Earl realized that Jane was a beautiful soul. It was also clear that she loved Earl unconditionally. She exuded an aura of simplicity and openness. She said what she meant.

As days became weeks, Earl began to hope that perhaps Jane was the woman he was waiting for. They spoke about the possibility of marriage. Jane, for her part, knew that she would have to return to England, resign her job and inform her family of her decision to return to India and make it her permanent home.

About a week before her departure for England, Earl noticed a wan look on Jane's face. Confused and concerned about her well being, he kept his fears to himself until after she had left the country. Verna then confided to Earl that Jane had asked her to accompany her to a gynecologist to discuss a problem. The prognosis was not encouraging. The doctor felt Jane could have no children. Earl was torn between his love for her and his desire for fatherhood. As always, he prayed for light.

Earl opened his heart to Jane and frankly told her in a letter that he couldn't marry her because of the fear that she could have no children. Jane was devastated, but respected his decision and replied with a brief note. Her unwavering principle was to go only where she felt welcome. She would move on with her life, to wherever fate would beckon her. But moving on was no easy feat for Earl or Jane. They each had to clear the past and press on with the future – a future untethered to memories or their raw emotions.

Some years later, Earl received a photograph and another brief note from Jane. She had since married and had a little girl. Her marriage, however, had ended in divorce. Earl would later confide in me that one of the most poignant experiences of his life was receiving Jane's news. He had been engulfed with many complex emotions – life was never simple and trying to find a simple explanation for what had happened between him and Jane was pointless. The turns their lives had taken were painful and depressing to look back on, but it was as it was meant to be. All his experiences with broken relationships would ultimately help cement the man he was meant to be.

Earl moved on from this letter too. His trump card of "God's Will" was always in the back of his mind. He began to put distance between himself and his past broken relationships. He made every attempt to convince himself that he wasn't in any way compromised – that he was indeed still desirable and sought after. Anchored by his Christian faith, he would enter a new era in both business and in his relationships. With his immutable, constant, honest self, he would launch into a future full of promise.

Four

RETURN FROM ABROAD

SISTER FELICIA AND I MILLED OUR WAY through the thick crowd in the Santa Cruz airport in Bombay. It was now mid-June 1967 and after several years abroad, both of us were excited at the thought of seeing our families. From a distance, I glimpsed the convent Sisters who had come to take us into Bombay, our temporary residence for a few days. Then I caught sight of my own sister Doris, my beloved mother, my brother-in-law Claude and another young man with them. With arms outstretched, I ran to my mother. It was six years since she had seen me – and never in the religious habit. Tears streamed down her cheeks. I wiped them off with my bare hands.

I hugged Doris and Claude, then moved on and stopped in front of the young man. I looked at him and hesitated. Could it be? His face had somehow vanished from my memory like the sands seeping through the slender neck of an hour glass. "That's Earl," said my sister. I put my hand out nervously and smiled. I quickly returned to Doris, who was standing a few feet away. "Isn't he married?" I whispered. "No, child," she responded, "He cannot find the right girl."

The words sank deep into my heart and soul. Earl's signature broad smile and sparkling teeth were still there. His dark mop of curls had thinned but his physique was taut and well toned. The last time we had met was a dozen years before, when he had come over to my house to drop off the trigonometry book.

Now it was time to once again say goodbye to my family and to Earl as I rejoined Sister Felicia and the others. As the driver deftly maneuvered the van through the cacophony of Bombay's unrelenting traffic, I kept telling myself that Earl's bachelor status was no business of mine. I was now a "Bride of Christ," a "Handmaid of the Lord." I had made my temporary vows of poverty, chastity and obedience.

On reaching the convent, I went to the chapel to thank the Lord for bringing me back to India, where I was going to serve my people as a missionary. As I knelt in prayer, I was able to unravel a sequence of events, minor yet significant which ultimately brought me to this surprising encounter between Earl and me a few hours ago.

PREPARATION FOR ITALY

I was returning to India after spending five years away, two in Italy and three in the United States. A few months after I had taken the habit, I had been summoned to the office of Sister Stefan, my novice mistress. She informed me that my superiors had decided to send me, with three other novices, to the international novitiate in Grottaferrata outside the city of Rome. We would first need to get some paperwork done – our passports would have to be processed and we would have to go through the required medical tests – but we were told to inform our parents of our imminent departure.

A few days later, our group left for Bombay. I had heard so much about the city but had never visited it. With its teeming millions, congested streets, high-rise buildings and incessant nightlife, Bombay was a classical metropolis of the third world and a dichotomy. The very rich shared the streets with the desperately poor. Families in chauffeur-driven Mercedes-Benzes drove alongside men struggling beneath the weight of heavy rubble on their backs, and passed half-naked children with hands outstretched begging for a few pennies.

Our Sisters ran two institutions in Bombay: a school for the upper class and an orphanage and school for the poor. In many cases, the income from the former subsidized the latter. We were sent to the convent that housed the orphanage. This experience reinforced my desire to be a missionary. I was most impressed by the orphanage supervisor, Sister Domenic. Originally from Malta, she was so dedicated to her young charges that she was fluent in Hindi, the language spoken by many of the orphans. I noticed her arms stretching out to touch a forlorn toddler craving affection. I noticed her easy smile, her gentle embrace. She had carved out a world of order for her orphans, a safety net to ease their faltering steps.

One day, while kneeling in prayer in the chapel, my head began to spin and I had to sit down. My upper arm began to itch. I tried to softly massage it and discovered huge festering blisters all over. I left the chapel and made my way to Sister Superior's office. A trained nurse, she quickly diagnosed chicken pox. I was confined to the infirmary for ten days and would not be able to return to Pune with the other three novices.

Little did I realize that only a few miles away lived the young man I had relinquished to the recesses of my heart and soul. His memory had by now almost faded into oblivion. I was now a novice and in the process of learning how to face the rigours of missionary life.

Once healed, I was ready to return to the novitiate. On the day I was to depart from Bombay, I was summoned to the main lobby of the convent. There, a few metres away, stood Sister Provincial – the Sister who had severely reprimanded me two days before I had taken the holy habit. I was told I would be her companion on the train. I mustered every ounce of courage and goodwill I could mobilize and, despite my apprehension, smiled at the Sisters who had gathered to bid us farewell. Fortunately, we scarcely spoke to each other during the trip. In the four hours of the train ride, she made only one remark to me. "Now don't make a scene; let's have our meal as quietly as possible."

During the trip, my thoughts turned to my family, especially my dear parents. I knew they would be proud and grateful that I had been chosen to go to a foreign land to be trained as a missionary. I longed for one last glimpse of their loving and caring faces before I left for Rome, knowing full well that it was impossible. My father had retired and finances were scarce. They would not be able to afford a trip to Pune to see me. Furthermore, I convinced myself that I no longer belonged to them. As a "Handmaid of the Lord," I was soon to be absolutely in His care. These lofty thoughts gave me solace and courage.

When the day in early May arrived to leave for Bombay enroute to Rome, we bade farewell to our beloved novice mistress Sister Stefan, and our Sub-Mistress Sister Teresa Ann. Once again, we were reminded of the privilege we had been accorded – to be trained in the international novitiate in Rome. The "Eternal City" conjured up many pictures in our young minds. We dreamed of seeing the Vatican, the Catacombs, the Roman amphitheatre, the Pieta of Michelangelo.

We embarked on board the *Flotta Laura*, an Italian sea liner that could hold as many as one thousand passengers, mostly Italians who had emigrated to Australia and New Zealand and were now returning to Italy to visit family. The journey was to take three weeks. We were now five Sisters who set sail. We had been joined by our mentor, Sister Domenica, who had served in India for thirty years, but was ailing and therefore returning to her homeland of Italy.

JOURNEY TO ROME

No sooner had the ship set sail than the scourge of seasickness struck us. As the *Flotta Laura* cut through ferocious waves caused by the tidal winds, the vessel jostled from side to side, mercilessly swirling her human cargo across the floors of the ship. Despite severe feelings of nausea, we hobbled along towards the dining room holding the railings of the deck for support. We had been advised before we left Bombay that despite the seasickness we should try and eat. We tried, but to no avail. As each one left the dining table, others followed and soon all five of us found ourselves in our cabin, too sick to even speak.

I recalled Sister Elsa Garreth, Sister Superior in my boarding school, who had recounted the story of her trip from London to India. "Seasickness was as close to hell as any human feeling felt!" she had exclaimed. Our own experience echoed hers. In the middle of the night, I opened my eyes and looked around the cabin. It was indeed hell: vomit everywhere, the floor a mess, our bedclothes in need of an immediate wash. The odour was stifling.

When daylight broke, I struggled to the bathroom. I managed to change into a fresh set of clothes and made my way to the deck, where I literally collapsed. A kind American couple noticed me slumped against the walls of the deck. They helped me to a chair and gave me a tablet. In fifteen minutes, I felt much better. The Americans then returned with some cookies and tea.

Energized, I asked if they had more tablets that I could share with my Sisters. I rushed to the cabin and insisted that each of the Sisters take one. I later sought out the pantry and asked for a few packets of cookies and tea. A few hours later, everyone felt better. We then got down to the chore of cleaning the cabin and ourselves. After lunch, we took a stroll on deck. It was the first time the others had ventured out of our cabin. It was spectacular. The clear blue afternoon sky, the navy blue waters of the Arabian Sea and our white-painted *Flotta Laura* presented a perfect picture postcard.

Now we could get down to the structure of a daily routine. The ship's chaplain, Father Bonaventure, a missionary who had done missionary service in Australia for several years and was now returning to Italy for a well-earned holiday, offered Holy Mass in the morning. After breakfast, we retired to our cabin, where we recited the Divine Office, primarily biblical excerpts. We then devoted ourselves to spiritual reading, such as books on the lives of the saints. No secular literature, such as newspapers or magazines, was allowed.

During this journey, I developed a strong friendship of trust and caring with Sister Christine, who also hailed from Kerala. We were both university-educated, she in social work and I in mathematics. She was a couple of years older than I and soon became a mentor to me. Our friendship would last a lifetime.

One night, standing on the deck, we exchanged thoughts about our families. Christine spoke about her brother who, because of ideological differences with their parents, had left home for England and had not been heard from for five years. As religious Sisters, the attachment you share with your family only grows stronger. Although you attempt to make your religious family your own, it never replaces your birth family. This is why a religious member of a family is always the uniting force long after the passing away of parents.

That same night, I looked up into the sky and my thoughts turned to Earl, whom I had desperately tried to forget because I wanted to give myself entirely to Christ. I looked around me and saw the endless ocean, the timelessness of space and our ship a tiny speck on this sea of darkness and infinite splendour. I confided to Christine the strong feelings of attachment I had developed for Earl since I was a young girl of twelve. Always the mentor, she tactfully but firmly reprimanded me. "Put these temptations out of your mind. God has called you to the religious life. He will take care of Earl."

One bright morning, it was announced on the intercom that we were to soon enter the Suez Canal. All of us five Sisters rushed to the deck, as did most other passengers. As we sailed through its tranquil waters, we witnessed the beautiful scenes on either side of us. To the east lay the Sinai Peninsula and we recalled the scenes in the Bible – Moses witnessing the presence of the Lord in the burning bush and later receiving the Ten Commandments. To the west we saw date palms swaying in the breeze and Bedouins tending their goats.

I recalled the classes of my high school teacher Barbara Pereira, who not only presented us with the geography of the region but also intertwined our instruction with the engineering and political aspects of the canal. We learned about the Suez in 1956, the year Egyptian President Gamal Nasser nationalized the canal, sending shock waves throughout the international community.

A few days later, we touched port in the Island of Malta, part of an archipelago of islands. Here again, I recalled Ms. Pereira explaining to us about Malta's strategic importance in the Mediterranean. I also remembered another teacher, Sister Luke, who related to us how Malta was a mixture of different types of peoples, much like India – a combination of European and mid-eastern stock.

ARRIVAL IN ITALY

Soon afterwards, we reached Naples. Early one morning, I witnessed the Italian porters rush onto the ship. With leather straps on their shoulders, each was able to carry four suitcases. Compared to the limited ability of our emaciated porters back home, this highlighted to me what a healthy and plentiful diet could do for the productivity of the average citizen. India of the 1960s was far behind the developed world.

By day's end, we were in Rome – the cradle of Roman Catholicism and the home of the Mother House of our Order. We were taken to St. Helen's Convent, situated on Via Giusti in the heart of Rome, where initiation would start after a night's rest. I was overwhelmed with the international dimension of my religious life. But my Lord Jesus Christ was ahead of me, smiling and beckoning me to follow Him.

A resplendent day dawned under a blue Italian summer sky. At chapel for Holy Mass and the Divine Office, we saw about three hundred Sisters, representatives from every corner of the world. We young novices were given the most junior seats, which in religious life meant the very first rows. The Mass was said in Latin, while the hymns were sung in French and Italian. After breakfast, it was time to be introduced to the Mother General, Mother Saint Agnes. She was a Frenchwoman who did not speak English, but was accompanied by a young, dynamic American, Sister Alma, who spoke fluent French and Italian.

One by one, we were ushered into the Mother General's presence. I must confess I was more impressed by Sister Alma than by the Mother General herself. Her personality, it was evident, was shaped by hard hewn principles that she had fearlessly cultivated. She brought freshness into a staid community. Above all, she was interested in the welfare of us young novices and exhibited a concern that came naturally to her. It was no surprise to me when I learned that she was elected the Mother General some years later – an American in an ultra-conservative French Order.

At noon, we entered the refectory, as the dining room was called. It was lined with rows of wooden tables and could seat two hundred Sisters at one sitting. The top tier was reserved for the senior Sisters. Then came the juniors and the novices were seated in the lowest tier. At the front was a small table at which the Mother General was seated. To her left and to her right were seated her six Assistants General.

Even to a novice like me, it was evident that Europe's structured society was echoed in the hallowed portals of the convents.

Superiors and those who wielded powers of governance generally came from the upper strata of society and were given privileges not generally accorded to the average Sister.

No wine was served to the community at large, but in front of the Mother General and each of her assistants stood two four-ounce bottles of wine, one white and one red. Beneath each of these privileged souls was a footstool to rest tired legs. There was a huge entrance at the end of the refectory leading to the kitchen. In the kitchen, the Sister in charge prepared trays of food. One tray was specifically prepared for the Mother General, who would be served by the Sister whose responsibility it was to see to her every need.

There was an established routine to serving the food. No sooner was the Grace said than the Sister in charge of serving the Mother General would enter the refectory and walk down the centre aisle with the tray in her hands. She would stop about three feet in front of the Mother General and bow to her. She then approached the table and gingerly placed the food in front of her. Two other Sisters (generally juniors) followed suit and served her assistants in the same manner. Afterwards, half a dozen Sisters bowed in front of the Mother General and then served the rest of the community. There was no distinction in the food served, and everyone ate off the same common plate-ware and with cutlery of simple aluminum. No talking was allowed during mealtime. A Sister was assigned to read aloud a spiritual book, often on the life of a saint.

Later in the day, we were told to get ready for the trip to Grottaferrata on the outskirts of Rome. This would be our novitiate, or house of training, for the next eighteen months. Before we left the Mother House, we paid our respects to the tomb of the Mother Foundress – Mother Hélène de Chappotin. She had started the Order in the late nineteenth century and her body was entombed in the Blue Chapel.

Tradition has it that the devil was so upset at her work that no sooner was her tomb completed than the craftsmen heard a terrible thud and immediately noticed a huge crack right across the marble pew alongside her tomb. The Sisters decided to leave it and a century later the crack was still noticeable. I kneeled by her tomb and prayed for the gift of perseverance. I asked her to intercede for me that I might continue to live as a member of her Order until my own death.

✣ GROTTAFERRATA (1962)

Vineyards and olive groves dotted the landscape enroute to Grottaferrata, a three hundred-acre estate where novices from around the world gathered. We were introduced to the Mother Superior and then to the Novice Mistress, who would be in charge of our training for the next eighteen months. She would decide whether or not we would make our first vows of poverty, chastity and obedience.

Sister Sagrado Corazón was a stunning Spanish woman with hazelnut eyes and rose-red lips. She was a deeply spiritual woman who yearned to model her life and that of her young protégées after her Master Jesus Christ. At recreation, she was the pinnacle of laughter and fun. She could converse in Spanish, English, Italian, French and Portuguese. Armed with these five languages, she was able to speak to almost every novice in her mother tongue. She approached her stewardship with calm and elegance. Her responsibilities were carried out with lazer like focus and adherence to the rules of the Order. Nothing – not even the glare of her young novices' expectations of her, the language barriers created by the international heritage of those in her care, or the evident loneliness of some of her charges – seemed to affect her. She skillfully dealt with all challenges while remaining the mother of her flock. We all shared the greatest respect and love for her.

The centrepiece of the convent was the chapel, which resembled a basilica and could hold as many as three hundred Sisters. Marble columns rose from floor to ceiling on either side of the chapel. A powerful pipe organ in the upper balcony was used to accompany a choir of fifty voices that sang Gregorian chants. As I listened to the haunting music, I felt as if I were in a dimension that transcended time and space. I was kneeling before the Majesty of God.

✣ CHAPEL IN GROTTAFERRATA (1962)

Now a world away from India, my life as a novice in Grottaferrata traced the same daily pattern as it had in Pune. We rose at 5:00 a.m., when a Sister exclaimed the traditional *"Benedicamus Domino."* As we got out of our beds and kissed the floor, we responded *"Ecce Ancilla Domini."* Then we were off to chapel for meditation, followed by Holy Mass and the Divine Office.

Our professional careers were put on hold as we novices took on jobs of housework and manual labour on the convent and its farm. There were only two leadership positions assigned to those novices who showed signs of ability in future governance: Guardian of the Postulants and Admonitress. During my year and a half at Grottaferrata, I was assigned to the kitchen, the laundry, the print shop and the pantry, as well as Guardian of the Postulants and Admonitress of the novices.

Despite the beauty of the Italian countryside, the splendour of Gregorian chants and the companionship of the other novices, my experience at Grottaferrata was a lonely one. I missed my family very much. International phone calls were uncommon; even letters were scarce. My mother kept in touch with me every month and let me know the whereabouts of my siblings and their families. My siblings themselves seldom wrote. One person whom I did hear from was my brother-in-law Claude. He initially kept me posted on his brother Earl, but with time he discreetly refrained from mentioning him.

FIRST VOWS

In November 1963, the Novice Mistress gave me the good news that my superiors had decided I was ready to take my first step towards a life-long commitment that I would make three years later. Twelve young novices who represented eleven countries – Argentina, Chile, Brazil, the United States, England, France, Spain, the Congo, Australia, India and Lebanon – were to make our first vows of poverty, chastity and obedience.

In the secrecy of my heart, I realized that this step would reinforce my commitment to Christ and further distance me from a liaison with Earl in the future. The more I prayed, the clearer it became that I was destined to be a missionary nun. All that I hoped and prayed for was that Earl too would find fulfillment in his walk of life. I did not look for an answer that would make my calling clear. The mystery of my love for Earl remained unsolved.

My faith in Christ, however, gave direction to my hopes for him. I was confident that God would not turn a blind eye to my concern. I knew He felt my pain and at the moment when I was called upon to make my first commitment, I looked upon Him as a God who had subjected Himself to suffering, pain and ignominy. I was now one with Him. In gazing upon Him on the cross I identified myself with Him and therein found solace. After having lived two years as a novice, I was now capable of seeing my destiny more clearly. With the help of my superiors and the guidelines they provided my future was now demarcated.

After a week of secluded prayer and silence, we were ready to take our vows. We each met with Sister Sagrado Corazón, who reminded us of our lofty calling: to be a Spouse of Christ, bound to him by the vows of poverty, chastity and obedience. The Order had set aside four days in the calendar year for ceremonies of commitment. On December 15, 1963, in a chapel decorated with white carnations and calla lilies, thirty of us walked down the aisle. Ten young postulants in their bridal gowns would take the Holy Habit, twelve of us novices would make our first vows, and eight others would make their final commitment. As the Bishop, assisted by three priests, sang *"Veni Sponsa Christi,"* we all prostrated ourselves on the chapel floor and kissed it three consecutive times. As I knelt before the Bishop to make my vows, I recognized it was a significant step to my final commitment.

Within a few days, those of us who had professed our first vows would be transferred to the other side of the novitiate – the section that housed the "Professed" Sisters. Some of us would be sent across the globe to bring the good news of the Gospel. I was thinking about what might lie ahead as I walked along the corridors of the convent one day not long afterwards when I felt the strong presence of someone behind me. I turned around but saw no one. Soon after, I sniffed the odour of cigarettes but again found myself alone. These episodes continued for the next three to four days.

A few weeks later, I received an unusually thick letter from my family. I recognized the writing as that of my Sister Phyllis. My father had passed away suddenly of a heart attack on December 22. I was the only child of the eight not at his funeral. As was customary in the Order, I spent the next day quietly. I wrote to my mother to offer her as much consolation as I could. I wondered to myself whether the unseen presence behind me those few days was the soul of my father reassuring me that all would be well.

As Professed Sisters, our next stage was spent at Saint Helen's Convent, our Mother House in the heart of Rome. I would spend another three months there, a period of time when I felt I was an unknown entity in a sea of seven hundred missionaries. Saint Helen's was a hub of missionary activity and zeal. Representatives from sixty countries or more could be seen in the hallways on a daily basis. The greater part of my day was spent either in scrubbing the marble staircase that linked the main floor to the seventh floor or folding clothes in a tiny room called The Pliage. I also spent three hours a day in prayer and an hour on study about the missionary activity of the Order around the world.

THE UNITED STATES

"Even the most insignificant act is of importance in the plan of God." I had almost given up hope of ever being assigned a missionary assignment of significance when I was reminded of the dictum so often uttered to us in our years of training. I tried to find fulfillment in my menial tasks. One day in March, as I was scrubbing the marble steps, the Sister Superior rushed down the steps and said, "Be ready to go out by 10:00 a.m."

Bemused by the urgency in her tone, I made my way to the front parlour, only to meet the two Sisters in charge of our travel bureau. Where was I to be sent? To my joy and excitement, the convent van stopped in front of the American Consulate. I was interviewed by one of the counselors there, who found my language skills in English satisfactory. Then I was returned to the two Sisters from the convent. During the entire trip to and from the Consulate, not a word about my going to the States was uttered.

Back at the convent, I kept the trip to myself. We had been trained never to discuss such initiatives with our peers. A formal announcement by our superiors would be made at the opportune time. I was reassured that the Order had plans for me, plans other than scrubbing steps and folding clothes.

The next day Sister Alma, Assistant General in charge of our missions in the English-speaking world, summoned me to her office. I was overjoyed at the opportunity of meeting a Sister who gave me a sense of worth, and felt that even a few minutes in her presence would be compensation enough for the many times I had felt ignored, even belittled. As was the rule in the 1960s, I knelt beside her. I didn't know what awaited me in the United States.

These fears were soon dispelled as she welcomed me with her broad smile. In my further studies, I was to pursue a Master's in Business Administration. The area of specialization would be left to my choice. We had been trained to believe that our superiors, under the guidance of the Holy Spirit, would always make the right decision. The long-term plan for me was to return to Madras, India, and help start a Faculty of Commerce at my alma mater, Stella Maris College.

Those of us at the convent who were about to leave for our future destinations were given an opportunity to visit the Vatican, the Sistine Chapel, the Forum, the Colosseum and other Roman landmarks. The convent left nothing to chance: it had its own guides in two Sisters who were trained for the positions and had many years' experience.

In a few days, accompanied by two very young Sisters from India, Sister Esmée and Sister Felicia, I would board the plane from Rome's Fiumicino Airport for New York's Kennedy Airport. I was the most senior of the three, so I was now mentor to the other two. Two American Sisters – Sister Claudette and Sister Paula – showered us with warm smiles and hugs and led us to the convent car. Much to my surprise, Sister Claudette was at the wheel! I would soon realize that the practice of nuns at the wheel was common in the States.

As we drove to the convent in the heart of Manhattan, I was awe-struck. I had learned about the differences between socialism and capitalism in my university classes. I was also a member of the debating team in my university when we held mock U.N. sessions. As a student, I was a socialist at heart, invariably on the side of the socialist bloc attacking the western world for its belief that the profit motive determined all economic endeavour. I had learned that capitalism was oppressive, caused discord and to a large extent dehumanized the individual.

To my surprise, I found real economic progress in the United States. This country had mastered skills and technology that had raised its people to a new plane. Surely, I thought, this was the desire of all mankind. I had always believed that capitalism exploited the individual, but here I found a culture where the individual was all-important. The class structure so prevalent in India was absent. Instead, a burgeoning middle class had become the backbone of American society. For those who aspired to "the American Dream" there was the wherewithal to fulfill it. I would now have to rethink my commitment to socialism.

The drive from New York to the American Novitiate in Fruit Hill, Rhode Island, presented a canopy of broad-shouldered maples and columns of firs that soared toward the light of the sky, reminding me of the steeples of the Roman cathedrals.

"Your superiors know best." I took a deep breath and remembered those words when I was introduced to my academic mentor, Sister Ruth. I wondered if a seventy-year-old could be even acquainted with the present curriculum in the universities. But my religious instincts came to my rescue. I would not have been assigned to Sister Ruth, I reasoned, if she were incapable of helping me. Indeed, she had already gone through the calendar of St. John's University in New York, where I was to pursue my MBA. She had spoken to the foreign students' counselor and was aware that I needed a few prerequisites before I embarked on my studies.

Within a few hours of our encounter, Sister Ruth suggested that we visit the public library to pick up textbooks in preparation for the two summer courses she had decided I should take. The books were *Economics* by Paul Samuelson and *The Practice of Management* by Peter Drucker. She could not have made a wiser decision. We met with the Sister Superior and together it was decided that I would be given four hours a day to study. The rest of the day would be spent in prayer, religious instruction, household chores and recreation. In four weeks, I had mastered both books from cover to cover.

Shortly thereafter, I was sent to Long Island, New York, where our Sisters ran a cardiac hospital. This was a large community of about fifty Sisters of whom I would be the most junior, and it would serve as my home for the next three years.

Upon hearing that a young Sister from India was coming to live with them, the community had conjured up bizarre ideas of my background. They assumed I couldn't speak English, would be uncomfortable with table settings, and unaware of table manners. Most of all, they assumed, or perhaps feared, that I would be a person "straight out of the jungle"! When I volunteered to read to the Sisters during lunch, everyone was aghast that I spoke and read in impeccable English, in a British accent to boot. Soon I was the official reader in the refectory.

When I arrived at the convent, the Sister Superior had been away. Her aloofness to me when we met a few days later was apparent. In my entire religious life, I had almost always encountered warmth, understanding and caring from the Sisters in authority. Sister Godfried was an exception. Was it because I was from India and she had never ventured out of the U.S.? Her condescending attitude toward me would surface ever more blatantly as time evolved. Her response to my outstanding marks in Economics and Management that first summer was typical: she told me to be humble and grateful. As time evolved, I didn't become callous or insecure. I felt alienated, not because of the community but because of her. I continued to find solace in the many friends I had made amongst the Sisters.

Sister Ruth, on the other hand, was truly happy for me. After completion of the two summer courses, I had returned to Fruit Hill for a short holiday. She continued to be my beacon of light. Knowing that I had majored in mathematics, she felt that accounting and finance should be my preferred areas of specialization. There would be a few more semesters of prerequisites and in the fall of 1965 I was admitted into the program.

Two more years of assiduous study followed, and I was then granted my MBA degree. I was on the Dean's list and was awarded a Certificate of Merit for outstanding scholastic achievement. No official announcement was made to the Long Island community about my graduation. But I understood Sister Godfried's dilemma. The other three Sisters who had started the MBA program with me had not completed their course work and hence were not ready to graduate. To ease their pain and humiliation, they were discreetly told to go on a holiday and my graduation was downplayed.

I felt guilty at my success – guilty that I had worked very hard; guilty that I was almost a decade and a half younger than the others and thus learning came more easily to me; guilty that the Indian educational system, with its emphasis on quantitative analysis, had prepared me for the MBA program. A Sister with little education and knowledge of English would accompany me to the official graduation ceremony and I was not able to share my success with anyone else in the community.

But I had one consolation: I was told that in a few weeks I would be returning to India. Very soon I would find myself at the Bombay Airport in the arms of my beloved mother and family.

Five

AN UNEXPECTED OCCASION

REAL LIFE IS OFTEN A HIGHWAY OF INCESSANT TRAFFIC, interspersed with intervals of stillness. It can be as simple as a hand stretched out to welcome you, a hug of endearment, or a bird's twitter.

Seated in the convent van, Sister Felicia and I made our way to Villa Theresa, our convent in the city of Bombay. We made a short visit to the chapel and then met with our Sister Superior, Sister Bartholomew. An Englishwoman, she had been a missionary in India for over twenty-five years. After a warm welcome, she accompanied us to our rooms and informed us that after a short nap, a shower and a hot meal, the convent van would drop us off at our respective family homes. Our curfew was set at 9:30 p.m.

✣ MERCY RETURNS TO VILLA THERESA CONVENT (2007)

My destination was Bandra, where my sister Doris and her husband Claude and family lived. My mother was also staying with them for a few months. A predominantly Christian community in the 1960s, Bandra was a desirable suburb: tennis courts, swimming pools and gymnasiums were all amenities available to its residents. Claude had recently accepted the position of Manager of Earl Bihari, and moved his family from the south of India. Most of Claude's family lived nearby.

Soon after my arrival at their house, we went on a round of visits. First on the list was Hazel, one of Claude's sisters. A vivacious and articulate woman, she held a senior administrative position in a British company. Her husband Herbert had already emigrated to Canada, and Hazel was in the midst of packing up the household to join him.

After a few pleasantries over a cup of tea, it was time to visit the home of another sister – Verna, who was married to Bihari, Earl's business partner. They lived in a mansion with an exceptional garden of manicured lawns, rows of flowers and exotic potted plants. Verna was a beautiful woman, sophisticated and perfectly put together. Like most wealthy Indian women, she was decked out in finery and jewels, although she somehow contrived not to look ostentatious.

In their ornate living room, I spotted Earl, brother of Claude, as well as Hazel and Verna, who also lived at Bihari and Verna's house. Earl shook my hand warmly and remarked that he would be driving us back to Doris and Claude's place for dinner.

As Doris rushed upstairs to set the table, I sat down on a couch in the living area of my sister's small flat. Earl entered the room, looked around and decided to sit next to me. My heart was throbbing. I was now seated side by side with the man I had for years tried to forget. I did not have the courage to look at him, but discreetly cast my eyes down. Gently, he put his left arm on the back rest of the couch. I could feel his arm behind my neck. I gave in to my sentiments and leaned my head on his arm. Did he realize it was deliberate? I didn't care. It felt wonderful. I would savour the experience for as long as it was possible. I had suddenly become tired of the unspoken rules of religious decorum. I was both angry and excited about my lapse of judgment.

Sitting next to him, I realized that Earl, too, was seeing the sparks fly. From the expression on his face and his body language, the truth was clear – he no longer saw his love for me as a stumbling block. It was no longer a moral issue. He was determined to let me know that he cared for me as much as I cared for him. My religious status was not going to be a barrier to the attention he was determined to show me.

I soon realized that in this small room of relatives, Earl's attention was more and more focused on me despite the fact that he tried vehemently to contain himself. He was weighing his every step; emotionally calculating his every move; he wanted to first win my attention and perhaps later my confidence. Only a short time ago his pursuit of me seemed impossible, now it seemed plausible. I realized it may in fact be happening.

A few minutes later, I took a pen from my purse and put it into Earl's shirt pocket, explaining it was a gift from me. "Can I give you a kiss for it?" he asked lightly. Keeping my eyes focused on the floor, I offered him my cheek. Then I looked up. Behind a curtain dividing the living room from the bedrooms stood my mother peering at us. The moment she saw Earl kiss me, she shook her head, visibly upset, and quietly slipped away.

At dinner, Doris and I sat on one side of the table, Claude and Earl on the other. As we said Grace, I noticed how fervently Earl said the prayer. We made eye contact several times, and for the most part were relaxed in each other's company. Evidently, he was enamoured by the contrast between my simple demeanour and my vibrant looks – features he later insisted, had always impressed him.

At the end of dinner, I said farewell to my beloved mother, assuring her I would let her know when my next home visit was to take place. Earl, accompanied by Doris and Claude, would drive me back to the convent. As I started up the steps, Earl called out. "Mercy, can I pick you up tomorrow and take you for a drive around the city? We can stop at a restaurant for dinner. I'll drop you back."

I was stunned. Didn't he realize I was a nun in a white habit? "I'll have to ask Sister Superior," I answered. He gave me his business card and asked me to call him. I was so confused that I dared not look back. I hastened to the chapel. "What's happening?" I asked the Lord. "Should I dare ask Sister Bartholomew? No!" I said to myself. "I will not ask Sister – I'll just forget Earl's request." On second thought, I said to myself, "Maybe I'll sleep on it! Maybe I'll leave the decision to the morning!"

Morning dawned. I went to the chapel for meditation, Holy Mass and Divine Office. As I emerged from the refectory after breakfast, I immediately encountered the Sister Superior. "My brother-in-law's brother would like to take me for a drive around the city and stop for dinner somewhere," I said. "He will then drop me off." I couldn't imagine the words had escaped my lips. There was no premeditation. To my utter dismay and surprise, she responded, "Fine, but be back by 9:30 p.m."

I was confused! How did this ever happen? Initially, I had been reluctant to even harbour such a thought and now I had been given permission without much ado. I went to the chapel and again confided to the Lord. "Why is this happening to me?" In a few seconds, I whispered, "Your will be done." From the chapel I went to the sisters' common room to telephone Earl. "Sister says it's okay for me to go out, but I must abide by my curfew." "Fine," replied Earl. "I'll be there by 5:30 p.m. I'm looking forward to seeing you again."

Earl, I knew from his reputation, was one of the most intrepid fighters for a woman's attention. As a man he was hard to define. He had many dimensions: the brilliant and hard-working engineer, the fun-loving romantic, the shrewd businessman, and above all the committed Christian. Why, then, was he inviting me out? Perhaps, I thought, he was attempting a balancing act, positioning himself as one who could win my heart while steering clear of a sullied soul. I would wait and see.

While trying to suppress my confused emotions, I spent the greater part of the day visiting my fellow Sisters, whom I had not seen for over five years. Towards evening, I donned the formal habit, went down to the parlour and informed the Sister there that I was expecting a visitor and would be waiting in the Community Room. Exactly at 5:30 p.m., I was summoned. There was Earl, standing at the head of a flight of steps, hands in his pockets, sporting his signature broad smile. He was impeccably dressed in a beige suit that combined elegance, modernity and sophistication. A tie in copper tone and dark brown shoes completed the ensemble. Ever the gallant gentleman, he opened the passenger side of the car and helped me into my seat.

For the second time in twenty-four hours, I was seated next to the man whom I had idolized since I was a young girl of twelve. For the first time in my life, I was alone with him. There was both an aura of intimacy that drew him to me, as well as an inner sense of religious decorum that yanked my soul away from him. Despite these mixed feelings there was a sense of peace that seemed to be engulfing the two of us. I had reached a newer dimension in my inner being.

I would later recall that this whole incident was supposed to be a "date", which to me, as a nun, wasn't even part of my vocabulary. Viewed from my own perspective of the time, I had agreed to a sightseeing trip. The occasion remains one of the great moments in my life. A man I loved deeply was seated next to me. My life and all its events flashed by like a film.

Earl had decided that he would take me along the Marine Drive – also called the Queen's Necklace – a strip of road with the Arabian Sea on one side and a stretch of buildings on the other. The buildings, he said, had once been handsome. However, to me they were an eyesore. Dilapidated, unpainted and bearing the scars of severe monsoons, they were a far cry from the beautifully maintained buildings of Manhattan. My confusion about the legacy of socialism again surfaced. Is this what socialism does to the human spirit – crush it? Give it no incentive for human betterment?

Suddenly, Earl turned to me. "So, tell me all about yourself. What did you study in the MBA? Tell me all about the States." Despite his attention to Bombay's heavy and unrelenting traffic, I was aware of his intent interest in every word I uttered. Every now and again, he would turn to me and we would make eye contact. I sat coyly at his side, but it was clear to both of us that we were experiencing an undiluted sense of belonging.

As these thoughts surfaced, I fixed my gaze on Earl for several minutes at a time. He looked handsome and exuded an aura of confidence. He was articulate, sophisticated and classy – attributes every woman admires in a man. I tried to focus on our conversation, giving him a synopsis of the MBA program and the courses I had taken. He was baffled that as a nun I would choose to major in accounting and finance.

By now, we had arrived at the Khyber restaurant. It was teeming with diners, but we were soon led to a table for two. All eyes were on us. I felt more than a little awkward. What was a nun doing out in the evening with a young man? Earl, on the other hand, was most relaxed. I had never been to a restaurant as an adult. He helped me with the menu. We said Grace and I noticed again how devoutly he closed his eyes and said the prayer of thanks.

As we waited for our entrées, we spoke about the different economic systems that prevailed in the U.S. and India and their respective impacts on human existence. He was a fiercely loyal Indian, although he did not hold socialism in any great esteem. In fact, he was highly critical of the burden of bureaucracy that socialism generated.

Soon our respective plates were set in front of us. He had ordered steak, potatoes and vegetables. I had rice, fish and vegetables. When it came to dessert, he suggested that I should try the leechees with ice cream. As he paid the bill, he suggested that we take the route through the Hanging Gardens, another landmark of Bombay.

By 9:15 p.m., we were back at the convent. I stepped out of the car and Earl hastened to my side. "Thank you for a lovely evening," I said demurely. In return, he took my head between his hands and planted a quick kiss on my lips. To this day that event remains emotionally raw and confusing, yet one of the most meaningful and tangible events in my human experience. I was mesmerized. I turned around, totally confused, and with tears streaming down my cheeks, I dared not look back at him.

⁜ Mercy in front of Villa Theresa porch (2007)

I hurried to the chapel. There I tried to say my night prayers and spend some time with my Lord Jesus Christ. What was happening to me? It was difficult to experience the truth of what had just happened, for I had come in contact with a deep human and spiritual challenge. I truly was in love with this man, the thought of whom I had tried to stifle for many years. Like an avalanche it overwhelmed me.

With my thoughts, my feelings, my emotions and all my passion now focused on Earl, I turned to my Lord Jesus Christ. I knelt in the chapel and turned to Him. "What do you want from me?" I felt comforted. He would show me the way. I told myself this spiritual and emotional crisis was temporary. I retired to my cell and once again knelt beside my bed. I would put my trust and faith in Him. I spent the entire night awake, frequently getting out of bed and kneeling down in prayer.

Earl would much later recount that he had stopped by his church after dropping me at the convent. Standing outside in the darkness of the night, he bared his soul to the Lord. He had just spent the evening with a young woman who offered him the possibility of great and profound intimacy. She seemed to have instilled in him a new hope – and the possibility of a new and everlasting love. And yet her religious vocation seemingly made her unattainable and unreachable. Yet he soon realized that this deluge of sudden emotion, this discovery which only a few months ago was but a thought, had now crystallized into a belief which he maintained within himself with awe.

The next day brought us back to the realities of our separate lives. Earl's daily routine included stopping by Doris's house to pick up the lunchbox she provided for her husband and brother-in-law. "I spent the most exhilarating evening ever with a woman!" exclaimed Earl. Doris, whom he respected, looked him in the eye. "Earl, if I were you, I would forget her! Go on with your life. There are so many girls out there." He pondered these words as he drove to his business.

My mother, on hearing about the early morning conversation from Doris, was livid. "Tell him not to tempt my nun daughter. Let him leave her alone." Earl acceded and continued to date other women in the months to come.

At the convent, Sister Felicia, who had flown back with me from the United States, noticed that I looked very perturbed. This was the day she and I were to fly to Madras, where I was to start teaching at Stella Maris College, while Sister Felicia was to become the principal of one of the schools in the city.

On the flight, I opened my heart to her. "I do not know whether I can continue – I love him so much." Her response was measured. "Don't worry! It will all wear off after some time. In any case, you are going to a different city and will not see him again. Pray about it and I too will pray for you." Despite her sincerity, I felt that Sister Felicia couldn't completely empathize with me. She didn't know what it was to feel the pangs of "being in love with a man." She didn't go to sleep each night only to wake up and feel her world cruelly divided. On the one side a world of religious calling and on the other, the love of a man beckoning her. This path to religious perseverance was a treacherous and slippery slope. Without absolute resolve, I knew I could slip and stumble into infidelity to my vows.

‡ Stella Maris College (1967)

Stella Maris was a university college opened immediately after the Second World War. Women in South India had started to flock to the universities, but demand outstripped supply. The archbishop of the city therefore turned to the Franciscan Missionaries of Mary, the Order to which I belonged, to start a university college. There was a pressing need for an institution of higher learning that would instill Roman Catholic principles to its students in a predominantly Hindu country.

As a faculty member in the Department of Economics, I immersed myself in my missionary work. I identified myself emotionally, intellectually and passionately with the world and the events of university college life. Despite all my efforts, I could not forget Earl. He kept dancing in and out of my mind – unseen yet real. He continued to be a beautiful thought – a thought that was both comforting and threatening. I resigned myself to the fact that in some way he would always be part of my day-to-day existence.

At times, I felt overwhelmed, but I was never devoid of hope. I realized that with the help of Christ, with the fulfillment of my teaching career, and the support of my community of Sisters, I would find peace and joy. Nevertheless, I decided to write a letter to my brother-in-law Claude. I would tell him of my feelings for Earl, praying that this opening of my innermost feelings would prove cathartic. I told Claude of the very strong love I felt for Earl, and of how I longed for his companionship. I wrote the letter, sealed the envelope and mailed it. Surely he could advise me, I thought.

I waited but there was no response. Strange, I thought. However, a few days after I had mailed the letter, my mother wrote to me, saying how happy she was to see me as a nun. She reminded me of how as a young teenager I had always aspired to missionary life. She was pleased that I had come full circle. She also emphasized that I had inspired some of my nieces to follow my example – my perseverance, therefore, was expected.

I wondered about the tone of the letter. But as the weeks unfolded and I did not hear from Claude, my confusion unraveled. My mother had evidently intercepted my letter. Seeing the sparks fly between Earl and me, she had become convinced I was in love with Earl and he with me, so she had decided to play the role of Divine Intervenor. She was determined that God had called me to be His own and that no man would distract me from that calling – not even Earl, for whom she had the highest respect.

TEACHING CAREER: EARLY DAYS

Nothing gave me greater fulfillment than stimulating young minds. I was allotted twenty hours of teaching per week – demanding by western standards, but the norm in India. My classes included Religious Instruction, English Literature and Economic Theory. I savoured every hour of my teaching. I soon became a very popular faculty member, with several extracurricular activities placed on my young shoulders. I toiled relentlessly, usually putting in seventeen-hour days.

At the convent, I had found "a house divided." We were a community of about fifty Sisters. The founding Sisters of Stella Maris College were still around, most of them now well into their fifties. Over the years, they had formed a clique and developed a sense of entitlement. Stella Maris College had been molded after the initiatives of these senior sisters. Most of them were from the United Kingdom or Ireland. Young Indian sisters were never able to penetrate the fortress the others had built for themselves.

‡ Stella Maris Convent (1967)

But this was the late sixties, an era after Vatican II, when religious communities were being encouraged by the Roman Catholic hierarchy of India to hand over positions of authority to capable indigenous members. Needless to say, there was resentment and backlash from the founding Sisters. But at that point in my life I was not engaged in idealism or intrigue. University politics, the shedding of principles of fair play, the desire of some to reach their lofty seats of power even at the cost of basic decency, all seemed the weaving of a radically new story line which I simply did not understand.

In order to make this transition possible, a relatively young, unsuspecting and deeply religious American nun, Sister Bennett – once a faculty member at the college – was chosen as Sister Superior of this community. It was a formidable task, one that would eventually prove too challenging a hurdle to scale.

Sister Bennett's first initiative was to transfer the powers of the Principal of the College from an Irish nun called Sister Sheila O'Neill to Sister Juliet, a native of India. Sister Sheila was magnanimous. In fact, earlier on being assigned the position of Principal, she declined to accept it preferring that the position be given to a qualified Indian Sister. So when the time did come for her to relinquish powers to an Indian Sister, she did it with grace and dignity. Hers was truly an example to emulate. But others were not as willing, as department heads were changed and powers of administration transferred to young Indian Sisters.

As can happen in religious houses, there was open discord. So apparent was the conflict that during the High Mass on the feast day of Sister Bennett, the senior founders stood tight-lipped in chapel, refusing to join in the singing of the hymns. To many of us young Sisters it was painful to see. My friend Sister Christine, from the Grottaferrata days, was part of this community and a faculty member, who would take over as Head of the Social Work Department. She advised me to steer clear of the clique and remain loyal to the Superior, not because of vested interests, but because it was the right thing to do. She reminded me that this was a directive set down by our Mother Foundress, who in her wisdom was able to foresee problems of this nature surfacing in the communities of her Order. I decided to continue to remain loyal to Sister Bennett.

About a month after my arrival, as was customary, I was summoned to Sister Bennett's office for an informal interview. She enquired about my teaching and college responsibilities, and then we discussed my religious commitment. She was my superior and as such, responsible for my religious development. And so for the first time, I discussed my love for Earl with one of my Superiors. She listened. She empathized. After all she was a young American nun. Perhaps she had experienced the same feelings at one time and had learned to sublimate them.

She told me in no uncertain terms that it was not wrong to have such natural feelings. However, she advised me that I should rise above them. "Christ is now your Spouse. Think of that," she said. They were not mere words to hide behind. They were words that truly captured the essence of religious life. With that sublime thought in my head, I decided I would do as she said. Every time Earl entered my mind, I would replace his face with the Face of Christ, my Lord and Saviour and my Spouse.

By the end of the academic year, it was evident that Sister Bennett could no longer continue as Superior. The forces of resentment, even rebellion, were far too strong. Her health began to fail. She was given the position of Superior in the convent at Ootacamund in the Blue Mountains of South India. Sister Angela Hurley from Ireland, who had spent almost twenty years in India, would now fill the position of Superior.

Tall, stately and trim, she commanded respect and loyalty the moment she entered a room. No sooner had she arrived than she won the loyalty of the senior founding Sisters. She played her cards so well that none among them felt she was a threat. She had an intuitive sensitivity to people and to situations, and seemed to transcend community politics while remaining the centre of the team. Through example and precept, Sister Angela showed us that if we were to be an effective community we had to put aside our pettiness and choose a path of solidarity, commitment and selfless service.

As for the younger Indian Sisters, they found in her not just a mentor, but also someone who was interested in their every need. These qualities were evident from the moment I encountered her. She skillfully made herself the focal point of the community. No other individual was as successful as Sister Angela in mobilizing a sense of loyalty and allegiance. And she did it with the utmost grace.

Sister Angela and I developed a deep understanding from the moment we met. Of all the superiors I had in my eleven years as a nun, no other individual played such a significant role in my development. To me, it was providential that she entered my life at its most vulnerable juncture. My trust and respect for her emanated not from adulation but from mutual respect.

With Sister Angela at the helm, community life took on a different dimension. There was laughter, music and excitement. Recreation was truly a time when we sisters shared our experiences with one another. Divisive politics were replaced with sisterly love and regard. These would prove to be the happiest years of my religious life and I soon became "the life of the community." I organized picnics on the beaches of Madras, movie nights, skits and plays during recreation. As a highlight, I also arranged for a Christmas tree to be brought in. The sisters delighted in the experience of exchanging small gifts.

THE "TRIALS"

It was now the summer of 1969. I was twenty-nine years old. I had just completed two academic years at Stella Maris and I could not have been happier. I had found my life's mission. I loved university college life, I loved community life, and I had grown spiritually. Following the advice of Sister Bennett, I had managed to sublimate all thoughts and desires of Earl. I was now ready to make my final commitment.

I was summoned to Sister Angela's office and sat down next to her. (The practice of kneeling down in front of our superiors had been discontinued.) In keeping with Vatican II directives, we each were renamed by our baptismal names in place of our religious ones. I was now Sister Mercy Jacobs, no longer Sister Agnes Romana. Sister Angela informed me that my superiors had deemed me fit to make my final vows of poverty, chastity and obedience. The date for this commitment was December 15 of that year.

I told her I was overjoyed that at last the wait was over. I was ready to make that commitment. I confessed to her about the strong feelings of love I had harboured for a young man out in the world. I told her all about Earl, the date in Bombay, and how he was still part of my everyday thoughts and experience. "For pity's sake, this is a country of about eight hundred million, half of whom are women, surely he can find someone!" she replied with her characteristic Irish humour.

A few days later, I was informed that I was to go to Ootacamund for what was known as "trials." This was a period of about two months during which sisters about to make their final vows re-enter novitiate training. They are assigned menial chores and spend the better part of the day in prayer and religious instruction. Before I left Stella Maris, some of the Sisters who had been through the rigours of these trials warned me about the nature of these chores.

Cleaning the washrooms was included in the rotation. "Ooty" was at that time suffering from an acute water shortage and the only time the flushing action of the toilets would work was for a half-hour in the morning. With about fifty Sisters in this convent, demand was high. I somehow knew without a shade of doubt that I would be assigned to washroom duty. I was right.

There was nothing I could do but do my best. The next morning, I ventured to my chore. The toilets had not been flushed for twenty-four hours so the odour was unbearable. Masks and gloves were unknown items in the India of the 1960s. The trick was never to pull the lever; if you did, all the excrement would overflow onto the floor. I had to fill buckets of water and pour it into the bowls from a height. This I did and successfully flushed out all the toilets. I then tackled the comparatively easy task of cleaning the floors and walls.

I left the washrooms spick and span and dreaded what assignments were to come. However, during the day I had a brainwave. In the laundry upstairs there were huge sinks of water for washing the Sisters' clothing. I realized that rather than being wasted, this soapy water could be used to flush the toilet bowls. With the help of the girls in the laundry, I then filled four buckets of water and left them alongside the washrooms, with a terse note "Please use to flush toilet." All through the day I replenished the empty buckets.

The sisters were pleased and the morning ordeal of washroom duty was now a thing of the past. After two weeks, I began to look forward to a change of chores. Sister Bennett summoned me. "Sister Mercy, everyone is so happy with the way you maintain the washrooms, and with such graciousness, that I have decided you will continue until you leave Ooty."

I smiled and left. Some in the community felt I was treated unfairly. But I took a sense of pride in the task. I had risen above the others; I had taken on a challenge and surmounted it. Very soon, it was not pity that I elicited but well-earned respect. By the end of my time at Ooty, I had endeared myself to the community because, as at Stella Maris, I had entered so wholeheartedly into community life. I prepared to return to the plains of Madras, back to my beloved Stella Maris. There I would continue to teach and be involved in university life.

FINAL VOWS

Back at Stella Maris, my first duty was to prepare myself assiduously for my final vows. I informed my beloved mother of the ceremony scheduled to take place in a few months. She in turn got in touch with my seven siblings and insisted that representatives from every family be present.

As the officiating Priest at the chapel of Stella Maris intoned the Latin chant *"Veni Sponsa Christi,"* the three of us – Sister Teresa, Sister Hilda and I – walked down the centre aisle. As in the past ceremonies, we would prostrate ourselves three times and kiss the chapel floor. An hour later, I would pronounce my vows of poverty, chastity and obedience. A crown of thorns would be placed on my head and a silver ring, with the inscription *"Ecce Ancilla Domini,"* would be slipped onto the ring finger on my right hand. The crown of thorns would signify my identity with Christ and His Passion, and would be placed on my pillow on my bed – a reminder that my life was now totally intertwined with that of my Lord and Saviour Jesus Christ. The ring signified that I was now a Spouse of Christ forever.

✣ Sister Angela Hurley (left) at Mercy's Final Vows (2nd from left, 1969)

My mother shed tears of joy all through the ceremony. The chapel was packed to capacity with Sisters, family and friends. I spent the remainder of the day with my family. After tea, my family members, about twenty-five in all, gathered outside the chapel to bid farewell to me. Sister Angela, my Superior, was with us, having a friendly chat, when one of the Sisters approached her and handed her an envelope that looked like a telegram. She opened it, looked serious, but then immediately broke out in a smile.

"Are your final vows final? – Love Earl," she intoned, looking at me with a mischievous smile and winking. The message was clear to my mother and siblings – Sister Angela was well aware of my problem. My mother didn't think the telegram was amusing. The others felt reassured that I had made my commitment with maturity and wholeheartedness.

My family left and I turned towards the convent that was now going to be my home forever. Within a short while, it would be the Christmas vacation. As the Economics Department Head at Stella Maris, I was scheduled to leave for Delhi to attend a two-week convention on centralized planning, the heart of India's socialist economy.

I left by train for the day-long ride to Delhi, traveling third-class. I was alone and had time to reflect on my commitment to Christ. There was no turning back. Earl's telegram indicated that he was still single. I didn't know his exact age, but I did know he was well into his thirties. I continued to pray for him. As usual, he danced in and out of my mind. I tried to stifle thoughts of him. Sometimes I succeeded, but often I did not.

After a tiring journey, I reached Delhi early in the morning.

Rules had changed and nuns were now no longer pampered with vehicles waiting to pick us up and drop us off at the convent. We were expected to find our own way, provided it wasn't too late at night. After a short rest, a shower and a hot meal, I left for Delhi University, where the convention was to be held for faculty from all over the country.

One evening, as a few of us were relaxing in the courtyard of one of the hostels, a faculty member who prided himself in his knowledge of astrology ventured into palm reading. Everyone else congregated around him while I sat far away watching the proceedings. My Roman Catholic faith prevented me from dabbling in any such dealings.

"Sister, may I read your palm?" asked Mr. Koshi. "No thank you." But by now he had risen from his chair and was seated next to me. Despite my protestations, he took hold of my right hand and held my palm right in front of his eyes. I did not want to be impolite. "You have made a commitment, haven't you?" he asked with assurance. Astounded, I could only nod yes. "Before three years are over, you will break your commitment," he continued. "Why would I?" I responded. "I don't know," he said simply.

My head reeled. I whispered a prayer and all that I could say was, "Oh, my God, Thy will be done."

Six

HEARTBREAK

EARL WAS AN IDEALIST. He was consistent. He was principled. He knew he had it in him to charm, even to woo the woman of his dreams, even if she did wear a habit. But he was as pragmatic as he was passionate. So he took Doris' advice and decided to look elsewhere for romance. In a short while, he would meet Penny Woolworth, the daughter of an Englishman who had abandoned her mother soon after Penny was born.

The moment Earl set his eyes on her, he was enamoured of her brown eyes, alabaster skin and shapely legs. As time went on and weeks turned into months, Earl noticed there was something elusive about Penny. One day he confronted her. Was there something wrong? "Yes," she replied. "I already have a man in my life, off and on – Dennis Alvarez." Earl understood her dilemma. He would continue to shower her with gifts and affection with one purpose in mind – to wean her away from Dennis.

Doris, always the respected elder sister, was convinced that Penny was playing games. "Earl," she would say, "she's not the girl for you." Earl, now a well-established businessman, was considered "a catch" and Doris felt that Penny was more in love with his money than with him. Dennis had an airline job that took him out of the country often; during these times, she would go out with Earl. At a certain point, Penny informed Earl that in a few days she would be leaving with her mother, aunt and Dennis for New Zealand. Earl was devastated. On the day of Penny's flight, he begged her to stay behind. "I'll go for a short visit and return," she replied. But Earl knew this was an impossible situation to accept.

As Earl drove away from Penny's house, he realized with some sorrow that over the past eight months he had learned to love her. Doris was busy getting dinner ready when Earl appeared, placed his head on her strong shoulder and wept. She whispered in his ear, "You deserve a girl who will give you unconditional love." Earl had watched Doris and Claude closely over the years. They had few material comforts but were a close-knit family with six children, and Earl dreamed of some day having similar joys. Claude was not surprised about the news of Penny's departure. With his characteristic humour, he consoled his brother. "Don't worry; there are many beautiful women out there. You can easily rope in one of them!"

On his way home, Earl drove to church, as was his practice in difficult times, and talked to his God. The following morning, he welcomed the new day with a sense of peace. A decision had been made. In a few months, he received a wedding invitation from New Zealand and sent Penny and Dennis his good wishes.

Earl was now in his mid-thirties. He decided it was time to move out of his sister Verna's house and live on his own. After Holy Mass one morning, he inquired of one of the older members of the congregation if she knew of a place to rent. He was in luck; one of her good friends owned a building and was looking for someone to rent the second floor. Soon after, Earl moved into an eight hundred-square-foot flat, which he furnished with pride. It was now his home. Although he continued to date, he also found time to travel, notably to Japan, Hong Kong, Thailand and

Singapore.

The succeeding years proved to be an increasingly intense time for Earl's business. As tenders were floated by the central government, he had to conform to the protocol. He would quote for the contracts and then submit the links for the routine firing test. He traveled several times a year to the capital city of Delhi to meet with army personnel. It was on one such trip that he met a young woman who had a profound effect on him.

A CHANCE ENCOUNTER

In May 1971, Earl was singing the "South Pacific" hit *Some Enchanted Evening* to a newfound love, whom he had met just a few hours earlier. In his rich, full-throated baritone voice, he was also singing the praises of Sheila Thornton, an American blonde whom he had spotted at the Delhi airport. Earl, a relatively short person, was attracted to women of about his height and Sheila fit the bill. Fortunately for him, he was assigned a seat next to her on the flight back to Bombay. Seated in the same row was a Russian technocrat by the window, with Sheila in the middle and Earl on the aisle. Both men competed for her attention. To Earl's satisfaction, she seemed more interested in him. Knowing that her flight back to the U.S. was later that same night, he invited her to dinner. She accepted.

He left Sheila in the Bombay airport lobby and rushed home to shower and shave. He then returned to the airport to take her to the restaurant of a five-star hotel called the Sun and Sand. There, by the pool, Earl wined and dined her with the sound of the waves dashing against the rocks, a clear blue sky above their heads, and the tropical red sun setting in the horizon.

They spoke of their individual lives and yearnings. Sheila appreciated his openness. She was a small-town girl from New York State who exuded an aura of simplicity. She had a high school education, was twenty-eight years old, and held a simple office job. There was so much chemistry between them that for a moment, Earl felt he had at long last met the woman of his dreams – a soul mate.

Earl suggested that Sheila try some seafood, perhaps oysters. This was followed by a steak dinner. She wasn't exceptionally beautiful. What was it then? Perhaps it was her blond hair and blue eyes that were so alluring. Like most Anglo-Indians, Earl believed these physical characteristics were a template of social status and power. Sheila, for her part, had never met such a romantic man. She had fallen in love instantly with Earl. More mature, he felt it was probably just infatuation. He would wait and see.

As they took their leave at the airport, he slipped his business card into her hand, and asked her to keep in touch. He made it clear that she would have to take the initiative. Earl was tempted to kiss her, but refrained. He turned around to take one last look at the woman who had captured his heart and, with strangely heavy steps, made his way to his car. Sometimes an exciting encounter can have dark shadows, he thought. He knew, however, that what bound them together went beyond "chance." He had fallen in love with Sheila.

Earl quietly returned to his flat, stopping at the church and whispering, "Thy will be done!" He prayed and put his trust in God. He would tell no one yet of this chance meeting. He knew enough from his own experience to let events take their course without building expectations.

Somewhat to his surprise, Earl received a letter from Sheila within ten days. She was in love. All she wanted was to return to India and share his life. Earl responded immediately. He shared the same thoughts and feelings she had expressed. His everyday life in the past few months before he met her had been dull and drab. Enthusiastically, he too hurled head on into this new relationship. He made it clear that she had become his beacon of hope, a woman who could set the course of his future endeavours. It was equally clear to both of them that he was suggesting that she become his wife. They had spent a total of six hours together – but the meeting was magical. Earl mailed his letter and immediately made arrangements with a florist to have a large bouquet of flowers delivered to Sheila's home.

Over the following three months, letters, cards, flowers and photographs would cross the oceans. Sometimes as many as three letters from Sheila awaited Earl in his mailbox all on the same day. Never in his adult years had he encountered such passion. As though to keep her presence alive, she enclosed photographs of herself with notes attached in each letter. One such note summed up her feelings towards Earl: "To my only Love – I miss you so much, Sweetheart. How much I want to be with you." It was time now for Earl to share this happiness, first with his mother and then with the rest of the family.

Finally, the day arrived when he received the news he was desperately waiting for – Sheila had packed her bags and would be arriving in Bombay in less than a week. In mid-August 1971, Earl, accompanied by Doris, Verna, Claude and Bihari, went to the airport to welcome Sheila. Earl had brought with him a bouquet of red roses. As Sheila entered the waiting area, she spotted Earl and rushed into his arms. They kissed passionately. She was then introduced to the other members of his family. Doris and Claude were somewhat disappointed. Earl had dated far more beautiful women. They recognized, however, that he seemed to be a very happy man.

Earl drove Sheila to his flat, where she would stay with him. She had visited India twice before as a tourist, but now she had returned to make her home here. The crowded streets, the suffocating traffic, the swollen crowds of people were all shocking sights. But she would weather it all – she had left America because she wanted to spend the rest of her life with this man. Earl told her that once they were married, he would purchase a larger flat. Her input, he assured her, would be essential in the purchase.

After dinner, he drove her to meet his mother and his sister Christabelle. His mother was overjoyed. At long last, she thought, her son had met his soul mate. Her prayers had been answered. If there were anything in life she wanted, it was to see this son of hers happily married.

Earl took great pains to introduce Sheila to his way of life. Every morning, he participated in Holy Mass and Communion and every night he said his prayers. He did not believe in pre-marital sex and suggested they wait until their wedding night. Sheila, brought up as an Episcopalian, began to accompany Earl to Holy Mass. Earl was encouraged when one day she mentioned that she would like to convert to Roman Catholicism.

With this end in view, he introduced her to a learned Jesuit priest he knew. Sheila would attend instruction five times a week. Earl accompanied her on these occasions and later in the evening they would discuss the teachings together. Sheila showed no resentment toward the changes she was making in her life. On the contrary, both she and Earl seemed to want to belong to each other completely.

MARRIAGE ON THE HORIZON

It was now time to plan the engagement. Earl invited Sheila to join him on a trip to the jewelers' district in the heart of Bombay. There he asked her to choose whichever ring suited her fancy. Wide-eyed, Sheila looked at the array of rings. A cluster of eleven diamonds caught her eye and Earl bought it for her. Coming from small-town America, Sheila had never in her wildest dreams imagined the possibility of wearing such an expensive ring. They would now fix the date of the engagement and the wedding date. The engagement would be held on October 22 and the wedding on December 11.

Earl invited his extended family and a few friends, about thirty people in all, to his flat. In the presence of a Roman Catholic priest, Earl slipped the diamond ring on Sheila's finger. For a moment, their worlds stood still. Earl was at last engaged. He was thirty-nine years old. He and Sheila felt that they were meant for each other. Before the end of the evening, Earl would once again sing *Some Enchanted Evening* – this time to his fiancée. Life itself could not have been more enchanting.

‡ Engagement Ring

With the wedding only six weeks hence, Earl vowed he would

spare no effort to give Sheila the most beautiful ceremony she could hope for. The reception would be held on the lawns of Bihari and Verna's home for one hundred and fifty guests. Strangely, there was to be no representative from Sheila's family or friends in the United States. Perhaps the India of the 1970s was forbidding to small-town Americans. Perhaps they were bewildered that their daughter had decided to marry a man she had known for a comparatively short period of time. Earl later acknowledged that he knew very little about her family nor, curiously, did he care to find out more.

The wedding invitations were simple but tasteful, printed on bond. The ivory paper bore a pretty blue rectangle with a motif of two rings intertwined. Earl sent me one addressed in his own hand.

Soon after, Earl began to plan the honeymoon. He was going to take Sheila to the most exotic places India boasts: the Kashmiri Valley, Simla, Chandigarh, Delhi and Pahalgam. Sheila set about choosing her wedding gown of light chiffon inlaid with paisley-shaped lace. Sheila wanted the wedding announced in the local newspaper of her hometown. With Verna's help, she donned her wedding gown and went to the studio to have a formal portrait taken. The photograph was to accompany the announcement of her marriage to a well-established Bombay industrialist and was published in her local newspaper during the third week of November.

A few weeks after the engagement, Doris noticed something amiss with her brother-in-law. "Is everything alright, Earl?" she queried. "Yes Mrs. A." (his affectionate nickname for her.) Doris was not convinced. To her, it was apparent that cracks in the relationship had begun to surface. Earl was realizing that Sheila was not all that he had imagined in a future wife. She was an "elementary" person, he decided. He loved her deeply but beyond the physical, there was little else they shared.

At times, Earl felt as though he had just peered into the abyss of her deep-seated insecurities, causing him to draw back in fear. He began to realize that he would never be able to share his innermost feelings and thoughts with Sheila. Furthermore, she manifested traits that he disliked. She drank too much Coke and lived on potato chips except when they dined with his mother or went out for dinner. When he discreetly tried to remind her that this was not healthy, she was stung. "Oh! That's what I loved to eat back home." To a proud Indian, this was irksome. And her cooking methods were inefficient in the eyes of her engineer fiancé.

But these were minor irritations. The major issue was her inability to engage in sensible discourse. As days turned into weeks, this incompatibility became all the more evident. Beneath the layers of her willingness to adapt, beneath her pleasant laughter, there seemed to be an inability to openly communicate, an inability to touch her future husband's soul.

Sheila, for her part, began to feel totally inadequate. As she got to know Earl better, she realized that here was a gifted engineer with a brilliant mind. He was highly opinionated and articulate. His was a mind she could never emulate. She would never be able to share an intelligent, well-informed conversation with him.

Despite their differences, Earl tried to reorder his own value system and made every effort to triumph over his cold intellect with some degree of emotional intelligence. He tried to stifle the engineer in himself and use compassion rather than traditional logic. He tried hard to draw from the example of the married life of his parents.

His father shared no intellectual companionship with his mother, yet they had a successful marriage. He had rarely heard his parents discuss issues beyond domestic concerns. But then they had lived in a different era. Perhaps, Earl thought, he was being naïve, unrealistic and purely sentimental. He cared for Sheila deeply and she reciprocated these feelings. However, compounding these feelings of anxiety there was yet a series of unexpected events unravelling before them. In late November 1971 there were rumblings of war between India and Pakistan. The U.S. an ally of Pakistan was now an enemy of India and there was a growing fear that U.S. citizens may be instructed to leave India. Earl feared that Sheila to whom he was engaged and about to marry on December 11 could be asked to leave the country. They therefore decided to immediately enter into a civil marriage and Sheila seek Indian citizenship.

To this end Earl and Sheila drove to Verna and Bihari's home where the civil marriage was to be held. Earl dropped off Sheila and continued on his two minute drive to pick up Mr. Gonsalves the Justice of Peace who was to officiate at the civil ceremony.

However, on this two minute drive, Earl was literally jolted with the conviction which he later termed "a divine intervention". On arriving at the home of Mr. Gonsalves, Earl announced he had decided not to go ahead with the civil nuptials.

He returned to Verna's home and informed Sheila and other family members of his decision. Sheila made no comment. This lack of discourse was a forerunner of what was yet to come.

This was manifested in the fact that the great joy he had shared with Sheila when she first arrived was now turning into tension, even sadness. The picture of married life Earl had dreamed about was changing. As he looked into his future, his projections were bleak. His greatest solace was prayer. From the time he had met Sheila, he had prayed that God would guide him. Quietly, with Sheila at his side, he would continue with the marriage preparations. There were, after all, only ten days left before the wedding.

As the day approached, Earl realized that he needed to discuss these differences with his prospective wife. But he hesitated, bowing to an inner fear that Sheila was too fragile to handle such a situation. Instead, he would put his trust in God and hope that with marriage they would be able to overcome these hurdles together.

Over a cup of tea with Doris, Sheila talked openly about her fears. In her view, Earl was so set in his ways that she wondered whether she could ever become the wife he dreamed of. Doris, in her wisdom, thanked Sheila for sharing this with her and promised to keep her in her prayers. The only person Doris shared this conversation with was her husband Claude. They decided that together they would pray for Earl and Sheila and tell Earl nothing about it. They knew he was aware of these problems and they had full faith in his judgment.

On December 4, exactly a week before the wedding, Earl, tears in his eyes, walked into Doris' kitchen. "Sheila is gone!" he exclaimed. "I found a note and the engagement ring on the dining table when I returned from work. She said that she couldn't marry me. She gave no reasons."

"Perhaps it's all for the best, Earl," comforted Doris, adding that Sheila had spoken to her about her fears of the approaching marriage. At the office, a subdued Earl broke the news to Bihari and Claude, and later that day to his mother, who was almost as heartbroken at the news as he was.

At a family dinner that same evening, some strong opinions were voiced. Bihari was livid. Perhaps she had run away from Earl because India was at war with Pakistan, an ally of the United States. Doris mentioned Sheila's doubts about being a suitable wife for Earl. Earl himself was too devastated to comment. It was decided that a note would be sent to all the guests announcing that the wedding was "postponed." Earl still harboured a faint hope that Sheila would return to him.

A few days later, Earl walked into his office to find a letter from Sheila. She now wanted to return to India, yet gave no reasons for her departure. Earl was filled with mixed feelings. Sheila still seemed to be the affectionate, guileless person whom he had so taken to, and yet he knew increasingly she was not the person he could find happiness with. Sitting on the steps of St. Theresa's Church that evening, he said to himself: "If I must carry this cross, I'll bear it." He replied to her entreaty for reconciliation and welcomed her back.

Not long afterwards, in mid-December 1971, Earl's secretary handed him a letter. Although he didn't recognize the handwriting, the sender's address with "Stella Maris College" was written on the envelope. Earl was surprised beyond belief. It started with, "My very dear Earl." His mind began to race: "It is Mercy, she's writing to me."

She had heard about the postponement of his wedding and that he was devastated, and she was writing to console him. The first two paragraphs were soul-lifting. He had to stop reading. The first few paragraphs had already given him an insight into the writer's mind. It was of a higher dimension – a level that, sadly, he knew Sheila would never attain.

Despite the crisis in his personal life, Earl had not neglected his engineering business. That very evening, he was due to take the train to a military base in Verangoan, where his cartridge links were due for firing tests. In a few hours, he was on the train for the night-long journey.

He would now reread the two-page letter and savour every word the writer had written. Mercy had revealed how much she cared for him and, in her caring, had always prayed that he would find happiness. Despite her efforts to be dispassionate, she evinced a passion that was so raw and so genuine that it penetrated his soul. As he read on, he was able to discern that she maintained a lasting love for him – something she didn't explicitly write about, but which became evident at this time of his life as she empathized with him. She seemed to exhibit an unclouded happiness in her missionary calling, little knowing that she herself had unwittingly bared an unfulfilled longing. He read the letter a third time and decided to sleep on it. He would handle his response when his duties at Verangoan were completed.

During the following day, Earl was in and out of the firing field of testing. Other competitors' links were also being tested. The verdict came in the evening: his links had passed the test, surpassing all specifications. His company would be awarded a contract with the Indian Army.

Afterwards, he said a prayer of thanks and got ready for dinner and his response to the letter from Mercy. Dining on the lawns of the guesthouse, Earl sat at the table. The sound of crickets burst through the torrid air, while the smell of jasmine wafted through the breeze. Fireflies glistened; the setting sun sent rays of mellow light that embraced him. The Acacia trees rocked in unison.

He pulled out his letter pad and put his pen to paper. "Dearest Mercy," he began. Then he told her of his deep love for her ever since he had brought her the trigonometry textbook almost two decades earlier. Her simple demeanour had impressed him. Turning to his meeting with her when she returned from the United States as a young nun of twenty-seven, he confessed how much he was taken with her vibrant looks and brilliant mind. Never had he spent a more exhilarating evening with a woman, he swore!

However, he continued, he had reluctantly felt obliged to let go of his dreams. She was, after all, a consecrated virgin to the Lord. He had realized that she was the person who could be "all things" to him, but he dared not go to that place from which he had stayed away for so long, for "where she dwelt was hallowed ground!" He was afraid that if he ventured forth, there would be shattering, soul-wrenching disappointment on both their parts. So he would keep away. "Knowing how I feel about you and how you feel about me, what more can I say except that God's will be done. With love, Earl."

Christmas of 1971 was painful. Earl missed Sheila's presence. After all, he had hoped that this would be their first Christmas as man and wife. But she had promised to return in the New Year. He would go to the Christmas and New Year dances without an escort.

He prayed that this was the last year he would have to go alone.

In January, with Sheila set to arrive in a few days, Earl would start a novena to the Infant Jesus of Prague on nine consecutive Saturdays at a nearby church. This was a devotion that attracted several hundred devotees every week. Catholics, Hindus, Sikhs and Parsees all flocked to the church. Earl prayed to the Infant Jesus that, now that Sheila was returning, he would be guided in his decisions. Yet he was still confused regarding her incipient return. A duality presented itself: Sheila was clearly not the woman he wanted to spend the rest of his life with; Mercy, seemingly out of nowhere, now embodied his hopes and dreams, unattainable though she was. He would wait and pray for God's will to unfold.

Sheila brought with her Tupperware sets, detergents not available in India and recipe books. Earl noticed these items and was happy. Evidently, she was determined to fulfill the role of a suitable wife. Ominously, the pair would never discuss why she had left in the first place. For his part, Earl did what he thought was expected of him. He encouraged Sheila to talk openly, hoping thereby he could help her erode the stigma of her failed attempts to make their relationship work. Sometimes he thought he had succeeded, but more often her distant look disturbed him. Despite these dark clouds, the couple resumed their former lifestyle: daily Mass, dinner with his mother, restaurants, weekend picnics, dancing in the evenings.

Sheila seemed content. But as weeks passed, Doris still noticed a troubled look in Earl's eyes. With each day, he seemed more bewildered. The initial exuberance that Doris observed at the time of the engagement had evaporated. It looked as though he were haunted by phantoms of uncertainty, of confusion, of meaninglessness. He walked as a man without a soul. Doris would confide this to Claude. They prayed. They waited.

On February 12, Doris held a fiftieth birthday party for her husband Claude on the apartment terrace. Dancing had always been one of Earl's delights, but on this occasion he held back. The morning afterwards, a friend telephoned Doris. "Is Earl really happy? He seemed so distant last evening. Is he really planning to marry that girl?" Doris was troubled. "I don't know," she replied. "I hope he makes the right decision."

ANOTHER TURN OF THE WHEEL

Very soon, it would be March 4, the last of the nine Saturdays of Earl's novena to the Infant Jesus. Mercy's face kept surfacing constantly. He had begun to realize that it was she and only she who would ultimately fulfill his dreams. From the only letter he had ever received from her, he realized that he had become mesmerized by thoughts of her. Fortunately, he also realized that despite the distance and circumstances that separated them, he had become a constant in Mercy's life as well – unsanctioned yet persistent.

At the church, Earl prayed and placed his future in the Hands of the Lord. Despite his uncertainty, he planned to take Sheila out for dinner that evening to propose to her for the second time. He opened the door of his flat. "Sheila, Sheila I'm home." She would usually run to the door and kiss him. On that day, there was no sign of her. In a moment of déjà vu, he saw an envelope on the dining table and the engagement ring neatly placed on top of it. He said a prayer, opened the envelope and read the contents. For the second time, Sheila declared that she couldn't marry Earl. In her view, he deserved better. She was returning once again to the States.

March 4, 1972

Dearest Earl,

It breaks my heart to think you have to read this and know that I'm going back to the States tonight. I know you'll say that I'm homesick again, but this is not the case this time, for I've grown to consider this my home and the thought of leaving you kills me. You have made me so happy and I love you so much. But, because I love you so completely, I cannot marry you. Sometimes, like last night, you've seen tears in my eyes and wondered why. It was because in my heart I knew I was not worthy to be your wife. Please believe me when I say I love you above all else on earth and to have been your wife would have given me complete and marvelous happiness. But I love you enough to put your happiness before mine, and I want for you a woman whom you could be proud of. I will always love you.

Sheila

Earl would tell no one yet. He slipped out for dinner to a nearby restaurant, and then quietly returned to his flat. It was now clear that a new chapter had opened before him. Sheila's was closed forever. He recalled the sparks of the evening that Mercy and he had spent together five years earlier. He recalled her letter of a few weeks ago. He had a drink on his balcony and thought deeply about what could be after all these years. Facing the darkness of the night, he sat down at his desk to write:

> Dearest Mercy,
>
> Sheila has returned to the States for the second time. The relationship is over. I now turn to you and see you as my wife. We can have a great future together. I have been carrying your letter in my pocket for the past two months, even though Sheila was around. Your words "You have become a constant in my life" have been resonating all through this time. I know you have made your final commitment, but could it be that now it is time for you to pursue something that has always remained latent? Become my wife?
>
> I've always loved you, Mercy, and I know you have the same feelings for me. I have not seen you for the past five years, but I can still recall most vividly the ecstatic evening we spent together. Think about this and get back to me. Thank you for your letter of concern and your prayers during the past few months.
>
> God's will be done.
>
> With love,
> Earl

Seven

A CHALLENGE TO FACE

I RETURNED FROM DELHI with a deliberate and forceful desire to forget Mr. Koshi's prediction and focus on my vocation as a missionary nun. Astrology had never been encouraged by the Church.

I resolved to think instead about the content of the conference on central planning: I had returned with an obsessive need to focus on the failures of the market system, and as expected with no corresponding list of reasons to celebrate its success. Over the next few years, my life was focused on prayer and meditation, teaching, spiritual growth, retreats, conventions and student affairs. No wonder I put in seventeen-hour days.

Even after I received the news from Claude that Earl was engaged, I was calm – at least until I received the wedding invitation. The envelope, written in Earl's own hand, immediately took me back to the note from him on the front page of the trigonometry textbook when I was a schoolgirl.

I was happy for him, but I also felt I was losing a part of my soul. On my way to teach a post-graduate lecture, I stepped into Sister Angela's office. From a distance of about three feet, I hastily threw the invitation on her table. "Problem solved," I said, as I dashed out.

Several times during that lecture, I imagined Earl walking down the aisle with his American-born wife. It was painful. Afterwards, I hurried to the chapel for Benediction and Divine Office. As I was walking up the stairs to my cell, Sister Angela beckoned me to her room. "Isn't this what you always wanted for him?" she asked.

As tears welled up in my eyes, I rushed upstairs. It was a Thursday night and I always tried to make the Holy Hour. This was an hour of deep prayer from 11:00 p.m., before the Blessed Sacrament, a wafer consecrated during Holy Mass, which Roman Catholics believe is transubstantiated into the Body of Christ. The Blessed Sacrament is therefore the real presence of Jesus Christ.

I went to the chapel and thanked God that Earl at last was getting married. I prayed that I would have the courage to "let go." Ever since I had entered the convent, I was guided in my religious growth by prayer on the events of my everyday life. I had learned to listen to my God speak to me through these reflections. I remembered my Novice Mistress's advice that "a seeker is one who in her restlessness searches after the light until she eventually finds it." At midnight, I returned to my cell and made a note on my calendar. For December 11, I wrote "Earl's wedding."

A FURTHER DEVELOPMENT

On December 15, I privately celebrated the anniversary of my entrance into religious life. All the major events in that life had taken place on this date. Two years had passed since I had made my final vows. Stopping by my mailbox, I found a small envelope. Again, I recognized Earl's handwriting. All I found inside was a small card with the printed announcement: "Earl and Sheila regret to announce the postponement of their wedding."

My gut reaction was a sense of relief. Once again, I went to the chapel and bent my head in prayer. I saw a vivid picture in my mind of Earl and me – he looking radiantly handsome, I dressed as a bride. After chapel, I rushed to Sister Angela, the person in whom I had complete faith and trust. I gave her the card. "What!" she exclaimed. "It must be the war with Pakistan." Later, in my cell, I wrote in consolation "wedding postponed" for December 11.

I had work to do other than ruminate on the postponement of Earl's wedding. The university exams were to be held in a few months and the students had to be prepared for this grueling task. Claude soon wrote to tell me that Earl was devastated. Sheila had returned to her home in the United States, giving no explanation. He wondered whether I could write to comfort Earl.

As always with important decisions, I would first consult Sister Angela. As a Sister Superior, she was never coercive or overbearing and always extended an invitation for discussion. She was serene in her response to my question. "If that's what you feel, go ahead. Write him a letter." Such was her faith in the judgment of the sisters in her charge.

I quietly sat at my desk and took a sheet of paper from the Stella Maris letter pad. It carried the official logo of the college: a ship out at sea tossed by waves with a shining star guiding it. This star was meant to be the Blessed Virgin Mary, the Mother of Jesus Christ, and Stella Maris, translated from the Latin, means *"Star of the Sea."* I certainly felt tossed in a sea of confusion, and turned to the Virgin for guidance.

"My very dear Earl," I began, and then stated how deeply sorry I was that his wedding had been postponed and that his fiancée had returned home. I empathized with him. After all, I confessed, he had become part of my everyday existence after I had seen him again five years earlier, following my return from the States.

I went on to say that I had mixed feelings about his engagement, feelings of joy that at last he was getting married, but also of pain. I was now moving into uncharted territory. Was it wisdom or folly to confide in him? It was my heart, not my head that was now motivating me to continue. Was it a ruse to let him know how much I cared for him? I didn't know.

The words flowed, the sentences were structured, the paragraphs built. By the end of the hour, I had completed the letter. "I must frankly confess that over the years you have become a constant in my life. I have tried very hard to relegate you to the recesses of my heart – but with very little success. With every passing year and news of a new woman in your life – I've had mixed feelings – feelings of both joy and sorrow. Joy that perhaps you have found a soul mate who will bring you happiness, and sorrow that 'I must let go.' It's strange that despite the fact that I am a fully committed and consecrated religious nun, these thoughts should surface – but they do."

I read and reread the contents. They were words that bared my soul. It was clear that for a long time I had nurtured a strong attraction for Earl – an unwarranted attraction, given my vows, but real nonetheless. It was also clear from my letter that despite the separation, despite the distance and despite the silence, he had become a world of love to me. Regardless of my efforts to the contrary, he continued to be a reality I desperately tried to dissipate with little success. I did state that my commitment to my religious calling was total and final. I was willing to live with unfulfilled dreams of a life with him as long as he found happiness with another woman.

STELLA MARIS COLLEGE
MADRAS-600 086

S. India
18th Dec 1971

My very dear Earl

A few days ago I received a letter from Claude informing me that Sheila had returned to the States. Prior to that I received your formal announcement of the postponement of your wedding. From Claude's letter I have come to realize that you are devastated that Sheila had decided to return home a week before the wedding.

I can empathize with you dear Earl. All these years I have thought about you many a time & hoped and prayed that somehow you would meet the woman who would bring you happiness — something you so richly deserve. I had hoped Sheila was this woman! But God's ways are not our ways! Often it looks as though He leads us on in the pursuit of an objective only to leave us in the lurch — totally abandoned & confused. I guess you are in this situation now. Don't lose heart. You can count on my thoughts & prayers.

I must frankly confess that over the years you have become a constant in my life.

✣ Mercy's Letter to Earl, page 1 (1971)

I have tried so very hard to relegate you to the recesses of my heart – but with very little success. With every passing year & with news of a new woman in your life – I've had mixed feelings – feelings of both joy & sorrow. Joy that perhaps you have found your soulmate who would bring you happiness & sorrow that "I must let go". It's strange that despite the fact that I am a fully committed & consecrated religious nun, these thoughts should still surface – but they do.

I still remember fondly the evening we spent together when I had just returned from the States. It was an exciting, magical & meaningful experience. I know it was the same for you.

I will be leaving sometime in January to work as a volunteer in the Salt Lake Camp not far away from the city of Calcutta. I will be away from Stella Maris for about three weeks.

In the meantime take care of yourself & keep ~~trusting~~ in ~~the~~ Lord. Merry Christmas & all the best in the New Year! You will be in my thoughts & prayers always. God bless you my very dear Earl. Keep in touch

Sr. Mercy J.m.m.

‡ Mercy's Letter to Earl, page two (1971)

In a few days, I had his reply. In no uncertain words, he revealed that he too shared my feelings. He also had news. He had heard from Sheila again; she was coming back to India in a few weeks. On one hand, he said, he wanted her back; but on the other, he had doubts about their compatibility. In fact, he confessed, she had become "a cross" to carry; "a millstone" around his neck.

The news of Sheila's impending return, he went on, brought him both pain and happiness. He felt impelled by a desire to have her back. He surmised that perhaps she could be a suitable mate for him, and this hope buoyed him. He asked for my prayers that he be guided to what was good and right. Although he had profound feelings for Sheila, there was also fear and anxiety. He was afraid, he said, that by marrying her he would be missing his truest goal in life: marital bliss. His greatest solace was his trust in God. He believed in the intervention of His Creator. He believed in the guidance of the Holy Spirit. God would show him the truth and through discernment the road to the fulfilment of his innermost desires.

Earl displayed such a strong faith in God that I was consoled by the knowledge that whatever the future held in store, it would be in accordance with the Holy will of God. He concluded: "Knowing how I feel about you and how you feel about me, what more should I say except that God's will be done; with love, Earl."

I tucked the letter into a folder. I would read and reread it a few times more during the coming week. Every time I did so, I whispered a prayer that God's will be done. I would ask myself several times how I could possibly harmonize all the feelings that had been brought out in the past few days. My strong feelings for Earl, his for me, his strong doubts about Sheila – it was all absurd. Yet through it all, I believed God would weave a good and beautiful outcome. He was after all a perfect Being who would in keeping with His revelations give meaning not only to absurdity, but as well to the yearnings of a loving human heart.

SALT LAKE CAMP

The beginning of 1972 brought another kind of challenge into my life. East Pakistan had separated from West Pakistan and a new country – Bangladesh – had been carved. Many citizens had been displaced, and hundreds of thousands of refugees from East Pakistan were pouring into the State of Bengal. Salt Lake Camp alone housed two hundred thousand refugees. Volunteers were needed.

Sister Christine and I, together with two other faculty members and a team of student volunteers, would board the train and undertake the arduous journey to Calcutta in the northeast of India. It was a thirty-six hour ride across the east coast of the subcontinent. But we were a dedicated band of volunteers, prepared to undertake any task, no matter how daunting.

We arrived at the teeming camp situated on the outskirts of the city. Amenities were the bare minimum. Tents were pitched on the soaking mud and most people slept on thin sheets. On arriving at the camp, we were shown our quarters: fabricated, makeshift dormitories of corrugated iron and asbestos ceilings. No running water, no fans. Sister Christine and I would share a curtained-off space and sleep on primitive cots. But it was far more accommodating than what the refugees had.

After a short nap, we were assigned our various duties. I was given the geriatric ward – a large room with rows of cots. Many of these patients were suffering from tuberculosis, dehydration from diarrhea, malaria and other water- and air-borne diseases. Volunteers were each given a pair of gloves and a mask. I was assigned five student volunteers, who would help me administer medical aid under the expert supervision of two volunteer medical doctors. We had 120 old people under our care. Most were incontinent and dehydrated. We did our best to nurse them back to health.

Our daily routine started at 5:00 a.m. with Holy Mass and Communion. A breakfast of bread, tea and a banana followed. We worked until noon, when we broke for lunch – usually rice, lentils and vegetables. A short rest period followed. Sister Christine and I usually said our Divine Office during this time. Then we were back on our wards, where we worked until 6:00 p.m. The supper menu was invariably the same as lunch. Afterwards, we helped out for another hour. Recreation followed.

We met volunteers from around the country and the world. We sang folk songs accompanied by guitars; others danced. Beneath the starlit skies, we were, somehow, a happy lot, giving of ourselves generously without counting the cost.

One elderly refugee under my care was Prakash, whose body was wasting away from tuberculosis. He was in the last stages of his illness. I watched helplessly, knowing that little could be done to lessen his suffering. All we could do was to put him on strong painkillers and wait. About a week after our arrival, he passed away. I will never forget the reaction of his son, a young man in his twenties who had sat expressionless by his father's bedside all day. As he watched his father breathe his last, he stood up, placed his right hand on the eyelids of his dead father, closed them and quietly walked away. He didn't utter a word to anyone. As he walked down the long aisle, it became clear to all of us that it wasn't sadness but relief that characterized his gait. He never once looked back at us.

A patient named Lakshmi had an insatiable appetite. All day long, she cried for food. I wondered why she was in the ward of ill seniors because she was not old, nor did she appear ill. One morning as I was making my rounds, I discovered she was not in her bed. I enquired from the lady next to her as to what had happened. She whispered in a low voice that Lakshmi had passed away during the night and that her body was removed for burial early in the morning. I was shocked. Nothing seemed to have been wrong with her.

To my surprise and consternation, I found Lakshmi back in her bed the next morning. One of the volunteers told me that Lakshmi had gone into shock and was motionless. An orderly, thinking she had passed away, wrapped her body in a plastic sheet and dumped it in his truck together with the other dead. As was the practice in the camp, huge pits were dug where the dead were buried. As Lakshmi's body was dumped in the pit, her screams were heard. Quickly they retrieved her and drove her back to the ward. In a few days, Lakshmi was well enough to be discharged and happy to make the trek to her new country of Bangladesh.

At the end of three weeks, it was time for us to leave the camp. I was afraid of my own reactions once I returned to life at the convent. I had every reason to be: I had just experienced a truly ghastly picture of suffering. The refugees we were leaving behind at the Salt Lake Camp faced deprivation of a new dimension. Stateless, homeless and deprived of the basic necessities of life, they were a bitter reminder of what war does to the human person. These people were the spoils of war; voiceless and desperate; the collateral damage of a painful political process. Our lessons learned, and our experiences tucked away for the time being, we boarded the train and returned to the familiar and comforting confines of Stella Maris.

On my arrival, there was once again a letter from Earl awaiting me. Sheila was now back in India. "Pray for me," he said. "May God show me the path." I put the letter away into my folder and did as he requested.

Back to my routine of prayer, meditation, university teaching and the challenges of my missionary and teaching vocation, I was kept busy. Those of us who had volunteered at the refugee camp were also called upon by various groups to share our experiences.

In the midst of all this activity, yet another letter arrived from Earl telling me that Sheila had ended their relationship, and that he now felt free to ask me to become his wife. "I've always loved you, Mercy, and I know you have the same feelings for me," he wrote. "I have not seen you for the past five years, but I can still recall most vividly the ecstatic evening we spent together."

In the chapel, I asked, "What is your will for me, O Lord?" My innermost feelings were my deepest love for Earl, something I had learned to live with for the last fifteen years. I had made my final commitment, in good faith, to live as a nun in accordance with the vows of poverty, chastity and obedience, and I believed I could not break that commitment. I had done everything humanly possible to sublimate my thoughts of a life with Earl. But I now realized I was fighting a losing battle.

I kept the letter in my pocket for the rest of the evening, even taking it to the chapel for Divine Office at 8:00 p.m. As we filed out of the chapel, I whispered to Sister Angela that I wanted to see her. I showed her the letter. She seemed more concerned that Sheila had returned to the States for a second time than about Earl's blatant declaration of love. "Mercy, don't worry, this is expected! He's broken-hearted! It's a rebound."

I looked straight into her eyes. "You forget how much I love him, how much I have loved him, and how much I've prayed and wanted his happiness." To my ears, Earl sounded literally and figuratively sure of himself. His problem wasn't so much that he didn't analyze his own feelings, but rather that he was certain of what they were. He now felt compelled to act on them with utter confidence and determination.

Ever the understanding human being, Sister Angela realized how hard it was for me to grapple with these emotions. "I cannot reply to this letter immediately," I confessed. "But he will be waiting for a response. Can you do it for me? Tell him I have made my final commitment and the answer is no." She assured me she would write to him and to Claude. "Good night – try to get some sleep," she said. I pressed the letter into her hands and ascended the steps to my cell. I told her I didn't want to see the letter again.

Back in my cell, my head reeling, I knelt down to pray. "All I want is that your will be done, O Lord." Jesus now broke into my confused and pain-filled world. I somehow intuited that He was about to change the course of my life. I knew He would always be an integral part of my life. I would not have to walk alone.

The next morning, I whispered to Sister Christine that I had something to discuss with her. "What's it about, Earl again?" It had been ten years since we had stood on the deck of the *Flotta Laura* and I had told her of my deep love for Earl. How could she have known that the chapter would be reopened?

"I noticed a distant look in your eyes and was wondering whether Earl had re-entered your life," she said. "Don't be stupid! He'll find someone else. Remember, you've made your final vows." Somewhat chastened, I went back to my cell and got down to my lecture preparations. With the end of the academic year approaching, I tried to bury myself in my work.

Sister Angela informed me that she had written to both Earl and Claude. She felt that she needed Claude's help and cooperation so Earl could be supported and nurtured during this trying time. Claude had written to Sister Angela, assuring her that he would help his brother through this trying period. But he emphasized that the ultimate decision to leave or stay had to be mine and mine alone. Earl also replied to her, saying he was convinced that my love for him was strong enough to warrant me leaving the convent. However, he believed absolutely that God would show me His will.

EARL'S VISIT

March 31, 1972 has a special significance in my memory to this day. I was in my cell when the sister assigned to parlour duties informed me that there was a phone call for me. I rushed downstairs and picked up the receiver. "How are you?" asked Earl. "Can I come down to see you?" I hadn't heard his voice nor seen him in the past five years. "I'd have to ask Sister Angela," I responded excitedly. "Can you call me back in a half hour?"

Sister Angela looked up quizzically from her desk. "Earl phoned; he wants to come down and see me!" As was her custom, she turned the question around. "What do you feel?" "I'd love to see him!" I responded enthusiastically. "Then tell him to come down," she replied. As I turned to leave, she added in her dry Irish humor, "I too would love to meet him! He says he's forty years old. I wonder whether he's pot-bellied and bald!" She smiled her enigmatic smile.

I was standing on a dangerous precipice, hoping for a shared life with Earl, which I knew in the deepest precincts of my heart would bring me untold happiness. Yet I had to be true to my consecrated self: I knew I had to step back and take time to think and pray.

The next forty-eight hours was the longest period in my life. Good Friday and Holy Saturday are two of the holiest days in the Christian Calendar. I felt that I was able to truly identify myself with the Passion of Jesus Christ. I thought of Jesus Christ submerged in His own suffering. I faced not only the fear and folly of the cross, but also its mystical and impenetrable wonder and awe. For a moment I dared not listen to my cold and pragmatic mind but rather to the dictates of my loving heart – which over the recent months had somehow evolved into a true and trusting friend. Over the years, through my religious training, I had thought of myself as invincible. My mind had made me think of myself as a self-sufficient being. But today I humbly recognized the fact that I had become truly fragile – a vulnerable human being totally dependent on the merciful goodness of my Lord Jesus Christ.

On Good Friday, I waited patiently for God in His goodness to take over. This was the God of the Old Testament who had made a covenant with His people that He would never desert them. I felt His presence walking with me, suffering with me and enduring my pain. This was the day that I identified my suffering with that of Christ. My own suffering stood in parallel to His much greater suffering and death. In His suffering I felt reassured that with Him at my side there could be no darkenss, no turmoil.

In sheer abandon, I pursued my Lord Jesus knowing fully well that His light would guide me. To seek Him and to walk with Him was a sure path to peace and love. This clear path would now steady my faltering steps. Peace and love were now within my reach.

By now, many of the Sisters, especially those closest to me, were aware of my dilemma. They also knew of Earl's anticipated visit on Easter Sunday. The day arrived: April 2, 1972; later I would learn it was also his fortieth birthday. I was in my cell dressed in my formal attire, when Sister Leony informed me, "He's come." I rose from my chair, my legs faltering as I descended the steps leading from my cell to the hallway that led to the parlour. I stopped by Sister Angela's room. To my surprise, she said she had already met Earl. "You did?" I asked. "Yes, just after Mass. Go ahead. I'll be there in a little while."

I opened the door and gazed into the verandah. After five years, Earl seemed not to have aged. At forty, he still had a thick mop of black hair, his teeth were as beautiful as ever and his physique was perfect. He looked tanned and toned. I later learned that his daily jogging and training with a Bullworker had kept him trim. He was dressed in an impeccably tailored suit and sported a knowing smile.

He looked at me, still wearing his dark glasses. Suddenly, he took them off and gave me a hard, confused look. I wondered why. I ushered him into the parlour, a sparsely furnished lounge. We sat on two separate chairs and momentarily held hands tightly. We looked at each other. There was nothing untoward or off limits in that gaze – just pure admiration and longing for each other.

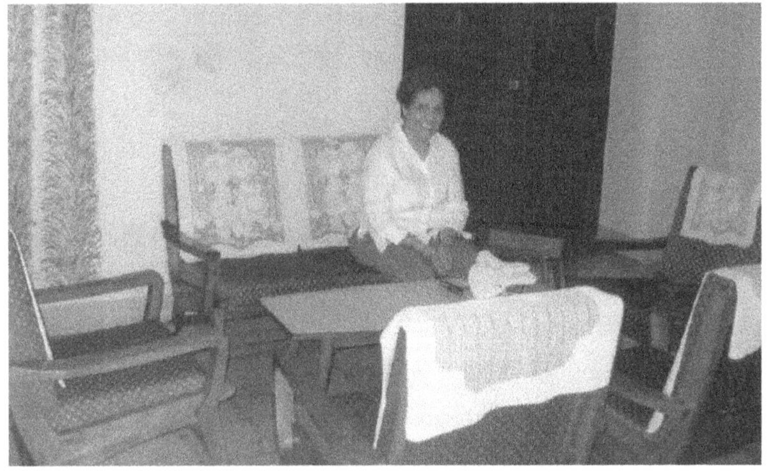

‡ Mercy visits Stella Maris Convent Parlour (2007)

Moments passed in silence. In the stillness of those moments, he entranced me. Did I entrance him? He later told me that I had physically changed from the vibrant, fresh-looking nun who had just returned from the United States five years ago. My missionary zeal, as well as my spiritual battle over the past few months, had taken a toll.

Earl spoke to me about the Easter celebration in our chapel and how much he loved the music. He commented on the size and beauty of the campus. Strangely, we did not discuss the most important issue for which he had flown down – my leaving the convent to marry him. Perhaps he felt it was best left unaddressed for the moment, which was far too exhilarating to be destroyed with any note of negativity. We simply savoured each other's company.

In a few minutes, the convent maid served him a light breakfast of toast, jam, fruit and coffee. He enjoyed it and commented on the finesse with which it was served. Earl always had an eye for detail and style.

A few minutes later, Sister Angela came into the room. "So how do you find Mercy?" "Rather washed out, Sister," he replied. She shook his hand while her back was turned to me. A few seconds later, she turned to me, smiled and winked. She chatted with us for a few minutes. She too refrained from any pointed discussion about the reason for his visit. These were uncharted waters that none of us for the moment dared to sail into. We let it be.

I was so proud of Earl. Sister Angela, I knew, had sized him up. He possessed an aura of charisma despite standing only five feet five inches. The moment he walked into a room, everyone noticed him. He was articulate, well informed and sophisticated. I knew Sister Angela was impressed with him.

Very soon it was lunchtime. The convent maid served Earl's lunch in the dining room. Since it was Easter Sunday, I decided to have lunch with the community. As I walked into the refectory, all eyes were on me. By now, most Sisters knew I had a visitor and who he was. I had a hurried lunch and spoke very little. I left quietly to be back with Earl.

After a few moments of silence, Earl said, "So what have you decided, Mercy?" "You know I have made my final vows," I responded. "Yes, Mercy, but I love you very much and I'm convinced that we can have a great future together." "I know that, Earl, I know that very well. However, I cannot walk away from a commitment made."

He then leaned over the table and took hold of my hand, looked deep into my eyes and said, "If there's anything I want, it's that you do what you believe is right. Don't rush. All I want is that through prayer you discern what God's will is for us."

With that, he rose and walked toward the parlour. I followed. We sat down and once again he took my hand. "I'll be praying for us that God may guide us." He looked at his watch. It was almost time for his flight. He would have to hurry to his hotel and from there to the airport. He rose and held my chin with one hand and my hand with the other. "I'll keep in touch," he said. "Look after yourself. Bye for now."

I stood on the verandah and watched him walk away down the tree-lined avenue leading to the main gate of the college. I followed him with my eyes for as long as possible. He turned around twice, smiled and waved. The meandering avenue would curve and then disappear from my sight behind the college buildings. I craned my neck for one last glimpse of him. Would I see him again? It would all depend on my decision.

THE PAIN OF DECISION

My eyes filled with tears, I walked to the chapel and poured my heart out. "I love him, dear Lord. I want to spend the rest of my life with him. Help me. I cannot be your spouse any longer. It's clear to me I must be his. I put my trust in You." At that moment, I realized how powerful a light true love is – it can create a fire storm, searing the soul and reducing it to cinders.

I recalled my meeting with Earl. For those fleeting moments, kneeling before the crucified Christ, I once again decided to abandon the eloquent wisdom of my mind and instead listen to the cravings of my heart. "Jesus," I whispered, "My heart wants to belong to him, but my mind says no. What is your will for me?" Jesus, I knew was no cunning and manipulative god influenced by only a cold mind. He was the Biblical God of Love.

For the first time in my life, I faced the fear and wonder of marriage – a world apart from my role at the convent. Although my imagining did carry the trappings of romanticized images from movies and novels, it also conjured up scenes of the realities I could encounter in the future. I knew that there would be no path I would have to walk down without Earl at my side.

Once again, I made my way to Sister Angela's room. As I sat on the chair opposite her desk, she leaned over. "I can see why you are so crazy about him." I nodded. "From the age of twelve, I've been crazy about him. For almost two decades, I've been struggling to forget him with no success."

Sister Angela looked straight into my eyes. "You have made your final vows. You cannot walk away from that commitment so easily. Think about that." She added, "You and you alone are to decide whether to break them or not. It's a decision that only you can make. Don't rush. Pray and we will all pray for you. After meeting Earl, I can see how difficult it is going to be. But I do know that if you decide to stay he will go on with his life, accepting your decision as God's will for you and for him. And if you decide to leave, we will continue to respect you. We will not condemn you.

We will accept it as God's will for you."

This was a fine example of Sister Angela's method of governance. She never overpowered me, only helped and guided me to see the light. And because of her open-minded approach to my situation, I never had to huddle shamefully in my cell. She constantly invited me to open a dialogue in which I was able to explore my innermost thoughts, feelings and impending fears. Although there were times when I experienced emptiness, loneliness and sometimes a sense of defeat, her maternal and friendly understanding helped me rise above my human foibles and experience the power of God's guiding light.

✣ Mercy visits her cell in Stella Maris Convent (2007)

During the following weeks, I would spend many a late night seated alongside Sister Angela on the bench in the convent garden. I would even weep on her strong shoulders. She never once told me I should stay at Stella Maris, nor did she tell me to leave. She insisted that I and I alone must make the decision.

Earl wrote to me soon after our visit. In short, he said he loved me dearly; he had always loved me but pursued other women because I was unattainable. He said he had been happy to see me after five years, but was concerned about my health. He regretted that he had become a source of stress to me. "Pray, eat well and sleep well – please, Mercy, look after yourself. I never ever imagined I would get a wonder like you! I love you, and all that I want is to continue to love you, to hold you and have you. Love, Earl." I showed the letter to Sister Angela, who returned it to me. It joined a growing number in my folder.

RETREAT TO THE ASHRAM

In a few weeks, the college would close for the summer vacation starting in May. I decided to make a one-week retreat and, in the process, find out for myself whether I would continue to live as a missionary nun or leave Stella Maris and marry Earl.

I had heard of the Reverend Bede Griffiths, an Englishman who had converted to Roman Catholicism while a student at Oxford, and later embraced the Benedictine Order and became a monk. He had opened an ashram called Shantivanam in India, where he incorporated Christian asceticism with Hindu philosophy.

I mentioned my choice to Sister Angela, who encouraged me to go ahead. In a few days, I left Madras for Tanjore, about three hundred kilometres south, where our Order had a convent. It was a convenient pause for the journey to the ashram, located thirty-two kilometres west of the town. The Sister Superior of the convent was none other than Sister Elsa Garreth, the nun who had first nurtured my religious vocation when I was a young teenager in boarding school. Sister Angela had phoned her to discuss my plight. Upon my arrival, Sister Elsa greeted me and spoke to me at length. She was most sympathetic. She advised me not to rush to a decision. "Think, pray and decide."

The following day, the convent chauffeur drove Sister Elsa and me to the ashram through the stunning teak forests of South India. The ashram was situated on twenty acres of land dotted with thatched huts. I was awestruck by the austerity of the place. In a few minutes, the Reverend Bede entered. A tall, lean man, he sported a white beard and his deep blue eyes penetrated your soul. He walked barefoot, a loincloth covering the lower part of his body and a saffron-coloured shawl on his shoulder. Every inch an ascetic, he had an aura of mysticism about him.

Sister Elsa said her farewells and promised to return in a week's time to accompany me back to the convent in Tanjore.

In addition to the Reverend Bede, the ashram housed eight monks, young men from around India who had committed themselves to a life of prayer and meditation and lived under his spiritual guidance. I would now, albeit briefly, be part of this ascetic group.

My cell was eight feet by ten feet, equipped with a cot and a quilt, sheet, pillow and stool. There was no plumbing other than a few communal washrooms outside. We rose at 4:00 a.m. and soon made our way to the Room of Prayer, where Holy Mass was celebrated. Unlike a Catholic priest who stood at the altar, the Reverend Bede squatted on the floor in front of the table. Marigolds placed in brass plates decorated the altar. The room was engulfed in the smell of incense and flowers. We meditated for an hour. The Reverend Bede read passages from sacred scriptures of both Christian and Hindu religions. At 5:30 a.m., Mass was said, followed by the Divine Office, based purely on Christian scripture.

Breakfast consisted of chapattis (Indian flatbread,) lentil soup, black coffee sweetened with brown sugar and a banana. Individual chores came next: I was assigned to help in the kitchen and the kitchen garden. A simple lunch of rice, lentils and vegetables, in keeping with the vegetarian practice at Shantivanam, was served at noon. The afternoon was spent in meditation and quiet reading. Supper was followed by a short recreational period. Meditation and prayer followed, after which we retired to our individual rooms.

Although the monks were able to meet many of their needs by growing most of their own produce, I remembered a lesson which had been taught to me in my early years of religious training: we are totally dependent on God. Life and all that sustains it comes from beyond oneself. We are therefore not self-sufficient in the truest sense of the word. This awareness had been somewhat eroded during my years of university teaching. I was now reawakened to its relevance.

DECISION TO STAY

I spent the week in quiet meditation and prayer. When my time at the ashram was almost up, I met with the Reverend Bede. He counselled me to remain a nun. "Mercy, we feel drawn to various walks of life, but we can only choose one. I, for one, would have loved to have the love of a woman and children, but I cannot. I have chosen to be a monk, and so too have you made your vows. I think you should persevere in your religious life."

I wasn't happy with this advice, but he had spoken and I accepted his reasoning. I left the ashram in a state of more confusion than when I had arrived. My inner self began to rebel. Reverend Bede's advice went against the very fabric of my inner self. Yet I told myself that I would abide by it. If I had had the opportunity to write to Earl at that moment, I would have said: "My very dear Earl, The decision is made: I will stay where I am… Is it a decision based on conviction? No, Earl. It is a decision based on faith. Earl, dear, as I write these lines, believe me, tears flow profusely. There were only two occasions in my religious life when I wept bitterly and both were for you – the other was in 1967 when I had met you and realized how much I loved you."

On our drive back to Tanjore, Sister Elsa commented that she didn't find me at peace. I replied that I would make a valiant effort to continue in my religious vocation.

After a pause of two days at the Tanjore convent, I left for Ootacamund in the Blue Mountains of South India. As was the custom, superiors from the south usually gathered here for retreats, discussions regarding future initiatives for the Order, transfers of Sisters, and general administrative issues. Sister Angela would be present and I wanted to let her know my decision.

As I walked into the community room, many of the Sisters remarked on how gaunt I looked, and some commented on the acne on my face. I hadn't looked at myself in the mirror for over two weeks. Sister Angela, far from being pleased about my decision, as I had expected, seemed perturbed. "If that's what you decided, it's alright with me. I'll continue to pray for you."

But she was not convinced that I had freely chosen to stay. It was clear to her that my living hell was a reality that would continue. I asked her to inform Earl of my decision. By contrast, the

Sister Provincial – the head of all the Order's institutions in South India – was overjoyed. She had always felt my leaving would be a blow to many of the younger sisters, who held me in high esteem.

After two days of rest, I left to return to Stella Maris, my beloved home in the plains. It was May, and there were only two weeks before the start of classes in the new academic year. I went up to my cell, pulled out the drawer, opened the folder that contained all Earl's letters and quietly tore them up. I was going to stay and there was no need to hold onto them. I also had three pictures of him, which he had enclosed in some of his letters. These I lacked the courage to destroy. Tears streaming down my cheeks, I looked at the photos and quietly tucked them back in my drawer.

A few days later, I received a letter from Earl, who evidently hadn't received Sister Angela's letter informing him that I had decided to stay. It was again a short note, dreaming of our life together. He described his flat in Bandra and enclosed a Lloyds Bank cheque for "a million kisses to be cashed in the privacy of our home." This, too, I tore up.

DECISION TO LEAVE

By mid-year, I was immersed in my work, preparing my lectures and new initiatives for the academic year. One evening, two faculty members visited me to discuss administrative matters. As the discussion progressed, I realized that I felt totally detached from these issues. I no longer had the motivation to work in this environment. I abruptly left the meeting, promising to get in touch with them later in the week.

It was now almost 8:00 p.m. and time for the Divine Office. I went to the chapel and waited for the rest of the community. Very soon, I was joining my fellow nuns singing verses from sacred scripture. Suddenly I had the inner conviction to leave my religious calling. I had heard no voice, seen no light. I just felt a sense of certitude that this was my path. For the first time in years, I felt happy and liberated.

After the service, my friend Sister Christine and I took a short walk, during which I told her of my plan to leave. She bravely supported my need to be true to myself. I then stepped into Sister Angela's room. "I've decided to leave," I told her. Without the slightest look of surprise, she said, "See me in the morning."

A complete inversion in my value system took place that night, although it was a long time in formation. Marriage, something I had rejected as a young woman, was what I now desired most desperately. My religious vows I would abandon. In my mind, I reconciled this seeming contradiction. My acceptance of the status of marriage to a loving man would, I knew, empower me and, in that sense, exalt me so that together with Earl I would continue to find Jesus.

With these thoughts in mind, I had a sound sleep. I was now, finally, at peace – no longer torn between my religious calling and my very strong love out in the world. After breakfast, I met Sister Angela, who informed me that she had already spoken to Sister Provincial, with whom I would later meet. Sister Angela felt Earl should not be informed until I had spoken to my mother. Despite her heavy responsibilities as Sister Superior and Chief Administrative Officer of the College, she decided it was more important to accompany me on this arduous journey to Ootacamund and from there to Fort Cochin, where my mother lived.

A formal announcement regarding my departure was made to the community. Many came to my cell and offered their good wishes. No one passed judgment. A number of the Sisters sobbed.

I had not been in contact with Earl for about six weeks. I knew he would be confused, since he had heard only from Sister Angela and not from me. However, a good friend of mine since novitiate days, Sister Cecilia, was leaving shortly for Bombay to further her studies at the University. I asked her to inform Earl as soon as she got to the city that I had decided to leave the convent. However, I gave her strict instructions to let him know this was confidential, since my mother had not yet been told.

Another important date on my calendar: June 10, 1972. When it came time to depart, a group of about thirty Sisters gathered near the gate of the convent. I hugged each of them. It was painful and tearful. Stella Maris had been my happy and fulfilling home for five years. I was leaving the security of the convent for a suspicious, violent world – yet a world of love with Earl. Therein lay a much stronger call beckoning me, a love I had nurtured for almost two decades. This love was to set the course of my life in the future.

I went once more to the chapel to kneel in prayer. This was the hallowed spot where I had pronounced my vows. Today was the day that my God and my love for a man took over my destiny. This was the day when my future would be chalked out by the God of love. I was turning my back on a vocation I cared deeply about. I was renouncing my vows of poverty, chastity and obedience, which I had promised to keep for the rest of my life. Was I taking the right step? I knew I was.

‡ Mercy visits Stella Maris Chapel (2007)

Eight

VISIT TO THE SISTER PROVINCIAL

The changes in people's lives sometimes bring with them tremendous burdens. I realized that if I were to be authentic in my choices, I would have to be well grounded. The chaotic beginnings of my new life demanded that I develop a sense of order and structure to guide me through the transition from nunhood to marriage.

In June of 1972, Sister Angela and I took the train from Madras to the plains of Coimbatore. Our third-class compartment was packed with travelers – all women. As was the custom in the convent, our hamper was packed with sandwiches, cookies, fruit, juice, water and a thermos of coffee. We were always advised never to purchase anything from the vendors for fear of infection. This was a strict rule and we were expected to conform to it.

Although it was a fourteen hour journey, my companion and I spoke very little. I was in a state of both sadness and joy: sadness at leaving my Sisters at Stella Maris and joy at the prospect of soon becoming Earl's wife. Sister Angela knew I was going through a traumatic experience and sensed that I wanted to be left alone. We had only enough room to prop ourselves up against the hard panels of the compartment. From time to time, we managed to doze off and catch a few hours of sleep.

By mid-morning, we had arrived at the little town of my school days. I recalled the memories of my childhood and teenage years and the place that had nurtured my religious calling. I had been a lucky child, secure in my family and interested in school. I thought of my life in the boarding school, where I had been Head Girl for almost three years. It was a caring institution that welcomed many broken children, some of whom had inherited a menacing burden of unsavoury experiences. With devotion and love, the missionary Sisters opened up a more promising future to these less fortunate students.

From Coimbatore, a shuttle train took us to the hill station of Ootacamund – the site of my "trials" three years earlier. Sister Angela and I had come up here to see the Sister Provincial. Sister Klemens, an Austrian who had devoted almost thirty-five years to her missionary calling, was Sister Superior of all Sister Superiors in the Southern Province of India. On this occasion, Sister Angela met with her first and emerged after half an hour. I was then summoned into the office.

Sister Klemens wasn't pleased with my decision. Throughout my ordeal, I had encountered only empathy and understanding from the Sisters. But this meeting was different. Sister Klemens told me in no uncertain terms that if I were to leave the religious life, I would be doing wrong. I would be reneging on a commitment made in full faith. I listened. Then I emphatically explained that I was aware of my commitment and that by leaving the convent, I knew I was breaking my vows. I told her that after all these years, I was now convinced that my future was with Earl.

In frank terms, I described to her that I was no longer able to fulfill my religious vocation. She handed me a clipping from a religious magazine featuring a picture of the weeping Madonna. "The Virgin is weeping for your sins," she said sternly. "I don't think I'm committing a sin, Sister," I replied. I left her office not unduly flustered. I was now at peace. I had embarked on a road that would eventually take me to my life with Earl. The thought was soul lifting. All the pain, humiliation and embarrassment I was experiencing seemed trivial in comparison.

Every detail of that day is still clear to me. I made my way to the refectory to have a late lunch. I was alone with two Sisters who were clearing the tables. After a very long time, my appetite had returned and I relished the meal. As I went out to the corridor, Sisters Myriam and Leena, who had completed their trials at the same time as I did, were waiting. They were anxious to know the details of my decision, and assured me of their understanding and prayers.

I spent the rest of the day outdoors in the convent's estate, walking through the long avenues lined with eucalyptus and pine. Beneath the majesty of these ancient trees, I nurtured a deep expectation of hope at the choices I had made with respect to my future. A new value system had evolved within me. A system that brought with it the conviction that God speaks even to a troubled soul. I listened. As a result fear and anxiety were soon dispelled.

God's love had always been a constant in my life. I realized that loving Him was not always easy. Throughout my religious life, I had tried hard to put Him first – but ultimately there emerged another love, my love for Earl. I found no contradiction here, only total fulfillment – that I could love my God and Earl both at the same time. I knew that in loving Earl I would find God's presence.

No longer was there a sense of guilt or shame. I was no longer willing to acquiesce to the dictates of my mind. A transformation had taken place. I was now a slave to my heart. I realized that the gentle, inward power of my heart was taking charge of my future. I came to the realization that love means the preservation, not the violation, of one's freedom. I began to listen to the gentle entreaty of my heart – it was now time to do what it dictated to me.

After the Divine Office and night prayers, I retired to my cell and went to sleep. The next few days were to be my greatest challenge: I needed to break the news to my beloved mother. The following afternoon, as Sister Angela and I prepared to leave the convent, Sister Klemens was more conciliatory towards me. She blessed me, asked me to rethink my decision and assured me of her prayers. At Coimbatore, we changed trains for Palluruthy, where we would stay at Our Lady's Convent before arriving at the nearby town of Fort Cochin, where my mother lived in the home of my sister Lillian and her husband James.

More and more, I was convinced that there was no turning back. On the train, I began to imagine my new life. What would it be like? I was a woman in love. As the train jolted from side to side along the narrow tracks, I thought of Earl – very soon to be "my Earl," "my husband." As I thought of him, I imagined his strong arms around me – he had a most beautiful physique! I imagined us as man and wife in his Bombay flat. I imagined him caressing me, kissing me and making love to me. After so many years, I no longer had to repress these thoughts, which represented the natural progression of all that was happening in my life. I knew he would be a tender and caring lover. I imagined having children. I imagined playing on a beach, a happy family: Earl, me and the kids playing softball on the Huksar beach. In fact, Earl had sent me a picture of himself in swimming trunks standing on this beach.

I dozed off and opened my eyes when we were almost at our destination. We took a cab to the convent in time for Holy Mass, followed by the Divine Office. After breakfast, Sister Angela made a call to

Lillian, who was just about to leave for her job at a British oil company. Sister Angela gave her the news and I watched as her face paled. She knew it was going to be an immensely challenging ordeal for me. Lillian told Sister Angela she would send the car and chauffeur to pick us up. In the meantime, she was going to break the news to my mother.

FAMILY DISCORD

My sister Lill was waiting at the entrance of her house to greet us. Sister Angela was no stranger to her. As we entered, Lill, visibly upset, turned to me. "What is wrong with you? The sisters have done so much for you – how could you turn your back on them? This is just a mid-life crisis." While Sister Angela tried to calm her, I said, as steadily as I could, "Lill, I love Earl dearly and I cannot continue in my religious vocation. I know my future is with him – there is no turning back."

✢ *Halcyon*, Lillian's house (2007)

Lill then blamed Earl for tempting me. "Why did he make that trip? Why didn't he stay away from you?" "Lill," I implored. "I'm no child. I cannot be swayed by a man I met only for a few hours. I assure you that I love him dearly." "What do you know of him?" she retorted. "Mercy, you are in love with love."

Sister Angela tried to intervene. She assured Lillian that my relationship with Earl was an ongoing saga and that I had given it a lot of thought and prayer in which I had tried to discern God's will for me. "He's forty years old and so set in his ways," Lill continued, undeterred by Sister Angela's defence of my decision. "You are thirty-two. You have lived a religious life for over a decade. You two are going to make a mess of your lives. Take my word. If I were you, I'd just go back to Stella Maris, where you've been so happy all these years."

We stayed at Lill's house for a few more hours, but my mother stayed in her bedroom with the door locked. She refused to see Sister Angela or me. Later in the evening, Sister Angela and I returned to the convent in Lill's company car. Early the following day, my mother and Lill visited the convent. As Sister Angela and I entered the parlour, my mother threw herself on her knees in traditional Indian fashion. "Do not send my daughter away!" she begged. Sister Angela leaned forward and helped my Mother back on her feet. "Mrs. Jacobs, we are not sending Mercy away – she feels she needs to leave us."

I returned to Lill's house with my mother and sister. Sister Angela was to leave the following day for Stella Maris; it would be another four years before I saw her again. I spent the rest of the week at Lill's place. Throughout this time, my mother refused to speak to me. She had meals alone in the bedroom. She did not venture into the living room, where I spent most of my time. Meanwhile, Lill continued to bombard me with insults. I took it all in silence and fortitude.

At the end of the week, Lill accompanied me back to the convent at Palluruthy, where I would continue to stay for another month. Life at the convent was a pleasant change from Lill's house. She was the eldest of us eight children and I the youngest, and I had always admired and respected her. In my early years, when my father was unemployed, it was she who opened her home to me and my sister Phyllis so we could start our education. We lived with Lill for almost five years until my parents could afford to send us to boarding school. She paid for our school fees, uniforms and books. It was a financial strain because she had five children of her own.

Lill was a highly driven individual who was talented, bright and focused. After high school, she had joined the Indian wing of the Women's Auxiliary Corps. At war's end, she left to get married. Consequently, she had no saleable skills. She couldn't afford to attend commercial school, so she bought herself an old typewriter and a Pitman's shorthand book. While raising her five children, she taught herself the skills needed for the commercial exam. Soon she was employed by a British tea company, then an oil company, where she rose to become the administrative assistant to the C.E.O. Thanks to her ambition and drive, she was able to educate all her children through university.

Given the admiration I had for Lill, and the moral debt I felt I owed her, it was painful beyond belief when she reprimanded me severely and predicted my downfall. I, on the other hand, had hopes and visions of a rewarding life. I realized that challenges can come to an individual through the people we love as well as through situations and circumstances. I was afraid however, that this sad encounter may leave me scarred for life.

Yet I dreamed of a life transformed by Earl's love for me. Lill's rhetoric, difficult as it was to unravel, did have an effect. A fierce debate raged in my mind: what was right, my remaining as a nun or my impending marriage? Time and time again, Lill had said that I had no feelings for my mother, that I was selfish, and that I thought only of myself. I realized I would have to trust my inner instincts. I believed that God Almighty, the Ultimate Truth transcended my limited experience. I trusted in the workings of His Holy Spirit and in His Healing Grace. Despite my family's objections, I had an incredible power at my disposal – God's guiding light.

Lill left me at the convent. "You are being stupid! Go back to Stella Maris. There is nothing glamorous about married life; just rethink your decision," she said in parting. I turned away and quietly found my way to the office of my new Sister Superior, Sister Isabella. She was a Spanish nun who had lived in India for over 30 years. Like Sister Angela, she knew I was having a most trying time. "You are not expected to do any work at this point," she reminded me. "Just pray and rest." I was so thankful to her. I would spend the next three and a half weeks quietly in this community. I knew only two of the nuns, Sisters Helen and Vincent, and confided my situation to them. They passed no judgment but were very sympathetic.

CALM AFTER THE STORM

Over the next few days, I wrote to all my other siblings to inform them of my decision. Fortunately, Earl was well known to them all. Everyone had been closely following the whereabouts of this gifted individual, a brilliant engineer and successful businessman from the Anglo-Indian community, still single despite his efforts to meet the "right" woman. They were also aware of his deeply Christian convictions. My two brothers in Australia refused to cast aspersions. They realized that both Earl and I were mature adults who had not rushed into an engagement. Lillian and Phyllis were the most vocal in their criticism. Eric and my sister Lovey kept their opinions to themselves. Doris, wife to Claude and sister-in-law to Earl, was deeply compassionate.

Increasingly convinced that I had made the right choice, I now knew that no matter what the reaction of my family, I would continue to live and labour on the side of the light afforded to me. But Lill's prediction that married life could sometimes bring shattering disappointments haunted me. I continued to pray and in prayer I found solace. I began to realize that human love is often an entangled love and that beneath this type of human feeling there can be fearfulness and hostility. Goaded on by the twin notions of independence and vulnerability, I was now more attuned to the foibles of a heart in love. True Love can be enslaving. With faith and hope, I now had to find solace. Through all this turmoil, I struggled to remain calm.

There remained a lurking spiritual question. By renouncing my religious calling and opting for marriage, was I seeking a way of life that was less sublime, less exalting? I now began to acknowledge that I still had a battle within me to overcome. In my confused state of mind, this question came to the forefront. One day, it dawned on me to contact a brilliant Jesuit priest named Father Samuel Ryan. In the 1960s and 1970s, he was considered one of the great theological minds in the country. The Jesuit House informed me that he was going to be in town for just one day, a forty-five-minute walk from the convent. I hastily made an appointment to see him and was granted a one-hour slot.

On my way to the tiny cottage where he lived, I rehearsed the question I would ask him: "Am I settling for a less sublime calling by renouncing my religious vocation and my vows of poverty, chastity and obedience, and getting married?" His response, when I met him, was heartening. "We are all called to live in accordance with the greatest commandment 'to love the Lord your God with all your heart and with all your soul and with all your mind.' This is the great and first commandment. And the second is like it: 'You shall love your neighbour as yourself.'"

Father Ryan pointed out that the call to Christian love was all-encompassing – pure, selfless and liberating. The walk of life we choose to attain this goal is our choice alone. "It would be presumptuous and condescending to assume that because I'm a priest I have chosen a more sublime route than my mother," he continued. He emphasized that my call to Christian holiness would still be my fundamental calling, but that how I chose to attain it was my choice. "All this while, you sought to fulfill your Christian calling through your religious life. Now it's time to pursue it through married life, if that's what you feel your calling is. I find no contradiction here."

I was now at peace. At last, I was free to love Earl with my whole being. I was free to become his wife.

As we rose from our chairs, Father Ryan took me by my hand and led me to the verandah. There we stood facing the dark monsoon skies and the torrential thundershowers. Still holding my hand, he looked at me. "Now go in peace and when you hold Earl in your arms, remember he is God's gift of love to you." I stepped out of the verandah, oblivious of the fury of the showers.

Back at the convent, I changed into dry clothes and sat down to write to Earl for the first time in four months. I informed him that I had decided to leave the convent. I told him how encouraged I felt after my discussion with Father Ryan. I said my leaving was imminent, perhaps only a matter of days.

Within a couple of days, Earl phoned. From his voice, I knew that he was pleased and excited that I was now at peace. He said he wanted to be with me during this trying time. I mentioned that he would have to give the Sister Superior some money to shop for clothes for me as well as to purchase an air ticket to Bombay. I didn't want to make the long and arduous journey by train. From now on, my love for Earl would chart the ebbs and flows of my life.

Within a few days, I received Earl's letter reassuring me of his love. "Really, my love, what I most look forward to is having you as my wife, to love, to have and to hold – whose company I enjoy, who fills me with happiness, to whom I want to give happiness. God bless."

'72 July 05

My dearest Mercy,

The way you've said it at the end of your letter, I'm certain that you feel as happy as I do. It's providential that you met Fr. Ryan. We must thank God together, when I meet you on Sunday.

I informed my folks yesterday and today. My Mother is very happy — I could tell from the chat we had while I was driving with her tonight. Naturally, Claude, Doris and girls are overjoyed. So are Donagh and Eddie. I called Bilari over to my place last night and talked about it for a long time. →

.... Really, my love, what I most look forward to, is having you as my wife, to love, to have and to hold — who's company I enjoy, who fills me with happiness, to whom I want to give happiness God bless!

Yours, Earl.

‡ Earl's Letter to Mercy (1972)

SOLACE IN REUNION

I was in the chapel, my head bowed in prayer after receiving Holy Communion. I looked up to see Earl take his turn. I remember the exact day July 11, 1972. He was dressed casually in a pair of beige slacks and a short-sleeved shirt. It was less than thirty-six hours since he had promised to come down and see me.

"Was that him? He's so nice," whispered Sister Helen. I quickly went to my cell and looked across the yard. I saw him talking to Sister Isabella. He was wearing his dark glasses, facing the morning sun, his hair blowing in the wind and, as ever, looking strikingly handsome. I waited excitedly.

Yes! Earl in your love for me I have found a new delight – and it is so true that in each other's love we find a truer expression of God's love for us. There is so much I want to tell you – so much I can tell you – so much that must be told. I'll keep it all for later. This is only to tell you that in your love for me I find peace – in your love I find fulfilment – in your love I find Him who is Love. You are no longer just "Earl" to me, but rather "Earl, God's gift of love to me".

Yours

Mercy [illegible]

⁜ MERCY'S NOTE TO EARL (JULY 1, 1972)

⁜ MERCY VISITS COURTYARD IN OUR LADY'S CONVENT, PALLURUTHY (2007)

A few minutes later, Sister Isabella informed me that I could go to meet him. I hurried to the parlour. Earl noticed that my unrest had disappeared, replaced by something unique and enchanting. We were at last free to be each other's. He realized that our mutual love for each other had brought with it deeper perspectives. As I gazed at him, I recalled Father Ryan's words: "And when you hold Earl in your arms, remember he is God's gift of love to you." I was still a nun and couldn't take him in my arms yet. But I was satisfied to just hold his hand and look lovingly into his eyes.

A few minutes later, Sister Isabella inquired whether we would like to spend the day together. Earl said he would like to take me out and that we'd be back for dinner. He was staying at the Malabar Hotel, the best one in town. He always lived in style. He had a beautiful room with a large bay window overlooking the backwaters of Cochin.

He put his strong arm around me in a tight embrace. "May I see you without your veil?" He was astounded by my head of rich and glossy hair. "You have such beautiful, healthy-looking hair. What do you use?" "Lifebuoy soap and cold water," was my response. He smiled. Lifebuoy soap was the cheapest soap on the Indian market! "I guess it's the veil that has protected it from the scorching tropical sun," I said, to make conversation.

Quietly but firmly, he took my head and held it between his hands. "May I kiss you?" For the first time in my life, I realized the presence and beauty of love. He asked me how I had learned to kiss. "It comes naturally to a woman in love," I responded. In that kiss, I realized the dimensions of human love – that each of us belonged to the other. In that kiss, I also realized God was speaking to me. At long last, I was not running away from the reality of my love for Earl.

Love meant being faithful in my relationship to Earl, just as I knew I could count on both his fidelity and respect. Despite our emotional involvement, we were two mature individuals, and we individually respected the chastity of courtship. We kept a healthy distance from the total surrender of ourselves to each other, which we would fiercely guard until the night of our wedding.

Earl wanted to take a drive around Fort Cochin. He had spent two years in the little town after his expulsion from the Jesuit College in Madras, where he had played truant and failed his first year in university. Later, at a local college here, he had worked hard and secured the grades needed to make it to Engineering. We walked around the corridors of the University College and peeped into the classrooms. We saw the cricket fields where he had played as captain of the team. We then visited a tiny cottage not far away, which he had rented during exams. Had it not been for this quiet retreat, he might not have achieved his academic objectives.

It was now time to get back to the convent. We had spent a total of eight hours together. In that time, I had become all the more convinced that Earl had kindled in me the hope of giving myself to him completely. My enchantment with him had opened my eyes to his unique goodness. I loved this man from the depth of my being. In those few hours, God gave me such a profound insight that I knew I was making the right decision. Leaving the convent was a pivotal decision in my life and I was able to make it with a great sense of clarity and freedom.

Earl would once again meet with Sister Isabella, giving her money to buy me clothes and my airfare to Bombay, plus a generous donation for the orphans in her care. I followed him to the waiting cab. He squeezed my hand and as the cab drove away, I looked upon the man soon to be my spouse. From the airport, he wrote me a short note: "My Love, you have made these days I spent with you exquisitely happy. It is a quiet, sustained happiness which makes me thank God for making it possible, which includes a desire to share it with others and for which I must thank you so very much. I know that these have been equally happy days for you. That knowledge adds to my joy."

Cochin Airport.
72 July 12

My Love,

You have made these days I spent with you, exquisitely happy. It is a quiet sustained happiness which makes me thank God for making it possible, which includes a desire to share it with others, and for which I must thank you so very much. I know that these have been equally happy days for you. That knowledge adds to my joy.

Parting was not sad, because I have so much faith and trust in you, and so much love for you. I feel as though you are with me right now. Yet I look forward to Sunday, so much.

Jim has just arrived, so I guess I'll close. God bless you my love.

Yours,
Earl.

‡ Earl's letter to Mercy from airport (1972)

I went to the chapel for the Divine Office and then retired to my cell. I had such powerful thoughts of Earl. Lill's prediction that "you two are going to make a mess of your lives" seemed futile and empty. I had experienced the most tangible nature of love – human, erotic and also a gift from God. I soon fell asleep and then welcomed the new day with an excitement I had never before experienced. Sister Isabella and I set the date of departure for July 15. I contacted my brother Eric, who lived in my parents' home, Millowen, not far away from the convent. I asked him whether I could spend that night with him and his family. My flight to Bombay was scheduled for 7:00 a.m. on the sixteenth.

DEPARTURE FROM THE CONVENT

I spent the next few days quietly preparing for my departure, devoting much of my time to prayer, meditation and walks in the garden. Most Sisters respected my privacy. By now, it was clear to the community that I would be leaving soon. Except for Sisters Helen and Vincent and Sister Isabella the Superior, I spoke to no one else. On Saturday, July 15, I woke up to my last day as a religious sister. I fulfilled all my duties of prayer and household chores. I knew in a little while I would walk out the doors of this hallowed institution, which had been my home for over a decade. These Sisters had nurtured me from my early years. They had educated me; they had instilled in me the values that would shape my life forever; in fact, it was they who had molded me into the person who endeared me to Earl. I was now walking away from them.

Some Sisters leave the religious community because they are unhappy with the environment within, but this was not the case with me. I loved the life and I loved my Sisters. But there was a greater love out in the world beckoning me. All through the years I spent within these walls, I had quietly told my superiors and friends that, "if ever the day came that I would decide to leave, it would be for one and only one reason – my love for Earl." This prediction had now come to fruition.

As the day progressed, my anxiety turned to excitement. I packed a bag with all my belongings, including the few clothes Sister Isabella had purchased for me. I left behind my Divine Office book but kept my missionary crucifix. With the deepest of emotions, I removed the silver ring from my right hand – the symbol of my betrothal to Christ – and placed it at the feet of the statue of the Virgin Mary in the Prayer Room. I said a prayer of thanks to her for watching over me all these years. I now placed myself and Earl in her care as I walked out into a new world.

⁜ The Virgin Mary before whom Mercy placed her ring (1972)

By 5:00 p.m. in the afternoon, my brother Eric had arrived in a cab. Coincidentally, it was he who had accompanied me eleven years earlier when I left my parents' home for my religious calling. He would now take me back to my parents' home. Dry-eyed, I bade farewell to Sister Isabella, promising to keep in touch.

My father had passed away almost a decade earlier. My brother and his wife were candidly disappointed that I had left the convent, but at the same time they respected and supported me in my decision. I would spend the night in my parents' former bedroom. As I lay down to rest, I recalled once again my childhood years. I was the apple of their eyes. I was always the "smart" girl, the one who was a cut above the others, the one who was called by God to serve Him in the religious life. Now my mother was too upset by my choice to even meet with me.

I wondered what my father's reaction would have been. Recalling his last words to me, "Don't come back!" I knew that if he were around, he too would have been distraught. Like my mother, he might well have disowned me. But I consoled myself with the thought that there are times when you must stand alone in the decisions you make. My place was now with Earl. My future had now become an expanded arena and I was entering it with a clear conscience unsullied by the past. At this moment I was also bracing myself for the unknown, for unsuspecting outcomes, for threatening surprises. Because of a past of naivete, a past that had been specifically tailored for me by my superiors, a past that was totally devoid of irregularities, I was confused. I now found myself suddenly through destiny's making on the shores of life I had least intended for myself.

I tossed and turned in bed, waiting anxiously for the rays of the morning sun to reach the windows of the bedroom. By 4:00 a.m., I was up. I had decided to wear a sari. My sister-in-law would have to show me how to dress, as this was yet another new experience for me. I set my hair as best as I could, and with no make-up, got into the cab with Eric to go to the airport. We sat silently most of the time. Eric, I guessed, was probably wondering what lay in store for me. As for me, I knew Earl would provide for me and, most of all, would create a world of love for me. Seated in the aircraft, I realized that I was going to take off into a whole new world, one I had very little experience of. Yet I had a deep certainty of my future with Earl. Together, our love would protect us from our past dark nights of the soul.

As I looked out the airplane window, I remembered Mr. Koshi's words as he read my palm. "Within three years, you will break your promises." It was now exactly two and a half years later. It was either the lines on my right palm or he had the gift of extrasensory perception; I imagined the latter was true.

In two hours, I was in Bombay. At the airport, I spotted Earl standing with my sister Doris and brother-in-law Claude. I ran into Earl's arms and planted a kiss on his lips. It was an auspicious day. Exactly five years before, in July 1967, I had met Earl again after I returned from the United States. As Earl, Doris and Claude looked at me, they realized anew that I had been through very trying times. But they also knew I was at peace – a peace that brought with it stability. It was a peace barely tangible yet deeply grounded, despite all the doubts I had experienced. This peace, achieved under duress, was now mine to keep.

LIFE AS A COUPLE

Earl's flat, soon to be my home, was on the second floor of a beautifully maintained building in the suburb of Bandra, where his mother and siblings also lived. We sat together on the couch in the living room, where he kissed me passionately. It was a glorious introduction to our future life together. But there were many details to attend to before our wedding.

Doris's teenage daughters suggested, with Earl's encouragement, that I needed a new look. At a nearby hairdresser's salon, I had my hair cut and styled, my legs waxed, my eyebrows shaped. My nieces insisted that I borrow a well-tailored pant suit and use make-up. When Earl picked me up to attend Holy Mass in the early evening, he was visibly pleased at the transformation since my arrival at the airport

As a couple together at church, many curious eyes were on us. Others in the congregation wondered where I had come from. Just a few months earlier, Earl was seen in these very precincts with a foreign woman from the United States – now here he was escorting another woman they didn't know. People might talk, but we were truly in love and that was all that mattered.

After the Sunday service, Earl arranged to take me to visit his beloved mother. I needed no introduction. After all, I was "the girl from next door." Her older son Claude was married to my sister Doris and the two families were well known to each other. It was evident to her that her precious son Earl was at last happy. He seemed, finally, to have met his soul mate. All she wanted now was to see us married. "That will have to wait," said Earl. "Mercy must first get her dispensation from her vows. This will have to come from Rome." His mother smiled and said she was willing to wait as long as it took.

Our next call was to visit Earl's sister Verna. She and her husband lived in a stately mansion with perfectly manicured lawns and lush flowerbeds. The house was surrounded by a wall alongside which grew pine and Ashoka trees. As we opened the gate, I spotted Verna standing on the balcony overlooking the garden. Next to her was a relative, a nun called Sister Zoe. With trepidation, I held Earl's hand as we walked towards the house. Earl had warned me that Verna adamantly resented his liaison with me. She believed that Doris had been instrumental in getting us together and was not pleased with the prospect of two sisters as in-laws.

Verna was a veritable Indian fashion icon. Draped in an expensive sari, every hair on her head was in place, mounted by a switch so much in style in the Seventies. Her neck, hands and fingers were bejeweled. Earl had disciplined himself to be a winner in every situation, so he would do whatever it took to prevail. Positioning himself as the man determined to marry me, he kept his arm firmly around my waist. The conversation revolved around the tropical heat, the garden and the races. Verna's husband Bihari owned racehorses and was an avid race-goer. Verna paid scant attention to me except to say that I looked a lot different than when she had met me five years earlier. Sister Zoe said little, perhaps uncomfortable about an ex-nun dating a man so soon.

Back in the car, Earl kissed me on my cheek. "Don't worry," he said. "You will soon learn to handle Verna!" He then drove to a nearby restaurant called McRonnells. This was my first dinner with him since 1967. I was no longer in long white robes, but in modern street clothes. He ordered steak dinners for us both and together we said Grace.

During our meal, he spoke to me of Sheila for the first time. He had cared deeply for her. But as time went on, he had realized it was just infatuation. "You, Mercy, I've always loved from the time I brought you the trigonometry textbook almost twenty years ago. But we went our separate ways and I pursued other women. Over the years, you have become all that I dreamed of in a woman to become my wife. I cannot wait for you to become my wife." He added, "And soon, I hope, to carry my child!"

After dinner, we drove to the Band Stand, an elevated stage where bands played while the waves of the Arabian Sea splashed against the foundation of the stage. On this particular night, it was quiet and deserted. We sat on a bench facing the ocean, the starlit sky above us. Earl put his arm around me and again we kissed passionately. I summoned up the courage to ask him about his previous girlfriends.

He was brutally honest. He confessed to me that over the years he had kissed other women on this very bench! "The feeling is so different tonight, Mercy. Deep in my heart, I have the feeling: this is it! It cannot get any better. You are all that I ever wanted. Thank you for leaving the convent for me." I cried on his shoulder, realizing that here was a man who loved me totally. Over the years, he had tried to love other women, but had not succeeded. I had tried to give myself to Christ fully in religious life, but the time came when I realized I wanted to be Earl's wife. I now found no conflict between loving Earl and loving Christ.

Earl dropped me off at Doris's flat. This was where I would stay until Earl and I were wed. Doris was waiting for me. Almost fourteen years my senior, she was like a surrogate mother. When she asked me how the evening had gone, I described the restaurant by saying that a uniformed person had opened the door for us. She laughed. "All good eating places have a doorman opening the door for the patrons," she remarked, adding that I had a lot to learn about the outside world.

Very soon, I settled down to my new life, patterned after Earl's busy schedule. He met me each morning outside Doris's building and we went to church together for Holy Mass at 6:00 a.m. After Mass, I went with him to his flat. Earl immediately got down to exercising with his Bullworker while his servant Rajan and I prepared a breakfast of brown bread, a hard-boiled egg, a cup of yoghurt and sprouted peanuts. Safflower oil was what he used on his bread in place of butter or jam. It was different from what I was used to, but I had no problem adapting to the change. It was clear that we would follow a strict nutritional regime. I spent the mornings at his flat. Earl had given me the keys to the flat, the cupboard and the drawer. This was now my home.

Always thoughtful, Earl soon realized that I had very few clothes. He turned to our three nieces, Claude and Doris's daughters – Judy, Sally and Wendy. Together, the five of us went shopping for material. The young women excitedly chose patterns for me – dresses, pant suits, maxi-skirts, blouses – all part of the fashion scene in the seventies. A skilled tailor turned out an average of three outfits a day on Doris's sewing machine. By the end of the week, I had a complete wardrobe. Five pairs of shoes matching the outfits were ordered from a *mochi* (shoemaker) and were ready in a week. A variety of handbags completed my ensembles.

Every evening when Earl returned from his business, he insisted that I wear one of the outfits. We dined either with his mother, or at a restaurant, or at a friend's house. We were, I thought with an inward smile, a sophisticated-looking couple.

I spent the greater part of my days with my sister Doris. Very soon, my meagre frame took on a little weight. Earl was happy that I now no longer looked "washed out." Every evening after dinner, we went for a walk along the sea face. Afterwards at the flat, he usually poured himself a drink; scotch was his favorite, while rum and coke became my choice. We would sit on his balcony and share our thoughts and experiences. By 10:00 p.m., he would drive me to Doris's flat. We made no plans for our wedding until we had word of the Church's dispensation from my vows. Although we spent many an evening together in his flat, Earl and I never crossed that line which defined the chastity of courtship.

As days marched into weeks, I realized I had too much time on my hands. Earl didn't want me to take up a job; quite apart from any other reasons, he felt I had earned the right to relax. But I was always a highly motivated individual and had kept myself very busy. Now the days seemed to be far too long. It struck me that I could return to my own studies. Why not pursue a doctorate in economics?

That evening, when Earl returned from work, I mentioned the idea to him. Initially, his reaction was one of apprehension. He wanted me to be a wife and mother. Would pursuing a post-graduate degree be compatible with these roles? He asked me to do some further research and keep him informed. A car and chauffeur as well as any secretarial help I needed would be available to me. Within a few days, I met Professor Kamal, of the University of Bombay. He was willing to be my guide and agreed with me that the bulk of the work could be done from home. I assured Earl that my academic pursuits would not in any way interfere with my role as wife and mother. We decided that, for the moment, all I would do is register and then proceed with my studies after the wedding.

WEDDING PLANS

In mid-August, a month after I had left the convent, my dispensation papers – the official documents releasing me from my vows of poverty, chastity and obedience – were at last ready to be signed. The next day, we drove to the convent Villa Theresa in downtown Bombay. We met the Provincial Superior of the Northern Province, an Irishwoman called Sister Maura. Years later, she was elected Superior General – the highest position in the Order. She was markedly different from her counterpart, Sister Klemens, because she understood the workings of the human heart. Sister Maura understood that it was love and love alone that motivated my departure.

Without the slightest hesitation, but with deep emotion, I signed the papers. The bond between me and the Order was now finally broken. I was free to get married. Earl had booked a table for two at an exclusive restaurant. After dinner, he drove to the Parish Church in Bandra – St. Theresa's Church. The doors were closed. It didn't matter. We said a prayer of thanks outside that God had brought us together, and then kissed each other. We could now embark on our wedding plans.

The next day, Earl returned from his business early. We first drove to the parish office attached to the Church of St. Theresa. This was Earl's parish and the church we had decided on for our wedding. The earliest date the priest could give us was September 24. I was extremely happy, as it was also the feast of Our Lady of Mercy, after whom my parents had named me. As well, it was the day I had celebrated my feast as a nun. A business friend was asked to print our wedding invitations. She suggested a vermilion-colored rich bond paper, with the print in gold letters and a gold cross mounted on grains of rice – rich in Christian and Indian symbolism – on the inside.

Verna, who had now bowed to the inevitable, offered to accompany me to Esmée, the bridal dressmaker. Together, we chose a heavy brocade skirt with a bolero, studded with crystals, in delicate Swiss lace. I would wear the veil and headgear that were chosen for Sheila, and carry a similar bouquet of roses and lilies of the valley. Traditionally, the bridal outfit is paid for by the bride's side of the family, but this presented a dilemma in that my mother had disowned me. My niece Judy, in the work force at the age of twenty-one, generously stepped in to pay for the entire bridal outfit. She would also be my maid of honour.

While the wedding reception for Earl and Sheila would have been held at Silver Oaks, the home of Bihari and Verna, there was no such offer for our reception. It was clear to both of us that Verna's initial displeasure at Earl's involvement with me was the underlying reason. Earl therefore set about making arrangements at the Sun and Sand, a five-star hotel. One hundred and seventy-five guests were to be invited, most of them from Earl's side. There would also be a few from my side: an uncle, cousins and several friends.

At the same time, Earl set about planning a lavish three-week honeymoon. He would take me to exotic sites: Sri Nagar, Gulmarg and Pahalgam in the Kashmiri Valley, Chandigarh, an architectural miracle, Delhi and Simla. Everywhere, we would be staying in the best of hotels. Earl had worked hard all his life and was now going to enjoy the fruits of his labour with his bride.

September 8 is traditionally the feast of the birthday of the Blessed Virgin Mary. In Bandra, it is known as "Bandra Feast," the feast day of the Virgin of the Mount. Throughout the mid-twentieth century, the suburb was home to a large Catholic population. A huge basilica was built on a mountaintop overlooking the ocean and dedicated to the Virgin Mary. After attending Holy Mass on the Mount, Earl and I were to drive to Doris and Claude's place for breakfast. Earl took hold of my left hand and quietly slipped onto my finger the 11-diamond ring initially chosen by Sheila. "Keep it, it's yours now!" he said as he kissed me. He didn't need to ask me to marry him. That had been taken for granted the day I flew into his arms at the Bombay airport six weeks earlier.

That evening at dinner, Earl's mother noticed the ring on my finger. "You're engaged?" she asked. "Yes, Aunty," I replied. (Aunty is a generic term that younger Indians use when addressing older women.) "Is it a new ring Earl bought?" she continued. "No, Aunty. It's the same ring that Sheila wore." "No, no, no, my son!" she said. "You must buy her a new ring. This one will bring both of you bad luck." "No, Aunty," I declared. "It's alright with me! The ring is beautiful and don't worry; whenever I look at it, I will remember it was always destined for me, even though it may have been worn by another woman for a short time." It mattered little to me what the origins of this symbol of love were. That which held significance for me was the fact this cluster of diamonds was now a permanent symbol of our deep love for each other.

As our wedding day approached, I was in a state of peace and joy, one that I had never experienced in my life. The taking of the holy habit and the days I pronounced my first and final vows were days of great happiness. But deep down in the recesses of my being were the thoughts of Earl that I tried hard to repress. Now my dreams were fulfilled. I had come full circle with the true yearnings of my being – becoming one with Earl in the sacred Sacrament of Matrimony. I desired with all my heart to give myself to Earl and in so doing to give myself to him always. It is not easy for us given our limited human faculties to fully comprehend the implications of our all too human choices. But this event of my marriage to Earl which brought with it its significant characteristic of permanence was one I welcomed both with fortitude and an uncanny feeling of certitude.

WEDDING DAY 1972

I welcomed September 24 with excitement. I was to proceed to the church from Doris's flat, while Earl would leave from Verna's house. Verna would then escort him into the church, where I would be given away by my niece's husband Eddie. Doris's friends had decorated the church with tall vases of white roses, carnations and gladioli.

‡ Wedding Day, Earl and Nel (1972)

⁜ Doris, Mercy and Claude (1972)

The church was filled to capacity. Everyone there had heard that Earl Anselm, well-known bachelor, was getting married to an ex-nun. To the accompaniment of *Here Comes the Bride*, I walked into the church and saw Earl waiting for me, looking his ever-handsome self. His suit, as I would later learn, was sewn from material imported from the world-famous looms of Manchester, England. The pattern had no duplicate because Earl wanted to underline the uniqueness of his wedding day.

‡ Earl and Mercy (1972)

Very soon, I was standing next to him and in a few minutes the priest would declare us husband and wife – after we had promised "to love and to cherish each other in sickness and in health, in good times and bad; until death do us part." The ring Earl placed on my finger and the one I placed on his were the same ones molded for his marriage to Sheila. Her engraved name had been changed to "Mercy." The rings would stay on our fingers for the next twenty-five years, when we purchased new ones in recognition of our silver wedding anniversary.

Soon we were at the hotel for our reception. Earl spoke eloquently about how at last he had found true love. Ever the romantic, he sang *The Rose* in my honour. The guest list was almost identical to the list from his previously planned wedding to Sheila. One very special person in attendance was his sister Dilores, who had traveled from England for the occasion. In her magenta taffeta dress and necklace with opal pendant, a family heirloom, she looked almost majestic. She had come to witness her brother wed a woman who most guests agreed was the perfect choice for their dear Earl.

‡ Wedding Reception

‡ Dilores, Earl and Mercy (1972)

WEDDING NIGHT

At midnight, we walked up the steps to our flat. We were now man and wife. As Earl turned the key, we were touched to see that the place had been decorated by our servant Rajan. He had lovingly put up streamers, balloons and homemade signs reading "Welcome," "Congratulations" and "God Bless You." Earl stopped at the threshold and then carried me across the living and dining rooms and lifted me reverently and lovingly onto our nuptial bed, which I had prepared with crisp new white sheets.

Earl helped me undress. I got under the sheets while he undressed. His warm and beautiful body lay close to mine. I felt his warmth. We said our night prayers together while he embraced me. We thanked God for bringing us together. We kissed and kissed! I once again recalled the words of Father Samuel Ryan: "And when you hold him in your arms, remember he is God's gift of love to you." Earl, who all his adult years had led a disciplined life, then made love to me, his wife – a woman who had once consecrated her virginity to Christ and then gave it to the only man she had ever loved.

PART TWO

Nine

OUR NEW LIFE

The morning after our wedding, I opened my eyes and looked at the face of my loving husband. He was so much at peace. A series of utopian and make believe images marched across my mind. Surprisingly, each in its own dimension carried a significant meaning albeit subject to its own interpretation. But this morning they seemed to happily converge into reality. I saw us lying next to each other, man and wife. I no longer had to cling to the make-believe images I had formed of marriage. My husband and I were now committed to each other forever.

In a few minutes, Earl awoke and kissed me passionately, caressed me and we made love. We sensed a feeling of sustained happiness that engulfed the room. With hope and contentment we welcomed the new day. We got down on our knees in worship, as we would do for the rest of our lives. In due course, we developed a prayer unique to us:

> *"Lord, we bow down before You, we adore You. We thank You for all that You have given us: the gift of life, the gift of faith, the gift of each other and the gift of our lovely children. O Lord, bless this home, may it be a home where peace and charity prevail. We love you, Lord, and we thank you for everything. May our love deepen and may our love grow and may our love be based upon total self-forgetfulness and concern for the other. Bless our children, may they grow up in your love and in your grace. Mary our mother help us, St. Joseph protect us. Amen."*

The morning after our wedding, we were alone in the flat. Our servant Rajan had chosen to spend a few nights at my mother-in-law's flat. So Earl and I together prepared our very first breakfast as husband and wife. It was the same meal Earl had each morning: bread, boiled eggs, yoghurt and peanuts. I would now have to learn how to fetch groceries and start running a household.

Our honeymoon had been postponed by two weeks because of an important deadline in Earl's work. He was needed to supervise the installation of a state-of-the-art jig-boring machine, one of the few of its kind in Bombay at that time. I was not at all perturbed at having to wait for our honeymoon. My Novice Mistress had advised me that the most precious things in life are usually close at hand. Earl fit this bill. He too had at last found a meaningful relationship. Together we began to experience pure marital bliss.

The weeks following our wedding thrust me solidly into the heart of Earl's family and Earl into mine. We continued to dine each night with Earl's mother, and my sister Doris provided us with lunch each day. We spent as much time as possible with Earl's sister Dilores before her return to England. Everyone in his family was now grateful that our wedding had taken place without a hitch and that at last Earl had found true happiness. His sisters Aureen and Hazel, unable to attend the wedding, sent us beautiful cards and generous gifts. All the gifts and greeting cards had been taken to Doris and Claude's home.

The response to our marriage from my family was mixed. My sisters Lillian and Phyllis, together with my brother Eric, sent us terse telegrams with the message "God Bless." My brothers Victor and Alfred in Australia sent us cards and generous cheques. But my sister Lovey, also in Australia, took it upon herself to reprimand me by letter. "Pack up and return immediately to the convent," she admonished. "Too late!" quipped our nephew Michael, Doris and Claude's son. Earl and I took the negative comments in our stride, knowing full well that time would heal all wounds.

Sadly, there was no response at all from my mother. Because of her absolute refusal to be reconciled to our marriage, I sought and received solace and strength from Earl. He was a strong believer in Christian values and forgiveness, but at the same time he was a pragmatist who observed situations, and later with an independent spirit analyzed their true meaning. I knew that with his help I would be able to weather this storm of conflict.

HONEYMOON

Two weeks after our wedding, Earl's work completed, we left on our honeymoon. We flew first to Delhi. Although I had been in India's capital city as a nun, I had never had the opportunity to visit the sites of interest. Earl booked us into the Imperial, a luxury hotel. We visited the Red Fort where, on August 15, 1947, India's first Prime Minister, Pandit Jawaharlal Nehru, made his midnight speech at the dawn of independence. Parliament House, the President's House, the Gateway of India and Connaught Place (Delhi's best-known shopping district) were all included in our sightseeing. What is probably the most telling of my experiences of my honeymoon is the degree of oneness, of empathy,of sheer awesome interconnection of our souls – our very beings were now one.

⁜ HUMAYUN'S TOMB, DELHI (1972)

Our next stop was Srinagar in the Kashmiri Valley. Here we stayed in a houseboat called the Kutty Sark, complete with a living and dining area, a bedroom with a king-sized bed and indoor plumbing. The boat came with a maid, a bearer and a cook. The cook catered to our every desire: trout, duck and meatballs were some of the dishes we enjoyed. We also visited the little town of Pahalgam, to me the most beautiful spot on earth. From our hotel window, we looked down on a valley where we saw shepherds grazing their sheep, a forest of riotous colors and a rivulet tumbling down the rocks, while birds disturbed the stillness of the day with incessant chirping.

I was no longer living a make believe world of delusions. Here was I truly in the arms of the man I had as a young teenager dreamed about. It was no longer an illusion. It was a reality – a reality whose every moment I savored.

As I lay next to my husband; as I clasped his hand; as I lay my head on his chest and looked deep into his eyes – it was no longer a distant hope; but rather a hope that had now become a reality. This union with Earl was my destiny. No longer did I doubt it. I knew with each passing moment of our honeymoon that God in all His goodness had planned this path for me – my union with Earl in holy matrimony – albeit through the path of my religious vows.

✢ Srinagar (1972)

Gul Marg, another town we saw, prided itself on having the highest golf course in the world. Film stars and film industry barons were busy shooting scenes for upcoming Hindi movies. After about ten days in Kashmir, we flew to the city of Chandigarh, a place that bears the handiwork of world-renowned architects. We later drove through the "rice bowl" of India, the state of Punjab.

As our honeymoon came to an end, I realized how deep my union with Earl had become. We had welcomed each other into our very souls. Curiously, this intimacy brought with it a realization of the vulnerability that accompanies the role of wife and one day, I reckoned, the role of mother.

Uncertain of my ability to steer a course of moderation, I plunged headlong into my new role of wife. Fearful of falling into the mold of one expecting all household chores to be done by others while I indulged in intellectual pursuits, I decided with the fervour of a missionary to ward off all temptation. I pursued my new wifely role with a determination that surprised even me.

LEARNING TO COOK

Once home, I settled down to be the wife Earl had always dreamed of having. My sister Doris, in my eyes a wonderful wife and mother, was my mentor. "Love your husband! Spoil him!" she exclaimed. "Forget all this women's lib stuff. You want a successful marriage, make your home a cozy nest for your husband and children – forget your rights – concentrate on your duties. Forget yourself! Think of the others!"

I would take her advice. I, who had so much admired the social revolution of the sixties in North America, now saw changes taking place in my psyche. I had to balance the demands of the domestic front with my innate sense of independent living. After all, for over a decade I had been a nun with all my domestic needs taken care of by the institution. Now I had to redefine what I meant by being a "free woman" and where to draw the line between this freedom and my domestic responsibilities. I soon realized that there is an undeniable power in a woman who can deliver a stimulating economics lecture and at the same time serve up a plate of delicious rice, beef curry and curried vegetables to a hungry husband!

Doris, armed with some of her favourite recipes, encouraged me to start cooking and I gradually became less dependent on her and Earl's mother for our meals. As the convent had not exposed me to any culinary expertise, I needed help from my sister. Our first stop was at the butcher's. She educated me on what cuts of beef were suitable for each dish. And she was thrifty. "Insist that they trim the fat off before they weigh the piece."

From there, we moved on to the fisher women. This domestic transformation was not easily achieved. I realized I was entering a path that was bereft of past experience. My life in the convent was one of discipline, prayer and academic pursuit. Now the responsibilities of a spouse were thrust upon me. I knew I had to venture into the unbroken path and scale a ladder of high expectations. Most Anselm and Jacob women were expert homemakers despite the fact that many of them were simultaneously employed in the workforce. Anglo Indian cuisine is rich in variety - a combination of Portuguese, French, British, and Indian culinary art. It was a perfect blend of west meeting east. Doris offered me tips based on her own experience. "Don't trust these women. They will try to sell you fish that is not fresh. Open the gills; you must be able to touch the mucous membrane and the gills must look a healthy red." She pointed out the difference between a blood red and a dyed red and warned me that fisher folk were notorious for artificially colouring the gills of stale fish. "Don't accept the price they tell you. Always bargain!"

After a few days of Doris's tutoring, I became quite adept at the art of shopping. My mantra was never to trust the vendors at the market, and that realization cut to the core of the task before me. One thing was certain as my innate religious values of trust were thrown into a state of flux: the new way of conducting my life was taking precedence over the old.

Not long after we had returned from our honeymoon, I decided to put my newly acquired cooking skills to the test. First, I informed his mother that Earl and I would not be coming over to her place for dinner. My mother-in-law was clearly concerned about her son's welfare. "Do you know how to cook? What will you eat?" she asked anxiously. "Don't worry, Mummy, I'll cook something." My entire day was then spent in the kitchen. I prepared rice, beef curry and steamed vegetables.

Knowing Earl to be a person of taste, I laid the table for two using some of our wedding gifts, including a new set of tablemats, cutlery and crockery. As Earl entered our flat, he noticed the table and asked what was happening. "I have a surprise for you!" I laughed. As he emerged from his shower, he noticed three piping hot dishes on the table. He was thrilled at my efforts and thoroughly enjoyed the meal. Together we did the dishes, and before he sat down to his customary scotch, he insisted that we drive down to his mother's flat to let her know that he had just eaten a most delicious meal.

His mother was satisfied that I was making a gallant effort to become a suitable wife for her precious son. "Tomorrow, come back here for dinner – you must be tired, my girl, after cooking today." Earl and I agreed. But as days passed, I tried my hand at a variety of new dishes. Notwithstanding the fact that "Mummy" as I called her was a woman of few words, I knew full well that below this calm exterior was a woman of steely qualities, a woman who expected her son's every need would be catered to by his wife. These were standards that all Anglo Indian women were expected to conform to. Nel was no different.

A PROMISE FULFILLED

As I sat down one day to have tea with Earl's mother, she asked me to accompany her to the Church of Our Lady Help of Christians, about fifteen miles away. She added a note of mystery by urging me to keep the trip confidential. On the appointed day, we arrived at the church, where she asked me to join her in reciting the rosary. She then removed her gold chain and handed it to me. Summoning the priest-in-charge, she asked me to hand over the gold chain to him. This was a commitment kept: Earl's mother had promised the Virgin that upon her son's happy marriage she would donate her gold chain, something she treasured greatly, so that it could be sold and the funds used to help orphans.

Later, back in her flat, she took my right hand and on my ring finger she quietly slipped a gold ring with three semi-precious stones. This was her transformed wedding ring. She had had it melted and reset to give to Earl's wife. It was her way of showing us that her utmost wishes had come to pass.

These gestures made me realize that my relationship with Earl's mother, or Mummy Nellie as I called her, was a treasured gift. I knew that day that she and I had started a journey towards a lasting friendship built on mutual respect and love. What a privilege it was to be her daughter-in-law.

STARTING A FAMILY

Earl and I wanted to conceive a child as soon as possible. He was forty, I was thirty-two, and given our age we realized the sooner the better. However, while on our honeymoon, I had my period. It was clear that we could lose no further time. On our return to Bombay, we met with specialists who conducted routine tests and assured us that all was well. All we needed to do was to be patient, hope and pray. My gynecologist, however, advised me to track my basal body temperature so we could better anticipate the days of ovulation.

Every morning, Earl noted down my temperature. Months passed and still I was not pregnant. Doris, who had trained as a nurse, had suggested I undergo a dilation and curettage; a procedure she believed would facilitate pregnancy. However, Earl had noticed the persistence of my current high basal body temperature and concluded that I was pregnant; the doctor therefore declined to do the procedure. A few days later, Earl took my urine for the routine test. All day I hoped and prayed for good news. We had no telephone in our flat, so Earl had promised that the moment he had the news he would return home.

I sat impatiently at the bedroom window waiting for his car to appear around the corner. When he finally arrived, I knew it was good news: he leapt out of the car, threw his arms into the air and made a positive sign with his hand. I rushed to the door. He hugged and kissed me and rushed me into the bedroom, where he got down on his knees and reverently kissed my tummy.

Now we wanted to share the news with his mother and then with Doris, Claude, Verna and Bihari. Earl's mother sprung from her chair, kissed me and in the characteristic Anglo-Indian fashion, made the sign of the cross on my forehead, blessing me and my child. "Ma, if it is a girl, I am going to give her a pet name," said Earl. "It will be Buffy. I like the sound of it." The Anglo Indian community was a predominantly Christian Community and had adopted many of the customs of the Latin church. One such custom was the sign of the Cross on the forehead. This was both a sign of blessing and approval.

Each morning and night, we prayed that everything would go well with the pregnancy. A few weeks later, my blood work tested RH negative, while Earl's tested RH positive. This would have posed a major problem had we been married a decade earlier, before the advent of gamma globulin. When this drug is administered to the mother twenty-four hours after giving birth, it immunizes her from the build-up of antibodies that could endanger future pregnancies. The drug, not yet manufactured in India, could be imported.

I now realized how providential it was that Earl and I married at the time we did. Had we married earlier, we might have been able to have only one child. Earl took the news in stride. He had a mystical belief in the power of divine intervention. "We will leave everything in the hands of God," he said. In certain ways, he was as immutable as his father Simon, certain of his faith in the goodness of God.

As a father-to-be, Earl encouraged me to read widely about pregnancy and childbirth and to highlight relevant passages so we could discuss them each evening. Together we planned a healthy lifestyle and eating habits. Every morning, I did prescribed exercises and every evening we went for our accustomed walk along the sea face after dinner. At the same time, I continued my doctoral research at home, with occasional visits to the university.

With a baby on the way, it was now time for us to purchase a new flat with more space than our current abode. As well, Earl's mother had declared that she wanted to spend her declining years in Earl's home. I was the last of a large family and grew up amidst a large throng of nephews and nieces. Furthermore my life in boarding school and later as a nun gave me the required experience to accomodate the needs of others. I knew I had the skills to provide for an aged mother-in-law. She wasn't in very good health having suffered a major stroke a few years earlier.

As Earl and I set out looking at buildings under construction, I realized how thorough an individual he was. In a two-inch binder, he would file the blueprints of the various flats we had visited, along with their respective characteristics. From time to time, he would compare the pros and cons of each flat.

Earl's mother grew impatient with the perceived lack of progress in making a choice. "I guess you people don't want me to move in with you!" she said angrily one day. I looked at her. She usually had the face of one who absorbs information and tucks it away, perhaps to think about later. But today her face no longer looked so reassuring. I was perplexed and resolved inwardly to settle the matter with my husband.

The following morning, I asked Earl about the purchase of the flat. He once again explained to me that this was an important investment and would take more time. "Is it so complicated? Why are you dragging your feet?" I snapped. For the first time, I saw a different man. In a fury, he yelled, "Stop it! I don't want my wife to be a nag!" I jumped up, burst out crying and ran toward the bathroom. I wanted to lock myself in. Doris had warned me about Earl's bad temper, but I had never experienced it. Earl came running after me and grabbed me in his arms. He apologized profusely, but he also warned me in no uncertain words that he wouldn't tolerate a nagging wife. Chastened, I learned my lesson.

During the subsequent years in our married life, there would be many instances when I would fail. But Earl would always be there, nearly always the first to apologize. Just as fast as he would lose his temper, he would be composed. I vowed to learn from him and try to do the same. The sun never set on our anger. This is the hallmark of our married life. We fall and just as fast as we fall, we pick up the pieces and move ahead. Sometimes I was annoyed at Earl's predisposition to minutiae, but this was leavened by the knowledge that what mattered most was his unquestionable love for me. It provided the mirror that reflected my innate hopes and aspirations.

One day, Earl rushed into our flat with the news that he had found the most beautiful place and wanted me to see it immediately. He was right. It was the best we had seen in our search. At one thousand five hundred square feet, large by Indian standards, it was carefully planned, with a living and dining area, three bedrooms, servant's quarters and four bathrooms. The lot provided ample room for children to play. The building was eighteen storeys tall and we made the decision to purchase a flat on the second floor.

Our new home would take another four months to complete. I was now eight months pregnant. Excited, we made the final preparations for the baby's arrival. Doris helped me to purchase the baby's clothes, and Verna gave me a baby bassinette as well as a baby bed. Since we only had a double bed in our one bedroom flat I insisted that Earl get a good night's rest by sleeping on the pull-out couch in the living room. I realized that he needed the rest much more than I – since I was now a stay-at-home mom.

A MAN OF MANY FACETS

As months passed, I realized a certain truth about Earl, a trait that many had warned me about. Earl was a fastidious man, given to detail and passionate about even the most trivial of matters. In the beginning, it exasperated me. For instance, we differed about the temperature at which the pressure cooker had to be set: I wanted it high while he wanted it low. He wanted to open faucets at a trickle while I wanted to open them full blast. The house keys, according to Earl, had to be hung at a certain spot on the rack; I was content that they were on the rack at all. "It just doesn't matter," I would shout.

But with time, I realized it did matter to my husband. Behind most of his thinking was often a hidden logic. Earl was, for example, conscious of the environment well before others. "You know something; I'm the only woman who could have ever lived with you and that only after having spent eleven years as a nun!" I would say. He would grin and respond, "You're right!" He would then take me into his arms and plant a kiss on my lips. We were both strong personalities, but we were also maturely aware that if married life were to be successfully joyful we each had to be willing to accomodate the other's opinions and feelings. With this in mind we deftly navigated our differences with patience, love and understanding. Forty-six years later we still fight. And we laugh. And we kiss.

OUR FIRSTBORN

On December 19, I felt the first contractions as Earl and I took a walk after dinner. We rushed back home and I got my bags together while Earl got in touch with Doris. A few minutes later, Earl helped me into the car and drove to pick up Doris en route to the hospital. I would deliver my baby at St. Elizabeth's, an excellent hospital run by Roman Catholic nuns. Many of my experiences of this time are poignantly memorable. I realized I had become a vestibule of God's creative power. I realized that within me lay a beautiful human being – a child that would one day hopefully reflect our family heritage. Earl stood at my side and gazed down lovingly upon me, never leaving me for a second, and repeating the words, "breathe in, breathe out" in unison with the contractions. It was an immense help.

Labor pains are often labelled as the most acute suffering a person is subjected to. In the seventies in India medications to ease labor pains was unheard of. Rhythmic exercises that we had read about and practised offered me the panacea I so much needed. At 11:30 a.m., a nurse helped me onto a stretcher and I was wheeled away from the private room where Earl would continue to wait and into the delivery room. Doris accompanied me. At 11:50 a.m., I heard a baby scream – my own baby. I saw Doris run out to give Earl the news. He so desperately wanted his eldest born to be a girl. "Buffy" was the pet name he chose for her and here she was in all her beautiful baby glory. The nurse held up the baby for me to see – a beautiful seven-pound, fourteen-ounce girl.

A few minutes later, Doris entered with my baby girl wrapped in a pink blanket. I looked at her – she was so adorable. The nuns called her "Rose Bud." She had an olive complexion, deep pink and delicately shaped lips, pink cheeks, brown eyes, a thick mop of dark brown hair and the high cheekbones of her father. She was gorgeous!

I couldn't wait to hold her, but a complication had developed. A few minutes after the birthing, I began to feel uncomfortable and then the pain became excruciating. My gynecologist was on his way out of the hospital when one of the nurses informed him of the emergency. He rushed back into the labour room and realized it was a case of internal bleeding. He immediately made an incision and removed a clot of blood.

The Roman Catholic hospital where our little girl was born bore a large statue of the Madonna in the labor room. As I gazed upon her maternal smile I tried to recall the scene in that small room where the Virgin gave birth to the Son of God, having gone through the same pangs of child birth. I thanked her for helping me through the ordeal and saving my life. Recalling my very close encounter with death, I for the very first time realized the fragility of life, how it can disappear with just one human error.

When I finally held my baby, I thanked God for the gift of this new life. Earl held her close to his heart with pride and joy, never ceasing to admire his little Buffy. Looking deep into her eyes, he realized that all this little bundle needed was to be lovingly cajoled as she surmounted the challenges of life. At that moment as he looked into her eyes, he bared his soul and entered into a communion with his beloved little girl. He vowed his everlasting love and loyalty based on his paternal willingness to sacrifice his all so that she could bloom forth into her full potential.

That evening, Verna, Bihari, Claude and his family visited us at the hospital. Our baby was passed from hand to hand, each holder admiring her stunning looks. Earl's happiness was complete. His mother was overjoyed. Her beloved son Earl was now a father, something for which she had prayed for a very long time.

Ten days later, Earl and Doris accompanied us back to our flat. Doris carried our daughter in her arms throughout the half-hour trip. Baby-seats in cars were an unknown commodity in the India of the 1970s. At the flat, we laid her in her bassinette hoping she would fall asleep. But no! Very soon I was to taste the joys and burden of motherhood. Our little Buffy suffered from colic.

For the first three months, she cried intermittently during the day and non-stop from 6:00 p.m. to 9:00 p.m. Then, during the night, she would fall asleep out of sheer exhaustion, only to wake again after a few hours. Earl would help me in whatever way he could. Knowing the responsibilities of his business, I would encourage him to get some sleep, but vigilant spouse and father that he was, he continued to stay at my side. I did have domestic help – a woman who performed all my household chores, so I was free to concentrate on the baby. I did my best.

OUR FAMILY HOME

Our new flat was now ready except for last-minute renovations. With the little time I had, I packed our belongings into boxes and they were transported to our new flat with help from Earl's factory employees. On our very first night in the flat, our little baby surprised us – she slept through the night. I was grateful for the first night of unbroken sleep in two months. Buffy's baby bed had been placed in the large living area with bay windows that allowed the cool tropical breeze to flow in. She evidently loved it.

Being the thorough person he is, Earl set to work to make our flat an elegant place. Several years prior to our marriage, Earl had found success and wealth not by virtue of inheritance, not by shrewd cunning, not by exploitation but by diligent hard work and an unparalleled respect for each of his employees. He had four carpenters, two electricians, two tailors and a mason at work full time. The carpenters worked on the kitchen cabinets and the bedroom furniture, the tailors on ceiling-to-floor drapes, and the masons and electricians on the interior lighting. By the end of six weeks, our dream of a comfortable home had come true.

We had much to celebrate: the christening of our baby, Earl's forty-second birthday and the housewarming. We set the date for April 14. Our little baby was christened Anjali Helen – Anjali, a Sanskrit name meaning "an offering to the Lord," and also chosen as a name in honour of my Sister Superior, Sister Angela, who was central to enabling my relationship with Earl. Helen was Earl's mother's name and also the name of the foundress of my Missionary Order. We chose Bihari and Verna as godparents. They had helped Earl get his education and we wanted to show our appreciation.

‡ Godparents, Verna and Bihari with Anjali (1974)

‡ Blessing of our Home, Mercy, Earl and Anjali (1974)

Our extended family and Earl's close friends were invited to the party, and about fifty people enjoyed our hospitality. Earl spared no expense: a stuffed suckling, prepared by one of the top chefs in the suburb of Bandra, mutton biriyani (rice and mutton cooked with Indian spices,) chicken curry, pork vindaloo (a traditional Goan dish) and salad. Dessert was strawberry shortcake with the words "Buffy our joy," which Earl and I cut together. The Chivas Regal flowed. As a teenager aspiring to the religious life and conscious of one's commitment to the vow of poverty, material trappings were not what I sought after. However, married to Earl, a successful businessman, I realized there was no harm in sharing a life of affluence, which he was rightfully entitled to after years of committed stewardship of his God given talents.

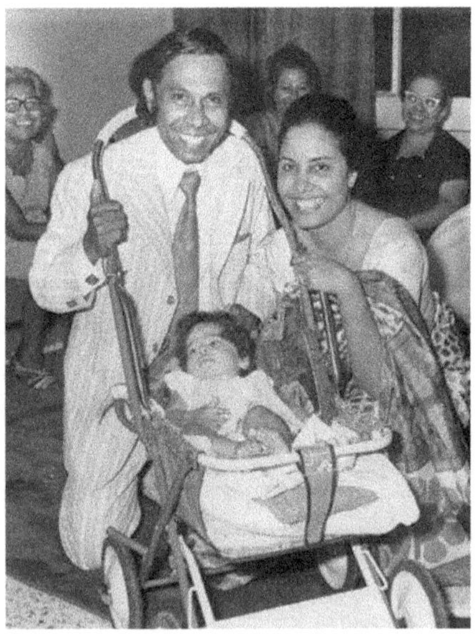

‡ Christening party: Earl, Mercy and Anjali (1974)

His beloved mother's dreams were finally fulfilled. She now lived with her son and his family and had become the central figure in our home. Hers would be the seat at the head of the table, while Earl and I would occupy the two seats to her left. Here we could enjoy the beautiful tree line that marked the edge of the property on which the building stood. Every morning and night, her son greeted her with a hug and a kiss on her cheek. We tried to model our home in accordance with the principles and values of Christian living, while at the same time reflecting our individual identities, our needs, our hopes and dreams and our challenges.

Despite the fact that Earl was a well-established businessman, we tried to avoid ostentatious acquisitions and concentrated more on prayerfulness and friendships. We continued with our Daily Mass, morning and night prayers, and we tried hard to foster a spirit of care and fellowship. Our spiritual growth was in progress.

As a nun I followed a daily routine of Holy Mass, Communion and the recital of the Divine Office (a combination of Scriptural readings) three times a day. In total we spent about four hours a day in prayer. However, once married we continued our prayer life, with Earl as my devoted companion in prayer. We started each day with Holy Mass and Communion. Every night we said the rosary. This latter was a Roman Catholic tradition which had become the central form of devotion in most Anglo-Indian homes. This devotion highlighted the special mysteries in the life of Jesus Christ.

As a wife and mother, I could manage our household with the help of Earl's mother and a maid. "Mummy," as I now called Earl's mother, would manage the kitchen. She was a first-class cook and, with the help of my maid Celine, turned out the most delicious dishes for our family. Frequently, Mummy would turn out favourite dishes that Earl grew up on; then with her own money and with the help of the building gardener she purchased the local brew. Nothing gave her greater pleasure than to see her family enjoy a meal she had cooked.

Life in our household was perfect. Anjali was growing healthy and strong with her milestones well in place. We continued to track my basal body temperature and the readings were promptly plotted by Earl each morning. This exercise of noting down my temperature was a strategy that was in keeping with Earl's engineering meticulousness. It was an exciting morning ritual. Observing the basal body temperature spike and then plummet offered him an insight into a woman's reproductive cycle – to him, an engineer, it offered him a poignant insight into God's creative wisdom.

One morning, Earl informed me that he felt I was pregnant for the second time. The test confirmed that I was. Anjali by now was only four months old. I wasn't perturbed. I knew I could count on the help of servants. We couldn't have been happier. Our little Buffy was poised to have a little brother or sister. We waited.

Because my doctoral research was progressing very slowly, there were times when I wondered whether I should pursue this venture. I was happily married, had a lovely baby with another on the way, and wondered whether my priorities were right. Perhaps, I thought, I should abandon my dream and concentrate on my family. However, I had a deep-seated urge to continue. I was not one to abandon a venture once I had in full faith undertaken it.

Despite the fact that I had left the convent, I found no reasonable inconsistency in this decision. I was convinced that God had chosen this path for me. On the other hand, abandoning the pursuit of my Ph.D. seemed an exercise in failure – failure to achieve a goal I had set out to pursue.

DARK CLOUDS

In September of 1974, I was frantically searching for a lost diamond from my engagement ring when Mummy noticed me rummaging through the sheets and pillows of Buffy's bed. "That's bad luck, my girl," she said, almost choking with fear. "Don't worry Mummy, Earl will take it to the jeweler and have it replaced," I replied. "That's not what worries me, my girl – a lost diamond is a sign of death in the family." "Oh, Mummy, don't believe in all this superstitious nonsense," I replied.

A few minutes later, I watched her as she walked down the road, walking stick in hand, hobbling her way to Verna's house. Mummy was now quite old, about seventy-five years, and time was catching up with her. Verna and Bihari were having their customary tea on their lawns. I would learn later that Mummy immediately gave them news of the lost diamond. "Maybe it's Bihari's Uncle Ram," said Verna. Mummy responded, "No, no, it can be me." "Why think of only old people?" asked Bihari. "Anyone can pass away – it can be me!" He was only forty-four-years-old and Mummy was visibly upset with this comment.

The following morning, Bihari rang our doorbell and walked straight into our bedroom to see Earl while Mummy and I continued to have our breakfast. Bihari emerged soon afterwards, rather unsettled from his conversation; bent down, took Buffy in his arms, held her up in the air and planted a kiss on each of her cheeks. He then put her back on the floor, kissed Mummy, said goodbye to me and walked out the door. "Bihari wanted me to accompany him to the races in Pune and spend the weekend there, but I refused," Earl explained. "The races are no longer a priority for me. My family and business are!"

The following day, a Sunday, was a work day for Earl, who returned in time for us to attend the evening service at our parish church. When we returned, Verna phoned with the alarming news that Bihari, his nephew Sunil and Claude had met with a serious road accident en route from Pune. Earl drove to Doris's flat and together with a family friend, drove two hours to the town near the accident site, where they found Claude, unconscious, lying on a bench at the police station.

Later in the evening, Verna phoned again. "My Barry's gone, my Barry's gone!" she sobbed, adding that Sunil had also passed away. I phoned Doris to give her the solemn news. Her immediate reaction was one of shock at the loss of Bihari and Sunil and concern for her husband Claude. Mummy was already in bed, but I knelt at her side and together we said a prayer. Earl was both shocked and saddened. He had lost his friend and partner and realized he was left alone to steer the ship *Earl Bihari*. However, what concerned him most was that his sister Verna was now left without a loving husband on whom she leaned to make most family decisions. Very soon, the news of the accident spread through the streets of Bandra. Bihari was a well-known and highly respected resident. For the next few hours, the phone was jammed with calls from concerned friends.

Claude was alive, but on impact he had been thrown twenty metres and suffered fractures to his hip as well as a severed jugular vein. Fortunately, Earl had the presence of mind to wait for the ambulance and not try to prop him up on the back seat of his car, which could have perhaps left him a quadraplegic. Claude, who at fifty-two was the oldest of the three men, was the sole survivor. The initial prognosis was not encouraging, but Claude was a fighter and that gave us hope.

What caused the accident? It appeared that Bihari had lost control of his car, which then swerved off the road and hit a tree. Bihari suffered multiple rib fractures, which penetrated his lungs. Claude and the nephew, who were not wearing seat belts, were thrown out of the car. Sunil hit his head on a rock and died instantly. Bihari passed away in the ambulance en route to the hospital. I realized life can be innately cruel and deal out suffering, most often unbidden. It is for those of us who are spared this ordeal to remain focused and calm and with grace turn it to our spiritual good.

Bihari's body was brought to his house for funeral services while Sunil's was prepared for the Hindu custom of cremation. Claude was brought to the city by ambulance to one of the most reputable hospitals, which boasted some of the country's top orthopedic surgeons. Over the years Claude would recall with fear and gratitude the fact that he was the oldest of the three travellers in that car to survive. He attributed his escape from death to the snap decision he made to switch seats and travel in the back seat rather than in front – even though Bihari had requested him to stay in the front seat.

Catholic funeral services were held for Bihari in their own house in Bandra; afterwards a well-attended cortege of mourners followed the coffin to the local cemetery. There, Bihari was interred. Eventually, the dynamics in the families that were responsible for the establishment and early successes of Earl Bihari would change, prompting some of them to leave India and migrate to Canada.

In the aftermath, Claude was faced with exorbitant medical bills. India in the seventies had no universal medical coverage. Earl stepped in and paid a generous portion of the bills for his surgery. This he did magnanimously and with the utmost grace.

A SECOND BIRTH IN OUR FAMILY

By January of the following year, the recent family tragedy continued to hang over us. But amidst the gloom, Earl and I were thrilled to welcome our second little girl into our family. Like Buffy, she was born with a thick mop of dark hair, large almond-shaped eyes and a captivating smile. We would name her Gita Agnes Romana. *Gitanjali* is Rabindranath Tagore's *Song Offerings* (a collection of poems.) Anjali translates into *Offering*, Gita into *Song of Praise*. It was also the name of a dear student of mine who served as a communicator with Earl during the weeks preceding my decision to leave the convent. Agnes Romana, my names in religion, would complement our new daughter's first name.

The birth of Gita soon brought to the forefront the caring person Anjali would grow up to be. The initial shock of a little baby lying next to me at the hospital, to her almost dramatic acceptance of another in the nest, afforded us with an insight into this little girl's personality. Anjali would grow up to be the rock of support in our family.

Unlike Anjali, Gita was a serene and placid baby. Perhaps I was a more experienced mother and better equipped to handle a newborn. She slept for the greater part of the day, as long as she was well fed. She would make rapid strides in her milestones, walking before her first birthday and uttering complete sentences before she turned two. Soon she became as much of a chatterbox as her big sister. I was now overwhelmed with the responsibilities of motherhood. Earl was busy at the business, and I had become totally dependent on my servants. For the moment I decided to temporarily abandon the pursuit of my Ph.D. and enjoy the fruits of motherhood. I looked upon my little family as a gift from God, a gift I had to lovingly nurture and mould. Gita was barely four months old when I conceived once again. We now waited patiently for our third arrival.

✣ Earl, Mercy, Anjali and Gita (1975)

Ten

DARK CLOUDS

SEATED AT HIS OFFICE DESK, Earl pondered the future of his company with growing unease. He had devoted almost twenty of the most productive years of his life into shaping Earl Bihari. It was his brainchild, his livelihood and his passion, but at the same time he knew his grip on it was slipping away.

After the automobile accident that killed Bihari and sidelined a badly injured Claude, Earl initially ran the business single-handedly. After a time, Claude was able to return to the company. Its finances were sound: Earl had established one of the finest tool rooms and production shops in Bombay, and his client base was wide and varied. But the winds of change would soon strike, first in the form of labour unrest, and then through events of a life-changing nature.

The company, with two hundred and twenty employees, had its own internal union. The personnel seemed content with their wages, and respected their manager, Claude, who was considered a person of integrity. He depended on crutches to move around and medication to manage the pain that he endured throughout the day. But he was a fighter and everyone knew full well that he would soon be back to his usual self.

It was at this time that a disgruntled employee, who was considered a leader of sorts, encouraged a group to vote to become members of one of the most powerful unions in the city, one that would not hesitate to bring employers to their knees. A short-lived strike was concluded by a new agreement. However, one of the terminated employees filed a suit in labour court. In a socialist country like the India of the seventies, scarcely any employer was known to have succeeded in legal proceedings against this particular union.

The case dragged on, sapping a great deal of Earl's time and energy. The management of the company was in flux. With Bihari's passing away, his role in the business was now assumed by his next of kin, Jonathan. Earl welcomed him. Jonathan began to learn about the business and assume responsibilities. He soon realized that Earl Bihari was a "gold mine" in Claude's words. Though his contribution initially was negligible, the family continued to draw the substantial income Bihari formerly drew. Earl was determined that Bihari's family would not suffer financially from the tragic event that had befallen them, and that they would continue to earn the same as when he was alive. Jonathan was now drawing Bihari's salary as well as their family share of other income which the company generated.

Since Earl was preoccupied with the legal proceedings at the labour court much of the day-to-day operations of the company were now assumed by Jonathan. Bereft of any technical skills he turned to Earl's deputy Dean. Earl had recruited Dean a freshly graduated engineer. Over the years he had acquired considerable training from Earl and was well versed in the technical know-how of all the products. Soon Jonathan and Dean became close friends. Initially, Earl was indifferent to this closeness realizing that Dean was closer in age to Jonathan than he was. Both were young bachelors with common interests, sometimes vacationing together. However, with time, the relationship took on the mantle of a threat to Earl. Bihari and Earl had shared a common trust; a trust that was implicitly based on mutual respect for each other. Within a few years Jonathan and Dean partnered to start a new manufacturing company which virtually became a direct competitor to Earl Bihari. Earl was angered and felt utterly betrayed.

He consulted a friend who, along with his brother had owned a well-established manufacturing company in the city of Bombay. Then a painful family feud erupted. Legal battles ensued. The families were ripped apart while the company went down in ashes. This experience was a learning moment for Earl. He knew his position at the company made him the eye of the storm. He had to act immediately. But while he considered legal action, he realized that a legal battle would plunge him and his young family into an expensive and time-consuming process. The resolution of civil suits in India during the seventies took years. He would look elsewhere for a solution.

Despite the goings-on at the factory, Earl tried not to lose his capacity for patience and endurance. He was angry; but was able to maintain a tranquil mind. This peace that he was gifted with, solely because of his immense trust in God, would follow him well into his old age.

Earl knew he had two options: offer to buy out his late partner's share of the company or start a new business. He would pursue both options. With this in mind he flew to Ahmedabad to touch base with his former employer Mr. Desai – now a very wealthy businessman. Yes, Mr. Desai was interested. He would buy Bihari's family's share of the company and Earl would continue at the helm of Earl Bihari. Fortified with this proposition, Earl approached Jonathan: "How much do you want for Bihari's share of the company?" "Fifty lakhs" was his response. Earl waited. He pursued the second option as well. With this end in view he explored together with an industrialist friend a new business initiative. A project report was prepared for the manufacture of light bulb holders for a growing Indian market. God would show him the path.

Earl at the same time knew he had to provide for his wife and young family. He began building a nest egg outside Earl Bihari. Whatever income Earl Bihari generated was no longer reinvested in it but rather in the stock market and elsewhere. These i nvestments s oon s howed signs of growth. He was encouraged. This would be his future focus.

In mid-1975, an old friend named Frank Lobo surprised Earl with a call. Frank was a very successful businessman whom Earl had learned to respect since their early University days and later as colleagues working for the same multi-national company. They arranged to meet the following day at the factory. Earl took him around the tool room, the air-conditioned area where precision machines and instruments were maintained at twenty degrees Celsius, as well as the press shop, the heat treatment shop and the phosphating and surface finishing areas. Earl had designed and built all of these processes.

"Earl, this is nothing less than a miracle," exclaimed Frank. "This place must be worth about one crore of rupees!" Given the exchange rate that pre-vailed at the time, that amount represented about one million U.S. dollars. "I'm not sure how much it is worth, but I guess it's around that figure," replied Earl. "As well, a certificate of excellence was awarded to the company from the state government," he added. Frank was also impressed with the client list, which included several multi-national corporations.

At dinner with our family that evening, Frank summed up his impressions of the visit. "Mercy, you must be so proud of your husband! The company is just fantastic!" I replied simply, realizing with pleasure that my husband's accomplishments had been acknowledged by a peer. "Earl has achieved it all in a tottering economy which has been growing so slowly and sometimes in negative territory," I replied.

MSFC

MAHARASHTRA STATE FINANCIAL CORPORATION

New Excelsior Building, 5th, 7th, 8th & 9th floors, Amrit Keshav Nayak Marg, Fort, Bombay - 400 001

M/s. EARL BIHARI PVT. LTD.
Kripalani Inds. Estate, Saki Vihar Road, Saki Naka,
Bombay - 72.
(Shri Earl Anselm, Director)

have been sanctioned aggregate loan of Rs. 10,95,000 from March 1964 to November 1973 by the Maharashtra State Financial Corporation for implementing their project for Electrical components, small tools, Automobile components The concern has progressed well during all these years and has been very punctual in honouring the commitments of the Maharashtra State Financial Corporation by way of payment of interest and repayment of principal. We, consider them as one of the best clients in view of their promptness regularity and progress.

In recognition of the above fact, we, the Chairman and the Board of Directors of the Maharashtra State Financial Corporation on the occasion of the 15th Anniversary of the Corporation have pleasure in awarding the "CERTIFICATE OF BEST PERFORMANCE"

TO

M/s. EARL BIHARI PVT. LTD.

Presented on this Second Day of January. Nineteen Hundred and Seventy Eight. i. e. the day of the main function with Shri. Vasantdada Patil, Chief Minister Maharashtra, as Chief Guest.

(M. R. KOLHATKAR)
Managing Director

(HOMI J. H. TALEYARKHAN)
Chairman

महावित्त

‡ Certificate from State Financial Corporation (1978)

TO WHOM IT MAY CONCERN

Mr. Earl Anselm has been associated with us from 1969 onward, when he pioneered on behalf of his firm Messers. Earl Bihari (now Earl Bihari Pvt. Ltd.), the manufacture of NATO type Link Cartridge 7.62 mm for machine-guns. He has developed his Company into the leading manufacturer of this item in the country, and is very well known in Defence Circles for high standard of quality and reliability. His Company has supplied over a billion links. He has also exported several millions of links which were inspected by us, and the Company was on two occasions awarded certificates for excellence in performance, by the Engineering Export Promotion Council.

In addition to Links, Mr. Anselm has developed several other stores for Defence, notably Charger 7.62 mm for Ammunition B, which has been supplied in large quantities, Hand-Guard Inserts for rifles, and Clip Q.F. Cartridge 2A. He has also supplied Browning Links to the Air Force and Clips to the Indian Navy.

I would strongly recommend him for the development, production and supply of high quality engineering stores.

(M R IYENGAR)
COLONEL
SENIOR INSPECTOR OF ARMAMENTS

INSPECTORATE OF ARMAMENTS
VIKHROLI : BOMBAY - 83
DATED : 08 APR '83

INSPECTORATE OF ARMAMENTS VIKHROLI, BOMBAY-400 083.

✣ Certificate from Inspector of Armaments (1983)

Institution of Industrial Managers

This is to certify that

Earl Anselm

has been admitted a

FELLOW

Given under the common seal of
the Institution of Industrial Managers

11th June 1983

MEMBER OF COUNCIL

SECRETARY

✣ Certificate from Institution of Industrial Managers (1983)

British Institute of Management

Certificate of Membership

THIS IS TO CERTIFY THAT

EARL ANSELM

WAS ADMITTED A FELLOW OF THE INSTITUTE

ON THE 21st DAY OF January 1983

Given under the Common Seal of the British Institute of Management

CHAIRMAN OF COUNCIL

CHAIRMAN MEMBERSHIP COMMITTEE

SECRETARY

This Certificate must be returned to the Institute on cessation of Membership

‡ Certificate from British Institute of Management (1983)

THE BIRTH OF OUR FIRST SON

In May 1975, just four months after the birth of our second daughter, tests confirmed that I was once again pregnant. We were overjoyed.

We considered each child a gift of love from God. We hoped for a son. We knew that with each child we had to recharge our motivational batteries and perhaps even reinvent ourselves. Love was to be at the core of all our endeavours and we realized that when it was focused on our children, we could together achieve the most unexpected outcomes – perhaps even the unattainable.

My obstetrician had calculated that my baby was due in the last week of February. By now, with three closely spaced pregnancies, my uterus had distended considerably. I was carrying a relatively large baby, and therefore had to have my abdomen strapped to my shoulders to ease the pressure on my spine. I had domestic help, but with two children under the age of two to look after, and Earl preoccupied about the company, life was stressful. Encouraged by Earl, I put my faith in God and trusted that all would be well. We continued our daily Mass and prayer. Despite all the events that were swirling around us, we maintained our belief that we would survive.

On February 29, I went into labour at 5:00 p.m. Earl, accompanied by Doris, drove me to the nursing home where our two girls had been born. As I was getting into the car, an elderly lady who lived on the third floor of our building shouted to me from her balcony. "This is a leap year. Don't have your baby today! Wait until 12:00 a.m.; otherwise, you will have three girls!" It is strange that despite my very strong Roman Catholic instincts I did buy into this superstition. Like most Indian women it was important to me to bear a son to carry on his father's name. I hoped my baby would be born on the first of March and bring into fruition this age-old superstition.

As it happened, our baby would not arrive until 5:00 a.m. of the following day. When I heard the infant cry, and saw Doris run out the labour room to give Earl the news, I knew we had our son: a bonny boy weighing eight pounds, ten ounces. When I inquired later of the hospital staff, I found out that all the babies born on Feb. 29, 1976 were girls. Those born on March 1 were boys.

Like his big sisters, our newborn had a thick mop of dark hair, but also a huge head. Earl's mother Nel was thrilled: her beloved son now had a son to carry on his name. "Big head – just like the father! Must be full of brains!" she exclaimed. We would name him Samuel Earl Bihari. His first name was given in tribute to the priest Samuel Ryan, who had advised me to leave the convent to become Earl's wife.

‡ Earl, Mercy, Anjali, Gita and Samuel (1976)

NEL

Nel was the centre of our home. Though small in stature, she commanded love and respect from her son, the servants and me.

She doted on her grandchildren and they showered her with unconditional love. With her chiseled features, perfectly coiffed white hair, over which she always wore a cap to ward off a cold, and walking stick in hand, she relentlessly wore what she called her "home frock" while tottering around our flat.

On one occasion, Earl returned from work and stepped into his mother's room to greet her. With his arm around her, he noticed huge tears in the dress under the arm and around the pocket. "Why do you continue to wear these tatters, Mummy?" he demanded. "Never mind, my son, this is my home frock." Earl was indignant. "At home, you should be decently outfitted." He then opened the door of her cupboard in which several lovely, yet barely worn dresses were hanging. "Why don't you wear one of these?" he asked. "No, my son, they are my church frocks." "Church frocks?" he responded. "So on Sundays you dress up fashionably in your silks, handbag, hat and feathers and the rest of the week you walk around in tatters!"

Mummy, visibly upset, focused her eyes on the floor and said nothing. About half an hour later, she stood at the entrance of our bedroom, her choice black felt hat precariously balancing on the fist of her right hand. "So are you happy now, there are no feathers on my hat?" The moment Earl had walked out of her room, Mummy had removed the feathers. She had not discarded them but safely tucked them away in her drawer. Earl was visibly moved. He grabbed her small frame in his strong arms. "I'm sorry, Mummy, I didn't mean to hurt you," he apologized. A few minutes later, the feathers were back on the hat. Mummy continued to wear her tatters at home and her silks for church. That's what made her happy, so he let it be.

Mummy belonged to the old school of Anglo Indians who

believed that all things "British" were beautiful. She was dazzled by Caucasian features. With this end in mind, Mummy supervised the baby's bath religiously. As my maid Kamu did the bathing, Mummy stood next to her and gave her instructions. The baby's forehead had to be massaged flat down; the bridge of the nose straight up; the cheekbones upwards. Good calves, she believed, could be developed by massaging the legs downwards toward the calves. This ritual was followed every day in the first eight months of the child's life.

As an ever-watchful Nana, Mummy was alert to her grandchildren's whereabouts. I attribute my children's safety to her diligence. On one occasion, when Sam was about a year old and had started taking a few baby steps, he crawled into Mummy's bedroom. He moved the chair stationed by her bureau, and dragged it toward the window. It was an easy climb for him to reach the windowsill. We lived on the second floor of the building, so the window was about sixty feet above the ground. Sam decided he would lie on his tummy on the window sill, which was about eighteen inches wide, and get a good view of the scene below.

Mummy, who was dozing on her bed, suddenly jumped up. She had the presence of mind not to shout and thus alarm her grandson. Having lost the use of her left side to a stroke, she needed help to save him, so she made her way to the kitchen and summoned my servant, who rushed to the baby's rescue. To this day, I have nightmares about this episode, and with loving gratitude think of Mummy Nel, who saved my little baby. Later, Mummy told me of her daily prayers to the guardian angels of my children to keep them safe.

Mummy moved in with us when she was in her seventies. Over the years, she had grown in wisdom and grace. She realized that in a country like India, where households depended on servants, the happiness of these individuals was tantamount to the stability of the home. Kamu was responsible for the smooth functioning of the kitchen. Mummy soon realized that she had a penchant for alcohol, and decided to win Kamu's allegiance by offering her a peg, but not more, every night. To this end, she asked Mali, the gardener, to provide her with a bottle of the local brew for a small sum of money every week.

This was kept a secret from Earl and me until Mummy was ill and bedridden. One evening, I opened her clothes cupboard and there, below her bed linen, was hidden a bottle of local brew. I was stunned. "Why would Mummy want a bottle of local brew when every day Earl offered her a glass of port wine, which she cherished?" I asked Christine, my other maid. "Oh, Aunty, night time Nana giving Kamu *daru* (liquor) – Kamu very happy." Therein lay the explanation.

⁜ Mercy, Earl, Nel, Gita and Anjali (1978)

‡ Daniel's 1st Birthday with Nel in the centre (1980)

‡ Mercy, Nel, Samuel, Daniel and servant Rajan (1980)

KAMU AND CHRISTINE

Life in India in the Seventies depended on servants. During my first three years of married life, the turnover of servants working for me was very high. I did some soul searching and came to the conclusion that I was not a demanding mistress. My training as a religious nun put the welfare of my servants in the forefront. I was not capable of exploiting them. What, then, was the problem? It was evident to me that they mistook my kindness for weakness. Needing help with three children under the age of three, I went to church and prayed fervently. I asked the Lord to send me two servants who would work for me indefinitely. Would He hear my prayer within the next twenty-four hours? "Please, Lord hear me, I implore!"

The following day, I opened the door to a woman in rags, her hair disheveled. She spoke only Gujarati, a tongue I didn't know. But she had heard I needed a servant. As I looked at her emaciated frame, intuition told me that she was the answer to my prayer. The only clothes she owned were the rags she was wearing. I welcomed her into my home and gave her a meal. She was hungry, not having eaten in the past day. I asked her to have a shower and wash the clothes she was wearing, to which I added some of my own old clothes. I had already won her gratitude and trust.

Then, in sign language and a few words in Hindi, I explained her duties. She would be in charge of the kitchen, under the supervision of my mother-in-law. I emphasized that each day by seven a.m. she would have to have the family breakfast and Earl's lunch box ready. Now, Kamu could not read a clock and consequently had no concept of time. However, like all village folks of India, she depended on her instincts. The next morning, I heard the flow of the kitchen faucet at 5:00 a.m. For the next eight years, that sound was as faithful a reminder of the time as the finest watch.

During the time she spent with us, Kamu developed into a

confident and powerful matron who saw to our every need. The well-being of our home revolved around her. Every three months, she visited her village, about two hundred miles away, laden with gifts for her family. She was now able to send her own two boys to school, so they no longer had to work in the fields. She also found jobs for her two daughters in Bombay. As time evolved, Kamu adopted all the trappings of sophistication that city life offered. It was a marvel to see her leave for her village, draped in a beautiful sari, her hair dyed, fingers manicured, a ladies' handbag hanging from her shoulder, sandals on her feet and sporting the sunglasses that were so much a signature of affluence in India.

A few weeks after Kamu knocked on my door, a pretty teenager presented herself. Her name was Christine. "Aunty Stella sending me," she said by way of introduction. Aunty Stella was a friend of mine whom I had asked to help me look for a servant to help with the kids. Christine was from a nearby slum, one of a family of ten children. Despite a life of poverty, she looked healthy and strong. She had unblemished glowing skin, perfectly white teeth and a captivating smile. She was hearty, jovial and friendly – great assets in someone who was going to be responsible for the well-being of my children. Christine danced and sang for them and became a kind of elder sister. She took great pride in dressing them up each evening, braiding Anjali and Gita's hair with colourful ribbons.

From four to seven in the evening, Kamu and Christine, together with my children, got together with the other servants and children from the building. While the children played, the servants gossiped. These servants were expert forecasters and predicted which couples were headed for divorce; which lady in the building was a hated mother-in-law; which married man was having an affair and with whom; which family was facing severe financial problems. I was always amazed at their accuracy.

After dinner and night prayers, the children got ready for bed. Christine also entertained my children with scenes from famous Bollywood movies. Often we heard loud laughter from the bedroom late into the night.

‡ Kamu, Christine, Gita, Samuel and Anjali (1978)

THE PHD CHALLENGE

After a hiatus of four years, I discussed with Earl the possibility of returning to teaching. My doctorate was going nowhere. I had done some preliminary research, but beyond that, I had shelved the effort. Sam, like Gita, was a very contented baby. I had trained him to follow a meticulous schedule. Christine was skilled enough to look after him as well as my two little girls. I reasoned that if I were to return to university teaching, I could kick-start work on my thesis and complete my doctoral requirements. I have never been one to abandon a half-finished objective. Earl agreed, with the caveat that my teaching did not jeopardize my primary role as wife and mother.

When I was offered a job as a lecturer at a local university college, I was overjoyed. I loved teaching, and opted for the morning shift from 6:30 a.m. to 11:30 a.m. Under Mummy's supervision, Kamu and Christine, with the help of a part-time cleaning service, kept my home well-organized.

A few months after I had returned to teaching, I dipped my toes into my doctoral research. I was determined to complete it within the next three years. I would try to postpone having another child. However, we wanted a little brother for Sam, so Earl and I discussed the possibility of adoption. We had a desire to open our home to a deprived child. For the moment, however, concentrating on the three little ones, teaching and research were my priorities. A good friend of ours had invested in a flat on the third floor of our building and allowed me to use it for my research. Every day, while the kids napped and later played downstairs under the supervision of my servants, I worked on my thesis. For five hours a day, I was able to focus on my research with no distractions. My doctorate came closer and closer to reaching fruition.

A TURN OF EVENTS AT EARL BIHARI

Earl's professional life, which had given him so much fulfillment, was now starting to cause him great distress. He realized his grip on day-to-day matters was quietly eroding. In early 1978, another turn of events presented itself. Claude was fifty-seven years old, the age of retirement for all Indians. Despite the excruciating pain that he still experienced from the effects of the accident, he worked assiduously to carry out his responsibilities as Office Manager. Nevertheless, his retirement was called for by Jonathan. Earl faced a dilemma: Claude still had three dependent children. Furthermore, the company had no provision for pensions. Also Bihari had assured Claude at the time of his leaving the Indian Telegraphs that he could continue working at the Company indefinitely. Earl was convinced that this commitment had to be honored.

SUMMER AT LONAVALA

The summer of 1978 provided a respite. As was our custom, we rented a bungalow in one of the hill stations close to Bombay. That year, we decided on the scenic town of Lonavala, about 100 miles to the east of the city. The children loved the countryside, so different from their urban life. The servants had a relaxed time with few schedules to keep. We savoured every moment of our stay; hiking, walking and picnicking all added to our enjoyment. Friends with young children visited us from time to time, providing a pleasing diversion for our own brood.

‡ Bungalow in Lonavala – with our ambassador cars in foreground (1978)

‡ Christine, Mercy, Anjali, Gita and Samuel vacationing in Lonavala (1978)

WINDS OF CHANGE

No sooner had we returned from our holiday than our phone rang. Doris was sobbing. She had always been the sister in control of a situation; I was the one who turned to her for help and advice. Whatever had happened? It transpired that while we were away, Claude had been let go.

Earl insisted that Claude be re-instated; but the experience was short lived. Jonathan, who with his family had a majority of shares in the company, gradually stripped Claude of much of his responsibilities. Claude began to feel more and more unwanted. He soon gracefully left the company, never to return. There was little Earl could do. Legal action was not an option since he held only a minority share. The best Earl could muster was a termination payment for Claude, a loyal employee for some fifteen years. Claude had long withstood Doris's arguments in favour of emigration, but now, jobless with three dependent children, he asked his daughters in Canada to begin the process.

BIRTH OF OUR SECOND SON

Our own children were now aged four, three and two. Earl and I felt ready to adopt a little brother for Sam, and visited an orphanage to talk to the Sister in charge. Earl continued to meticulously plot my basal body temperature, and one morning he announced to me in an excited voice that he thought I was pregnant. Nine months later, a beautiful baby boy was born. We named him Daniel Dominic Dennis: Daniel after Earl's maternal grandfather, Dominic after a Roman Catholic saint I had prayed to for a safe delivery, and Dennis after Claude's second name. With four children under our wing, we abandoned our thoughts of adoption and we prayed and thanked God for His gifts to us.

In June 1978, I received a card from Australia from my beloved mother. She had evidently had a change of heart. "Dear Mercy and Earl, How are you? How are the children? I hope all of you are well. I hope to see you in the near future. God bless you. Love, Mummy." It seems that while on retreat, a preacher had advised her to rid herself of the anger she had been harbouring. I must confess that after years of tepid indifference to my mother's feelings of anger at my leaving the convent, the card awakened strong filial feelings and my deep love for my mother resurfaced.

A few days after Dan was born, in April 1979, my mother visited us. She was thrilled that Earl and I had set up a happy home and that God had blessed us with four beautiful children. She was also very happy that her good friend "Nellie", Earl's mother, was living with us with all the comfort that only a loving home could provide. My children would develop a strong rapport with my mother, which continued throughout the next two decades. She lived to the age of 101.

Like all our other children, Dan had a thick mop of dark, wavy hair, beautiful olive skin, pink lips and his father's high cheekbones. Very soon, Mummy would call him her "Handsome Anselm." Although he was a relaxed baby and in apparent good health, around the age of seven months we noticed that he seemed restless from time to time and his sleep pattern began to change. The pediatrician checked him out and felt all was well. When Dan's restlessness continued, Earl insisted that we take him for another check-up. Our boy's heart was pounding at an unusual rate. He was suffering from paroxysmal atrial tachycardia, a condition in which the upper chamber of the heart begins to beat irregularly. We rushed to the hospital, where a team of doctors brought him back to health.

Throughout the ordeal, Doris stood at our side. She made a promise that if Dan were saved, we would take him to the Shrine of the Infant of Prague in Nasik, a small town about one hundred miles from Bombay. Devotion to the Infant of Prague has spread throughout the world since the seventeenth century, and the church in Nasik attracts thousands of pilgrims. My own faith had not faltered. I realized that God's power is made manifest not in force but in His faithful and quiet presence. When Dan was ill, I sensed that He was near me and would restore my child to perfect health. A few months later, we made the promised pilgrimage to Nasik, where we thanked the Child Jesus for His infinite mercy.

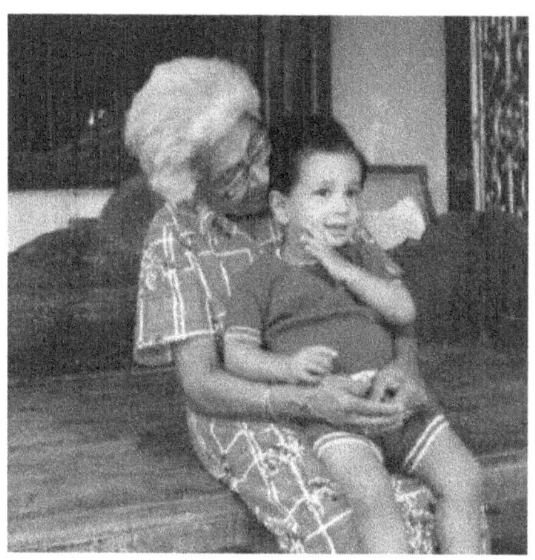

‡ Nel and Daniel (1980)

FAREWELL

At the end of 1979, an eventful year by anyone's standards, Doris and Claude arrived at our flat to tell us that their visas for Canada had arrived. The whole family would be leaving India shortly. Earl and I were speechless. This couple, which had been our greatest support in times of need, and were always there to share our joys and sorrows, would no longer be part of our daily lives. Within a month, Earl and I were at the airport bidding them farewell as they departed. For the first time, I witnessed Earl weep. As for me, I sobbed uncontrollably. I would now have to fend for myself, without my beloved sister nearby. Earl and I returned to our flat, devastated at the absence of our much-loved relatives.

Our family life now took on a new dimension. Without these two pivotal figures, the cruelty of those initial moments of solitude were a poignant reminder of the human drama and the realities of our future existence. We plunged headlong into the unknown path, prepared even for the unexpected when it did appear.

At the factory, Earl tried to patiently withstand the prevailing winds of discord, as his opponents relegated him to nothing more than a figurehead as a minority shareholder of 49% of shares. The strike which had engulfed the company sometime in 1975 was short lived and the employees returned to work. However, the dismissed employee with the backing of a larger and more powerful outside union continued his fight for reinstatement. The responsibility fell to Earl to fight him in court. The case dragged on for several years thus providing Jonathan and Dean the opportunity to consolidate control of the company. He would not accept this treatment, even if it meant substantial financial loss. He continued pursuing his options of trying to buy out his late partner's family's share or start a new company. Prayer ensued.

Each day I saw hurt and pain written all over my husband's face. I would also see a new man emerge; a man who under immense weight felt overwhelmed, pained and tortured by the betrayal of those he had welcomed and once so trusted. But he would soldier on despite the fact that he was being exploited by the shifting sands of power that prevailed at the company at that time. There were occasions when this turmoil spilled over to our home. Now and again I would see though very seldom, Earl`s anger seep through his otherwise calm demeanor. He had good reason to be angry. He searched for the right approach to these massive problems. Here was a man who would now put his family at the forefront of all his endeavours. These trying times were also a religious turning point that forged his views on family life. These were not just spontaneous reactions to situations over which he had no control. Rather, they would culminate in a template of rock-solid values that would be the guiding light to all his future challenges.

‡ Our four children (1980)

‡ Our children cycling on the building grounds (1982)

PEACE AND TRANQUILITY

The summer of 1980 provided us with a much-needed holiday. We rented a comfortable bungalow on the seashore in the rural town of Nargol, in the state of Gujarat. It was a large house complete with swimming pool. The property was peppered with coconut palms, mango and papaya trees. A large swing that could hold all four children hung in the front verandah. Alongside the swing, Earl built a rope ladder.

Our day would start with the entire family walking to the beach to wait for the fisher folk to bring in their catch. We would have our pick of fresh fish, shrimp, oysters and lobsters. It was Mummy's privilege to make the choice, while Earl paid for it. After breakfast, Kamu would clean the seafood and later cook it under Mummy's supervision. Earl and I, Mummy, the four kids, and the two maids were a happy household. For four memorable weeks, we were able to put aside our worries.

‡ VACATIONING ON THE BEACHES OF NARGOL (1980)

A TASTE OF THE WEST

We returned to Bombay in time for the new school year. My thesis was due within a few weeks. Earl for his part had received good news. The labour court had ruled in his favour. It was now time for him to visit the West. I would stay behind to look after the family as well as to do the finishing touches to my thesis. Earl planned a trip that would take him to Italy, the United Kingdom, Canada and the United States. Foreign exchange restrictions in India at the time meant that the average traveler could take no more than one hundred U.S. dollars. However, Earl was allowed to take four thousand U.S. dollars because he owned a company with special status as an exporter. The export of cartridge links that Earl had developed earned the country substantial foreign exchange, a scarce commodity at the time.

Our niece Wendy was to be married in December of that same

year, and she wanted Earl to raise the toast to the bride. Earl planned his itinerary accordingly. He would travel first to London and do some sightseeing. From there, he would travel to the north, where his sister Aureen and her ten children lived. From London, he would fly to Chicago and then to Rochester to visit friends, young engineers who had worked with him in his company in Bombay before they emigrated.

A four-week stay in Toronto with Doris and Claude was followed by a trip to British Columbia to visit friends. Earl also made plans to see the Boeing Manufacturing plant in Seattle, after which he would fly to Los Angeles, then on to New York. The next stop was Rome, where I had received my religious training.

Earl visited the Mother House, where Sister Angela, temporarily stationed there, extended the hospitality of the Order. He also met Sister Maura, the former Sister Provincial of the North Indian Province in whose presence I had signed my dispensation papers. Sister Angela then accompanied Earl to Grottaferrata, where I had done my novitiate, but found it disappointing. From the bustling centre of religious training it had been in my day, it had now become a "ghost house." With the decline of religious vocations, the corridors of this hallowed place lay virtually empty. Huge meeting rooms were now locked. The photos he took reflected the truth of his observations.

During his two months abroad, Earl studied life in North America in depth. What fascinated him was the sheer freedom and absence of bureaucracy in which the economies functioned. There were scarcely any of the "under-the-table dealings" or "black money" aspects he found so abhorrent in the Indian economy. He also longed to be free from the burden of the atmosphere that had developed in the company he had founded. He wanted to find a way to be rooted and have a purpose in life.

At age fifty-two, Earl decided to take a leap of faith – faith in another country. He knew he could count on me to adapt to a new environment despite its challenges. As for Earl the yearning to start afresh in some place he could call home was overwhelming. He knew without a doubt that this place was Canada. Earl's optimism about the future grew. He had learned from his past experiences to have an unshakeable faith in God. In the face of difficulty, he had faith in himself and his family; in the face of uncertainty, he had hope in God; despite the uncertainty of what life held for him in a foreign land, he knew he could count on the love of his wife to hold his family together.

Claude and Doris had succeeded in making their way in Canada and harboured no regrets about leaving India. Claude had an office job; Doris, despite her age, had decided to go back to school to secure her nursing diploma. She already had one from India, but needed to work towards Canadian registration. Four of their six children were well-employed, while their younger sons were still in school. They had also made a down payment on a spacious home and garden, a contrast to their crowded flat in Bombay. Earl saw the beauty of the country, and the freedom, transparency and openness of the culture. He became convinced that his family too should emigrate.

Earl realized a metamorphosis was taking place in his mind. All through his adult years, he had vehemently opposed his siblings' decisions to leave the land of their birth. "Why can't we Indians stay behind and build India?" he would ask. Despite his beliefs, he now had to look to his own children's future. He had no doubt that wherever they lived, they would each reach their full potential. He would have to give these matters serious thought.

Earl also considered that if he did leave India, he would have to start his business life from scratch. As in all matters, he would pray and trust that the Lord would show him the way. During this period of reflection, there was never a cathartic moment, a time when all the pieces fell into place. Rather, there was a growing sense of certainty that it was now his turn to leave his motherland to start afresh.

During Earl's two-month sojourn, his letters and phone calls made me realize that radical changes were taking place in my beloved husband's mind. I realized my Earl had begun to rethink the direction of our future. I prayed and waited for his return. I knew that whatever he decided, I would be there by his side to support him. As for Earl, he realized that although he was skilled at many things, the thing he valued most was a loving wife and family.

EMIGRATION LOOMS

In mid-December 1980, the doorbell rang. My beloved Earl was finally home after his travels. I had missed him so much. As I welcomed him in my arms, I knew instinctively that I was holding a man who had become deeply introspective. As we settled down to a cup of tea, he told me he would like to discuss many matters with me at the first possible moment.

After dinner, he poured drinks for the two of us. The children, excited to have their father home, were now in bed. Together, we said our night prayers and then he opened his heart to me. It was best, he began, that we prepare to leave India and settle in

Canada. The children would have great opportunities. With my doctorate almost complete, he felt I would be employable. As for him, he continued, he would keep his options open: perhaps he would start a small engineering business.

I then mentioned the company – the company to which he had given twenty of the best years of his life. "I will just walk away from it," was his surprising reply. "I will take whatever I can get as long as I do not have to go down a legal route that would jeopardize our emigration. God will help me!" What now mattered most to Earl was not the assets he had worked hard to build over the past two decades. What he truly wanted was to maintain his dignity and freedom. He decided that the time had come to walk away and start again.

Earl displayed his extraordinary gift for perspective, for balancing his professional life and his ambitions for his family. He knew the future called for dramatic action, but action prompted by reflection and careful analysis. He also knew he didn't have the luxury of time to think through all the angles of emigration. We spent the greater part of the night discussing what the future could hold for us and our family. I asked him about his beloved mother, now eighty years old and an integral part of our household for the past seven years. "Oh, Mummy will come with us wherever we go, our home will always be hers as well." As the new day dawned, so too did a new dream. Earl would now work on an exit strategy. We did not discuss the matter with anyone. We would hope and pray for the dream to unfold.

The following day, Earl walked into his office. He had decided that his mantra was going to be: peace at any price. Having been reduced to nothing more than a figurehead, his pride of achievement totally suppressed, he now looked elsewhere and the possibility of a life of true endeavour, achievement and pride. He had more important matters to plan for. Funds would have to be transferred to Canada in a clandestine way because of the prevailing money transfer restrictions prevalent at that time in India. Given the change in the company's direction, he was now prepared to leave it behind. Always a man of integrity, he would put his trust in God that he had made a wise decision. He decided he would accept whatever price he was offered for his share of the company and walk away.

The future, Earl came to realize, might very well be devoid of the assets he so painstakingly had built. His dignity meant more to him than anything else and he was determined not to get caught up in the weeds of what might be an unpleasant battle. It was time to start all over again. At the same time, he believed that this material loss would be balanced with the opportunity his children would soon have to fulfil their dreams in Canada.

As for myself, I felt Earl was too dispassionate and nuanced. I wanted him to fight for what was rightfully his. But, obstinately, he would have none of that. He explained to me that he had started the business with Bihari, "but the tables have turned." He wanted to walk away in dignity and start all over again.

PRIDE OF A DOCTORATE

I now worked assiduously on completing my Ph.D., all the more so to enhance my own job prospects. Within a few weeks, I submitted my thesis and awaited the date for my defense. With trepidation and excitement, I soon faced a team of seasoned economists, who questioned me extensively on the problems and possibilities of growth of the engineering sector in Greater Bombay. In a few weeks, I was notified that my thesis had been accepted and that I would be conferred with a doctorate in Economics at the next convocation.

In June 1981, Earl and our four children accompanied me to my convocation. The children, all under the age of seven, were too young to comprehend and appreciate my achievement, but they were excited. "Mummy is going to get a prize," they exclaimed. As I walked into the convocation hall in my doctoral cape and cap, I thanked God for having given me the strength to persevere in pursuit of this goal. Eight years and four children later, I was the happy and proud recipient of a doctoral degree. As Earl stood beaming, I knew I would never have arrived at this moment in my life without his reassuring presence at my side.

⁜ Doctoral Convocation,
Mercy third from left (1981)

PREPARATION FOR LIFE IN THE WEST

During the next three years, I began to get ready for a future in North America. My first step was to improve my résumé. I applied for a director's position in one of the Institutes of Management affiliated with the University of Bombay. I was soon called for an interview and a few weeks later, received my letter of appointment. From lecturer to director was a quantum leap. Both Earl and I were happy with this achievement. My hours of work were conducive to raising a family; the children were now older and the home front stabilized.

My next venture was to work towards a driver's license. Earl warned me that if we were to survive in North America, I would have to be able to drive. It wasn't easy. Bombay's unrelenting, disorderly traffic was far from a welcome arena for me to develop my driving skills. For years I found no need to get a driver's licence. When our chauffeur was unavailable, Earl did the driving for me. But once again, I applied myself diligently and in the space of six months, I had my license. Then I decided to take some cooking classes. Over the past several years I had altogether abandoned my initial attempts at basic cooking. With Earl's mother living with us and with the assistance of three servants there was no need for this skill on my part. But I knew I wouldn't have the luxury of servants in North America; therefore it was imperative to acquire this skill.

In September 1982, Earl again traveled to North America. This time, it was to attend the weddings of two of his nieces, as well as to finalize his plans for emigrating. He met with the Minister of Industry in Ontario, as well as a counterpart in New York State. Both Canada and the United States, he was told, would welcome him as an entrepreneur. He would be granted family immigrant visas. He opted to prepare a proposal for Canada because his siblings had settled in Ontario. Now he would return to India and wait.

Earl knew without a shadow of doubt that he would be welcomed into Canada. It was now only a matter of time. He concentrated on liquidating his financial assets. Before the end of 1983, we received our immigrant visas. Canada was happy to have us.

Unfortunately, we were now faced with a dilemma. Earl's mother, who was now eighty-three years old, had suffered a fall that left her immobile. Earl and I had decided that we were going nowhere without her. She, too, would be welcomed to Canada. Unfortunately, her health deteriorated and she spiraled into dementia. Sadly, Earl realized he would have to leave her behind in the care of his sister Verna. Leaving Mummy behind was a necessity. By now she was bed-ridden and despite his strong desire to take her with the rest of the family to Canada it was impossible. With the help of servants in India, Earl felt this was a decision he was compelled to make.

SOUTHERN SOJOURN

By the end of 1983, Earl had informed the Canadian Embassy that the family would be emigrating in June of the following year. As a farewell trip, we decided we would travel through the states of Kerala, Tamil Nadu and Mysore. Earl and I had both grown up in the south and we wanted our children to visit their roots. Earl's mother stayed at Verna's while we holidayed for three weeks, first visiting Tangasseri and Earl's ancestral home, *Loveapple Cote*, now in the hands of new owners. It was painful to see the majestic black wood main entrance, and the teak wood window and door frames, now painted in indigo blue. The moment rendered Earl distraught more viscerally than he ever imagined. Memories of his boyhood overpowered him. The garish color of the doors and windows was a catalyst of the impending change the family was to encounter – emigrating to a new land of unknown challenges.

We then visited my old haunts. One was a nostalgic trip to St. Francis Convent, in the little town of Coimbatore, where I was a boarder for seven years and where my religious calling was nurtured. It was no longer a boarding school. As a former head girl, I found that walking through the dining rooms, dormitories and even the corridors brought back happy memories of my teenage years. I prayed in the chapel and remembered the Sisters who had looked after me. Most of them had toiled in India for well over sixty years without ever revisiting their homelands in Europe. Such was their dedication.

These were sisters, de facto mothers, gifted both with a sense of vision and pragmatism. They could be ruthless in discipline and compassionate in understanding. Patiently they transformed the tottering, forlorn little girl into a stoic woman; the selfish adolescent became a generous adult open to the world.

At Stella Maris, the university college where I had studied for my bachelor's degree, and later worked as a faculty member in the Economics Department, my former colleagues were happy to welcome me back. It was at Stella Maris that I had made the decision to leave the Order and marry Earl. Now our four children frolicked through the portals of this institution. The sisters welcomed us. They had always supported and respected my decision to leave and marry Earl. Not once was I condemned by any of them. Over the years I kept in contact and some had grown to love my family, even though most of them had not met Earl nor my children. It was a true homecoming as the sisters showed their joy at seeing us. I realized that I had not really "left" the sisters but was now returning to their warm embrace with my children.

I had requested the Sisters to allow our son Sam to make his First Holy Communion in the chapel. This was the sacred place where I had made my final vows and wherein I had spent many hours praying for light regarding my future. However, the day before the ceremony, Sam's temperature soared to 104 degrees Fahrenheit. Amazingly, early the next morning, I found Sam standing by my bedside in the hotel room, beaming. "Mummy, I'm alright, I can make my first Holy Communion!" My prayers to the Virgin Mary had been answered. Sam and the rest of the family enjoyed good health for the rest of the holiday. After the service, a breakfast was served in the college cafeteria for about one hundred guests, which included the Sisters, our relatives and our friends. It was truly a homecoming.

The hill stations of Coonoor, Kotagiri and Ootacammund were next on the agenda. We traveled through the tea plantations and experienced the unique qualities of lush green forests, waterfalls and an army of women workers picking tea leaves; most of them carrying a child fast asleep on their backs. The town of Mysore, with its grandiose palace of the Maharajah, was a feast to the eye. Built in the fourteenth century, it had been rebuilt several times. The current palace was built in the late nineteenth century. The architecture was a blend of Muslim, Rajput and Gothic styles. The palace housed several Hindu temples. However, that which fascinated us the most was the Royal Wedding Hall with its stained glass ceiling of peacock motifs. We spent Christmas and New Year with my niece before returning to Bombay.

Mummy returned to our flat, staying with us until a few hours before we embarked on the plane for Canada. Earl knew he would be returning in a few months to settle various matters. He hoped to see his mother again. As for the children and me, we knew it was the last time we would see her. Earl's beloved mother had become a mother to me, and my children adored her. They sobbed when they realized they wouldn't see their Nana again. Fortunately, Mummy was unaware of what was taking place around her.

‡ Our children at Fort Cochin (1983)

‡ Mercy, Anjali, and Gita at Stella Maris (1983)

EMIGRATION

June 17, 1984 was the day of departure. My maid Christine and I helped our children get ready for the Sunday service at the Church of St. Anne's, our parish church. It would be the last time we would attend the service there as a family. During the service, I glanced at my children. The three older ones prayed fervently with eyes closed. I could see they were concerned about our journey to an unknown land. After Holy Mass, we stayed on for few more minutes. We first prayed as a family, knowing that all good things come from the Lord to those who trust Him. We then visited our pastor to bid farewell.

After breakfast, the children left to say their goodbyes to their friends. By midday, they were back in their room sorting out their stuff, placing what they wanted in their carry-on bags and placing the rest in a box meant for our two maids. Earl and I were in our bedroom, the door closed, as he made important last-minute phone calls. Suddenly and unexpectedly, the bedroom door was unceremoniously flung open. Sensing imminent trouble, I immediately left the room. Earl was handed a sheaf of papers by Jonathan who Earl later relayed seemed concerned that we might leave the country without having relinquished his position as Chairman and Managing Director at Earl Bihari. Earl, busy with moving a family of six within a few hours the same evening to another country had intended to formally resign but had not had the chance to do so. He knew he would have to return to India again to settle financial matters and had intended to take care of the matter at that time. He signed the papers, avoiding any confrontation that would jeopardize leaving the country in the next few hours. Years of dedication and self sacrifice to the beloved company he had co-founded had now come to an end. This event severed his official position in the company. Jonathan left immediately after. Earl felt sorely wounded but he carried on with preparations for the move with his characteristic undeterred focus. However, the exchange never sat well with me. I felt my husband had been betrayed. We were wounded; though not for long. We knew Canada the land of promise awaited us. What he was to receive for his forty-nine percent share was still not negotiated. In retrospect, I would like to believe that my reaction to Earl's decision to walk away from what was truly his had been philosophical and calm. But it was not the case. "You are fifty-two years old, we have four children below the age of ten, and we are leaving for a foreign land. What are we going to do?" I exclaimed to my husband in despair, fear and even anger. "Don't worry, God will take care of us," replied Earl tenderly. "Let's look to the future. We are leaving tonight and there are many important matters to be attended to before we leave. God will help us." I wanted to call out for someone to make sense of what was happening. Earl, for his part, had responded to the situation with ever-steadfast faith. In time, he believed, he would be rewarded with peace, dignity and respect, far more important to him than financial gain.

In the evening, we took Mummy to Verna's place. The children sobbed as each one hugged their beloved Nana. I stayed outside the room. The emotional goodbyes were raw and overwhelming. As my youngest child emerged from the room, I went in to kiss my mother-in-law. I knew this was the last time I would see her. With palpable sadness, we made our way back to our flat and loaded our two cars and two taxis with our twelve suitcases. We said a prayer, thanking God for all the blessings of the past ten years of our married life.

Our four children had grown up in this place. Three generations of our family had lived here in peace and harmony. My two devoted servants, Kamu and Christine, said their farewells to the family. I gave each a substantial monetary gift as well as many of my household wares. I wept with them. As the taxi pulled away, the ten years of peace and happiness lived in that flat, flashed across my mind. These two women had helped nurture my children. Would we see them again? Time would tell.

With the help of good friends, we were seen off at the airport. We stepped out into the unknown, armed with little more than our self-confidence and an unshakeable trust in God. Earl was my husband; I was prepared to follow him anywhere.

Eleven

A NEW LIFE BEGINS IN 1984

"MUMMY, MUMMY, LOOK! That building is touching the sky," enthused Daniel at the age of five, standing amidst the skyscrapers of Manhattan. Enroute to Canada, we spent three days in New York, taking in the sights: Rockefeller Centre, the Statue of Liberty and the United Nations. The children were too young to fully appreciate anything other than the iconic skyline.

The twenty-two hour flight, with a two-hour stop at Dubai, was surprisingly uneventful. The children were excited and handled the journey with a sense of maturity beyond their years. Anjali took charge of Daniel, while Gita took Sam under her wing. They settled down in their economy-class seats and without hesitation explored the novelty of earphones, music and news on the different channels, and overhead reading lamps.

Earl and I held hands and often prayed together. We dreamed of building a framework so our children could move forward, even if it meant that we would have to take a step back financially. Strengthened by Earl's mystical belief in divine providence, ours would be a home that provided our children with a springboard to success. Like a deep sigh, our lives were rolling from an era of certitude to the unknown.

On the morning of June 20, we left our YMCA rooms for Kennedy Airport to fly to Toronto, our final destination. It was a short flight and the children were grateful that at last they were arriving at their permanent home. At the Immigration counter, an officer welcomed us to our new country. It was a quiet, positive feeling. Our apprehension about the unknown was beginning to give way to an outburst of exhilaration.

As we ascended the escalator to the main lobby, it became clear that Canada, which had so warmly welcomed our family, had become a home to peoples from all over the world. With twelve large suitcases in tow, we met the extended family, who greeted us with a fleet of cars. As we snaked our way along the sixteen-lane highway, I could hear the cacophony of a never-ending sea of cars – each one respecting the right of way of the other. From an economic perspective, I began to realize it was these highways crisscrossing the North American continent that had made possible the stupendous economic growth of the past century.

Doris and Claude opened their home to us for the next two weeks. It was a chaotic existence, but we were two close-knit families and any inconvenience was far outweighed by the camaraderie we experienced.

The neighbourhood where Doris and Claude lived was typically middle-class, with both detached and semi-detached homes. Every family took pride in closely manicured lawns with ensconced beds of multi-colored petunias and impatiens. After the dull and drab, concrete high-rise buildings of Bombay, this was a feast to our eyes. Our children exclaimed how much they would love to have a home of their own with a garden to tend. Earl cautioned them that they would have to be patient.

Our extended family members then took turns introducing us to life in Canada. There was no logical path that connected our lives in India to our present-day reality. We were in a new world of uncharted waters. Our family ship, which only a few years earlier was on a course certain of her destination, was now out at sea, rudderless, tossed on choppy waters and dependent on the winds of change. Despite these insecurities, we knew we had to take root as quickly as possible.

Earl attended to getting his Ontario driver's license, whereupon he purchased a new car. Our family was now able to move around freely without having to depend on others. Before our arrival, Claude had purchased two bicycles from a garage sale, and this allowed Sam and Dan the liberty of riding around the neighbourhood. Chocolate chip cookies, cereal and ice cream soon became their staple foods – something we temporarily allowed them to indulge in.

A few days after our arrival, Earl and Claude began house hunting. Earl knew he would have to return to India several times to settle his matters, so it was agreed that we would rent a place initially. A house would be bought in due course. We soon found a suitable townhouse to rent, only a stone's throw from Claude and Doris's place. It had three bedrooms and a fully finished basement.

All we needed now was some furniture. At a garage sale, we purchased two headboards. Alas, there were no beds to go with them, so Earl and I made do with a sleeping bag. But then, we asked ourselves, what would we do with the headboards? Having grown up in large families, we had been taught frugality. So Earl decided to affix them on the wall along the main hallway, where they would serve as shelves for the children's gloves, scarves and lunch boxes. Years later, our children would recall with amusement and mock horror our first home in Canada with its two headboards nailed to the walls.

Yes, we had a lot to learn before we became fully fledged Canadians. In India, although we were privileged to live in a decent-sized flat, we didn't have the luxury of our own private garden.

Our new townhouse, much to the delight of our children, had a small front yard. It was already late summer when we moved in and therefore too late for any gardening. But the following spring found us at the nearby garden centre. Very soon, we had rows of beautiful petunias and Romano tomatoes. We harvested enough of the latter to be able to freeze some. All my Indian curries now carried the flavour of our very own Canadian-grown tomatoes.

One of my first tasks in Canada was to learn how to shop for groceries. Doris tutored me on the art of looking for the various "specials." This was important because we now had to live within a tight budget. With neither Earl nor I working and four young children to feed, every dollar was precious. Although we had been able to transfer a fairly substantial amount of money, we realized we had to be thrifty. We knew it was going to be an uphill climb to establish ourselves professionally. We decided to initially rent a townhouse. With Claude standing as guarantor, this was no problem.

With only a few weeks before the new school year, we had to hurry to get the house into a semblance of order. Our children, who had grown up with servants to look after their every need, now rose to the occasion. Anjali, now ten, and Gita, a year younger, helped me with the household chores. Sam was given the responsibility of looking after the car, and Earl instructed him on the various details of maintenance. Every Saturday, our son washed the car, checked the oil levels and monitored the windshield fluid. At eight years old, he developed a strong work ethic that would stay with him as he grew. Dan, our five-year-old, helped wherever help was needed, but he nearly always opted to assist Sam.

Our tiny household was now well-organized and Earl felt he could return to India once the kids were in school. We strongly believed that our aspirations for our family were sound and armed with this conviction, we decided to pursue these goals with moral integrity and human courage.

Our children learned everything about growing up in Canada within the four walls of that small townhouse. With time, we realized each was a beautiful painting, desperately yearning to break free through the portals of their own identities. Anjali, our eldest, became a surrogate mother to her three younger siblings. That house and the responsibilities that were born therein parachuted her into a new world of beginnings and possibilities. The future, with its tremendous opportunities, began to unfurl itself before her ten-year-old eyes and, through her, to her younger siblings. As time evolved, it was clear she had three obsessions: order, devotion to detail and the realization that in Canada her dreams would be fulfilled.

UNPLEASANT REALITIES OF OUR EARLY DAYS IN CANADA

Labour Day in early September 1984 was pivotal to our family. Our children braced themselves for their first day in a Canadian school. With our Indian mindset guiding our decision-making, we opted for their Sunday best, as they would have dressed on their first day in a new school in our home country. On Tuesday morning, our children found their way to the nearby Catholic school, the girls in slacks and blouses with frills and bows, the boys in dress pants and long-sleeved shirts. They all wore dress shoes.

They held each other's hands for comfort. When they returned at three p.m., they were a little agitated. "Ma, we looked odd today," exclaimed Anjali and Gita. "No other child was dressed like us. They all wore jeans and running shoes." "Fine," I replied. "That's what you will wear to school from now on."

Earl and I knew that there were many Canadians at that time who discriminated against South Asians, usually calling them "Pakis," so at lunchtime that first week we walked over to the school to check on our children. All four were huddled together standing in the corner of the playground. New to the school, their Indian accents were frowned upon, and no schoolmate was willing to risk befriending them. But at least they had each other. The demographics of the school was predominantly Anglo-Saxon, Eastern European and Afro Canadian. There were very few East Indians. However, despite this mix there were cliques and no new comer was welcome. My four children found themselves on the periphery of these cliques.

Two decades later, giving a speech at Sam's wedding, Dan would reminisce about those early days in Canada, when he had no friends except his brother. He recalled how he would roam the school grounds and approach every boy and girl pleading, "Can I be your friend?" Only his brother Sam had said yes. However, all four children weathered this rocky start. In the classroom, they proved to be far ahead of their peers because the Indian educational system had equipped them to excel, especially in mathematics and science. Since they were very often at the forefront of the class, other kids began to realize it was "cool" to befriend them.

Racist harassment continued to manifest its ugly self. On one occasion, a young lad at the water cooler spat water at Gita as she passed by. "Go back to where you came from, you Paki." She would have none of it. She walked straight into the principal's office and complained. Fortunately, the school janitor was a witness to the event, so the student was handed a suspension for a few days. Despite this kind of incident, I continued to believe that Canada would change; that the country would evolve with time into a new model of a multi ethnic Canada – a country that my children could truly call "home".

A month later, Earl decided it was time to return to India to follow up on unsettled matters. I still did not have a stable job. All I had succeeded in obtaining was teaching one course in organizational behaviour at a community college. The salary of $1,500 was all I earned in my first semester of teaching in Canada. "That's just enough to pay for your postal stamps to write to your husband!" remarked my brother-in-law Claude. I took these humiliations in stride, and as the years rolled along, my earnings would increase several fold. Far from being discouraged, I continued to seek teaching contracts, both at the university and community college levels. Little did I know that it would take about fourteen years before I encountered some form of stability and adequate compensation.

For the time being, I was alone with our four small children while struggling to establish a career with little success. These were some of the saddest days in my life. Without Earl nearby to share my concerns, and my children too young to empathize with me, I spent hours quietly seated in our living room looking out the large bay window. Often I wondered whether we had made the right decision.

Earl had walked away from a company he had so successfully built over twenty years of his life. It had provided us with an affluent lifestyle, and it had seemed that we were set for the rest of our lives.

I wondered incessantly what the future now held for our young family. Doris and Claude offered me encouragement and solace, but I knew that ultimately I had to brace myself for the uncertain future. Images of life in Bombay flashed through my mind: Mummy with walking stick in hand trudging through the length of our large living room; Christine, our teenaged servant, mimicking scenes from Bollywood movies while my four children applauded with raucous laughter; Kamu, our older servant, trying to bring about some semblance of discipline; and Earl at work while I eagerly awaited his return each evening.

To compound my anxiety, I had not succeeded in obtaining a driver's license. My first four attempts were failures. I have often relived this experience. What happened I ask myself? Why was I such a hopeless failure? I had been driving in India for about two years before emigrating; coupled with about a month of driving lessons here in Canada, that was ample experience I thought. My hopeless performance, I concluded, was stress related. Earl had left for India leaving me alone in a new country with four small children. It was difficult to cope all alone. Coupled with this was the fact that I was scarcely making inroads into a teaching career. I practiced a few more times and then attempted once more, only to be told I had failed again. Devastated, I made my way to Doris's house, laid my head on her kitchen table and sobbed. She asked to look at my temporary learner's license. "No wonder you are failing. When an examiner sees the number of times you have failed, he will not grant you a pass! Go and get a new one." "But how?" I asked. "Lie if you have to. Tell them you lost the original and hopefully they will give you a new one which doesn't carry a record of your failures."

A few mornings later, I presented myself for the driving test for the sixth time. Seated next to me, the examiner asked, "Is this your first attempt?" "Yes, sir," I replied. Twenty minutes and six kilometres later, I was presented with my driver's license. That evening, I celebrated with my children by taking them out for dinner at McDonald's.

RAYS OF SUNSHINE

Life's defining moments can be random and fleeting. Yet they carve an indelible mark in your memory. Toward the end of 1984, I received a call from Professor William Morgan, of the Economics Department of York University. He said he had studied my résumé and invited me for an interview. He suggested that I audit the Economics course he was going to teach in the next semester as well as the course of one of his colleagues. He also suggested that I work as his teaching assistant. This path, he said, would give me a foot into the world of academia in Canada. I was thrilled. I loved teaching; I knew I would make a success of it if I were only given the opportunity. And here it was.

Christmas was now approaching and so too was Earl's return after a three-month stay in India. It was to be our first *White Christmas*. The kids were excited, knowing that Earl would arrive with gifts for all of us. We had decided that we would, wherever possible, spend our rupees and conserve our dollars. Despite our financial burdens, we were determined our children would not be deprived of what would help them in their development. With this in mind, we enlisted our children in piano lessons and figure skating. The boys would join the local hockey team. On the day Earl returned from India, he was delighted when Anjali and Gita played a duet of Christmas carols as he entered the house.

Our first Christmas in Canada was a simple one. I set up an artificial tree, eighteen inches high with four little gifts purchased in India neatly placed beneath it. This was a tradition we practiced in India, which we would continue in our home here in Canada. After the traditional opening of gifts, we had a simple breakfast and then made our way to the noon service at the nearby Catholic Church. We thanked God for our first Canadian Christmas and prayed for a bright future. The traditional turkey dinner was held at the home of Doris and Claude, who showered us all with gifts.

A short time after his fifty-third birthday, Earl returned to India for a second time. Despite my fears about whether we had made the right decision, Earl remained confident and happy that we were in this glorious country. At last he had a soaring feeling of liberation from the restrictive practices that stifled the business person in India. He had sought guidance in prayer and knew that, with the help of the Holy Spirit, we had made the right decision to emigrate. He would stay in India until the beginning of summer to settle his matters. During the summer of 1985, we began to look around the suburban neighbourhoods to see where we would like to settle down.

In the fall of that year, Earl made a third trip to India. I had successfully managed to increase my hours of contract teaching and was now teaching at both the university and community college level. I had little to complain about except that I was not yet in the tenure-track stream. We continued to live a simple and frugal life, and my teaching contracts meant that we didn't have to touch our capital.

Earl's mother in Bombay, by now very ill, was living in her grandson Aubrey's spare flat after Verna decided to migrate to Canada in the fall of 1984. Mummy Nel was cared for by her daughter Christabelle, her granddaughter-in-law Lauraine, and a maid. In early November 1985, in the presence of her grandson Aubrey's family, Earl and Christabelle, Mummy peacefully passed away at the age of eighty-five. Her wish that her beloved son Earl be at her bedside during her final hours had been granted.

Earl returned to Canada in time for Christmas. In the early winter of 1986, we visited Woodbridge, Ontario – a half-hour drive outside Canada's largest city, Toronto – and conveniently located not too far from Claude and Doris's house. We drove along the streets until a *For Sale* sign caught our attention. The house, set on a ravine lot with a walkout basement, matched our hopes. Across the street was a park and tennis court. This was truly my "dream home." It was large – almost three times our spacious flat in Bombay. The children would now have separate bed rooms – the girls in one and the boys in the other. Shared rooms we realized would instill a spirt of cooperation and understanding. The fourth bedroom was transformed to a study. Each would have their own desk and chair. Very soon a shared computer was installed. We loved the house and dreamed of renovations we would undertake when finances permitted it. We decided we would move into the house in August 1986. Earl would now return to India for his fourth trip since our arrival to settle his matters.

RACIAL TAUNTS AT SCHOOL

Gita came home from school one day with a high fever. She was ill – there was no question of that – but she was also upset. As I put her to bed, she began to cry and related the events of the day. Her class had traveled by train to the downtown core of the city. Gita found herself seated next to two girls who only spoke to each other. She made an effort to join in the conversation, but was told, "We don't want to talk to you, you Paki." They then left their places to sit elsewhere.

Gita was having her lunch by herself when the class teacher invited Gita to join her. "All through the day, Mummy, I was just tagging along with the teacher. No one would talk to me. Why are these kids so cruel, Ma?" she asked. Earl and I had anticipated the possibility of such encounters. I comforted her with the words: "Don't worry Gita girl. Very soon you will know how to handle this stuff. Be patient."

The next day, I found myself at the office of my children's school Principal. His name was John Curry, a young man of Irish descent, who I estimated to be in his late thirties. To my delight, he seemed to know a lot about India, as his aunts and uncles had been missionaries in my homeland. That struck a familiar chord and I reclined more comfortably in my chair. I relayed to him the events of the previous day and he listened intently. "Mrs. Anselm, this is to be expected. At that age, children are insecure and therefore can be cruel. But let me tell you, give your children a few years and you will see the change. Your children will be leaders."

Time would prove how right he was. I walked home fully

confident that despite all that had happened, my children would not only survive but thrive in their new country.

In the meantime, it was not the end of Gita's setbacks. I wondered why my dark-skinned girl, so gifted, was subjected to such torture. When her class was asked to put on a play for the spring concert, the teacher asked for volunteers to come up to the front of the class and apply for the lead role by singing to their fellow students. Gita had played lead singing roles in India and therefore was one of the most confident volunteers. She sang *Feed the Birds*, every note on pitch. She was soon followed by another student, whom everyone in the class thought was "cool." Unfortunately, the teacher left the decision to the class by taking a show of hands. When the other student's name was called, every hand in the class went up. Gita was devastated! Not a single hand went up when her name was called. After class, the teacher approached Gita and tried to comfort her. "Don't worry; I'll put you in the chorus with the rest of the class."

‡ GITA SINGING AT A SCHOOL CONCERT IN BOMBAY (1982)

Coming from India, my children had never experienced racial taunts. A country of diverse groups – Sindhis, Punjabis, Sikhs, Bengalis, Maharashtrians – we Anglo-Indians had felt very much at home and considered ourselves children of Mother India. We all spoke English and savoured the same varied cuisine, yet worshipped at different churches and temples, a fact of life that didn't matter at all to our children or their friends.

But in Canada we found two distinct worlds – a white world and a black world. Every ethnic group, we found, was desperately trying to carve a niche. We Anglo-Indians considered it our birthright to create our own presence in the mainstream of Canada. It sometimes worked, but often it did not. As time evolved, our children would teach us a way out of this morass. "Ma, we are Canadians first with an Indian heritage. And we are proud of it." Gradually, they introduced their friends to this newfound identity. As they skated, swam and attended parties in school and social clubs, their circle of friends expanded and they were increasingly accepted on their own terms.

‡ Our children with friends (1995)

WORKPLACE EXPLOITATION

This was also a period when, for the first time in my life, I felt exploited. Teaching a fourteen-week course in a community college and driving thirty kilometres each way, I earned only a paltry sum. But there was no other way to get my foot in the door. Fortunately, after a semester of this humiliating routine, I secured a day contract. I was now teaching a full load – fifteen hours a week – and earning a modest salary. The catch was that I received no benefits.

I looked around and I found immigrants with Ph.D.s from all over the world struggling to make inroads into the university or college teaching profession. I had made my start, but I found the lack of benefits, combined with the lack of understanding from the administration of these institutions, appalling. I soon learned that a two-tier system flourished within these citadels of learning. A system of privilege was accorded to the tenured faculty while one of exploitation was meted out to individuals on contract, the majority of whom were immigrants.

On one occasion, my ninety-year-old mother in Australia became seriously ill. Fearing that I might never see her again, I asked for a week off. I was allowed to make the trip, only to discover on my return that fifty percent of my wages had been deducted. On another occasion, despite a doctor's note stating that I was compelled to rest at home from the effects of pneumonia, I lost seventy-five percent of my wages.

I became totally disillusioned with the system and for a time questioned Canada's pride in being "one of the best countries in the world." Emboldened by my faith, along with the encouragement of Earl and the children, I was given the gift of being able to see far beyond the turmoil and negativity of the present. I knew that this period of feeling taken advantage of would not be definitive. As always, I continued to pray and hope for a better future.

"WHEN IN DARKNESS NEVER DOUBT THE GOD OF LIGHT."

If I were to make it in Canada, I knew I had to prove my teaching skills. Professional success and meaningful parenting both take time, hard work and, more often than not, sleepless nights. At the conclusion of the two courses I taught in the spring of 1985, I was offered several more courses at the university and community college levels. My teaching evaluations were not just good but excellent. My total earnings had reached the average of most assistant professors, although there were still neither benefits nor job security. I realized that the western world still frowned upon degrees from third world countries and that my hard-earned doctorate from the University of Bombay was, paradoxically, an impediment to landing a tenure-track position.

As I mulled over these thoughts at home, the phone rang. It was my beloved Earl calling me from India regarding the price he was to be paid for his share of the company. He informed me how his sister Verna who had earlier emigrated to Canada but later returned to India, offered him her share in the Company. She felt that together with her share Earl would now have a majority hold which would enable him to sell the company as a whole and take his share, pay her dues and together they could start afresh in Canada. Earl refused. He told her that he did not want to create a wedge between her and her family. Family unity was more important to this man than financial well-being. He looked into her eyes and said, "I want no part in this deal. This will permanently fracture your family." He related this incident to me. I was angry. Why was he putting the welfare of others before his own family I queried. While I was thrilled that Earl and I wouldn't have to be separated again by his trips to India, I was deeply concerned for our financial future.

On his return, I confronted Earl on the issue. He informed me that he preferred walking away from the opportunity rather than be the cause of disharmony in his extended family and instead decided to sell his forty-nine percent of the shares to his late partner's family for whatever he could garner. My response was one of anger. I felt that we had thrown away our best – perhaps our only – chance at financial security. He insisted that he had done the right thing. I prayed for guidance, but everything now seemed dark and bleak. "Why is he being so stubborn and stupid?" I asked myself. Throughout the night, I wept and in weeping I found solace.

By 4:00 a.m., I had regained my composure. I returned to bed and immediately Earl wrapped his strong arms around me and kissed me. Quietly, the morning rays of the summer sun lit our window. He looked so handsome and peaceful. I knew it was the peace that only the just have the privilege of experiencing. Within a few minutes, we were making love. All was clear to me now. I had married an exceptionally virtuous man. Slowly, it dawned on me what a magnanimous person Earl had proven himself to be. Why had I been so blind to the truth? Perhaps, I told myself, it was the result of the strains that I was enduring as an immigrant.

As I lay there beside my beloved husband, I whispered, "Sorry," into his ear. "It's alright," he murmured as he embraced me, and was soon lost in a deep sleep. I continued to lie awake. I felt virtue emanating from his being. "Oh, God!" I prayed. "Why was I so selfish? Why couldn't I see his point?" I vowed then that someday I would tell the world of the unselfishness of this man. Lesser human beings would not have had the tenacity or temerity to do what he had done for the sake of peace in his extended family.

With the approach of morning, I made us each a cup of tea. As he sipped it, he said how happy it made him that I was able to discern the rightness of what he had done. "Don't worry," he comforted me. "Everything will be fine. Let's trust in God." And then he uttered words which would surface many a time when I was faced with misgivings: "When in darkness, never doubt the God of light." That morning, I placed one hand in the Lord's grip and the other in Earl's. Thirty-seven years of our life in Canada later, God has blessed us with a bountiful harvest of peace and well-being – a foretaste of His Everlasting Providence.

Earl's sister Verna, who had immigrated to Canada and then decided to return to India, now resolved to make Canada her permanent home. On her return, she worked on securing her Canadian registration as a nurse. She had not practiced for over thirty-five years, but was now obliged to make a living for herself. A woman of steely pride and grit, she would carve a life of total independence. She was almost sixty years old when she went back to school and worked part-time in a seniors' residence. This woman, who all through her married life had had a fleet of servants and a chauffeur-driven car at her behest, now had to depend on public transport and walk through snow-covered footpaths late at night.

But with dignity and grace she pursued her objective of financial independence. She became nurse-in-charge at the seniors' residence where she had been working. She was now free to pursue her other interests – bonsai gardening and ballroom dancing.

OUR NEW HOME

On August 15, 1986, the movers arrived promptly on our driveway at 7:00 a.m. Our new home, in the leafy suburb of Woodbridge, was located in a predominantly first-generation Italian neighbourhood. Nonos and Nonas spent their retirement looking after the grandchildren while their parents were at work. Sending children to daycare was an unheard-of concept among this group of immigrants. We felt at home in this family-oriented community.

Our new home was large – three thousand five hundred square feet – and the children were excited, especially Sam and Dan, who now found use for their "walkie-talkies." It was a memorable day. On the Roman Catholic calendar, it was the feast of the Assumption of Our Lady into Heaven. As one of the tenets of its faith, the Roman Catholic Church holds that the Virgin Mary was assumed into Heaven body and soul. Mary, as the mother of Christ, was thus preserved from the punishment meted out by God to Adam and Eve: *"Dust thou art and unto dust thou shall return."*

‡ Our home in Woodbridge (1995)

Within a few days, Earl, the children and I visited a reputable furniture store. Apart from the children's bedrooms, already furnished with decent second-hand furniture, we purchased items for the rest of our home. We also bought wooden icons from the store of the Sisters of St. Paul, including a three-foot-high statue of the Virgin and Child carved out of the trunk of a pine. It was a spectacular piece of art and we decided to mount it at the foot of the pine staircase because the Virgin was to be the centre of our home. Each morning, Earl and I started our day with a prayer at her feet. Two other icons featured the Last Supper and the Holy Family. These were mounted on the walls of the formal dining room and family room.

We now had the home we wanted and two good cars. We thanked God for his blessings and decided to celebrate. We gathered together our pastor and the associate pastor along with Earl's siblings. Our home was blessed and we placed it under the protection of the Holy Family of Nazareth, a model to all families.

We still had an unfinished basement, a scarcity of landscaping and a rustic porch, which I longed to convert into a sunroom. But these projects would have to wait – it was more important to us that the children continue with their piano lessons, swimming, figure skating and hockey. We wanted them to be exposed as much as possible to the Canadian way of life. They attended the local Catholic school, where the students, mostly of Italian heritage, seemed a better fit for our children. Very soon, they made friends, and as we witnessed their growing confidence and happiness, Earl and I were truly grateful that we had made the move.

OTIS

Over the years, our youngest son Dan kept asking us to get a dog. He did his research. The only breed he wanted was a French Bulldog – the price well beyond what we could afford. "No problem," Dan exclaimed. "I'll work for it." With this in mind, Dan worked long hours at his father's machine shop until he had saved up $1,500 – a sizeable amount almost equivalent to half his monthly salary! He then drove about 200 miles to the west of Toronto to the breeder's farm and brought home Otis, the most adorable little creature, who perfectly fit Anjali's description: "He's so ugly, he's cute."

We adored Otis and in our adoration, we spoiled him. He had the women of the home wound around his little paw. He had no time for the men, except for Dan, whom he respected and feared. Otis, though only fourteen inches off the ground and weighing about twenty-five pounds, concluded the neighborhood belonged to him. He seemed to have been trained in the martial arts – neither squirrel nor chipmunk could invade our property. Our commando Otis was on patrol.

Alas, these daredevil tactics finally took his life. Chasing a squirrel across the road, he was struck and killed by a passing vehicle. For months, we mourned his loss, while being grateful for the eight years he brought so much joy to our home.

‡ Otis on Sam's Wedding Day (2006)

CAREER PATHS

It was now time to work on our respective careers. I continued to teach on contract. Each semester, I found myself with a load of new courses. While a university professor typically taught nine to twelve hours a week, I was now saddled with twenty-four hours. With the demands of raising a family of six, funds were scarce and I was still not receiving benefits.

Earl continued to look into the possibility of starting a new business. Best-equipped to work in the manufacturing sector, he was determined to find something close to home, so as not to waste time commuting. This time around, he was interested in a sole proprietorship, unwilling to partner with anyone else. His experiences in India had taught him that it was best to be independent.

Within a few months, Earl found a machine shop that fabricated parts for the automotive industry. He felt a strong need to get down on his knees as he had done in the past, get his hands dirty, sweat a little and show that he was willing to trudge forward in pursuit of a viable business. Against all odds, he survived. His success demonstrated that he understood his innate potential and the possibilities implicit in it.

In search of capital for the business venture, we turned to a bank and offered the equity in our home as collateral. In the summer of 1987, Earl was fifty-five years old. At an age when most Canadians are looking forward to retirement, he found himself starting from scratch. All that he had worked for in his business life had slipped away. His magnanimity would continue to be the hallmark of his entire life. Never compromising his principles, he would press on. His faith in the providence of God continued unshaken. The new business sector was predominantly controlled by Eastern Europeans, who had migrated to Canada in the post-war years. They supported each other and were highly skilled tradesmen. He was competing against this tenacious group. Very soon, word spread regarding his workmanship: his reputation as a highly skilled engineer from India circulated to the nearby manufacturing units, and there were prompt requests to partner. But Earl fiercely guarded his independence.

✣ Coil Cars (1987)

✣ Gearbox (1988)

✣ Recoiler Mandrel (1989)

Orders now poured in, making it necessary for Earl's company to expand. He rented an adjoining unit and bought a new milling machine, again with a bank loan, which he cleared in less than a year. This early taste of success was encouraging, yet humbling. By mid-1990, the winds of recession would spread far and wide. Orders began to fall off, bankruptcies swallowed several of Earl's clients, and with the bankruptcies came defaulters. We had never experienced a recession because India, a socialist economy, was not subject to market forces. Earl's company, named Dadson Custom Machining, was one of the few in the industrial park in which it was housed to survive this painful period.

With the recession came another life lesson. At the time, our children were too young to take up part-time work as the legal age to become employed was fifteen, so the responsibility to keep the home fires burning fell on my shoulders. I worked as I had never worked before. No course was too insignificant to me; instead, I thought of each one as an additional source of income. We were now well into our middle age and realized that there were fewer sands in the hourglass than we were willing to believe.

Every dollar coming into our family coffer was precious. I refused to evaluate the cost and benefit analysis of each course. I was fully aware that several of the courses I was teaching were economically unprofitable. When I factored in the distance I covered, the gas consumption and the preparation time, I knew the remuneration bordered on minimum wage. Nevertheless, we decided that we would have to live within our means. Earl and I raised our children in keeping with the principle that "you are judged by who you are, not by what you own." I refused to be discouraged. However, I could often feel the bitterness of my working conditions lurking below the surface.

Why was a tenure-track position so elusive? A school is judged by its faculty. If even one member of the faculty were to have a doctoral degree from a third world country, the conventional thinking went, the prestige of the institution would come into question. As I continued to ponder my career predicament, and how I could change it for the better, I had a chance encounter on the university campus with the chair of one of the departments. He happened to hail from my part of the world, but had acquired his doctorate in the United States. He enquired how life was treating me.

"Not good," was my response. I elaborated about my inability to secure a tenure-track position. He looked me in the eye. "It's okay to work on contract. You are an excellent teacher and you will always be in demand." He went on to explain how staff on tenure track were saddled with a host of administrative duties. "You don't want that. Go ahead, teach as much as you can, and you can make a decent living." "What about the benefits?" I persisted. "Well, the university is looking into the matter. Very soon, you guys will be covered." As we said our goodbyes, I was somewhat encouraged.

FAMILY PRAYERS

Earl and I had grown up in strictly traditional Roman Catholic families. We believed firmly in the inherent role of family prayer. "A family that prays together, stays together" was often repeated to us by our grandparents and parents. Every evening in our respective homes, *Loveapple Cote* and *Millowen*, every member in the household would assemble before the family altar and recite the night prayers. The focus was the Rosary, a Roman Catholic devotion that highlighted the chief events in the life of Jesus Christ.

Earl and I decided that this tradition would continue in our own family. However, instead of the family rosary, which our children felt was too long, we read a scriptural passage, and then a member of the family would comment on it. Every day, this practice was carefully guarded. The children did not resent the time because it was also a time for family sharing of the day's events. It could become argumentative and sometimes Earl and I had to intervene to restore peace. But today our children look back on this family time as the key to the strong bond that exists among them.

Another practice we developed was family attendance at Sunday Mass. No matter how busy the children were, despite their studies and their part-time jobs, attendance at Mass was non-negotiable. It is heartwarming that even today, after all of our children have married and all four have left home, that they and their families still attend Sunday, Christmas and Easter services as often as possible.

A MEASURE OF STABILITY

One night as I returned home from one of my late classes, I found a note on my table left by my son Daniel. "Please contact Professor Edith, of Ryerson." I knew Ryerson to be a wonderful university located in the heart of Toronto. I soon accepted a contract position and spent years teaching there while continuing my contracts at York

University. Together my pay cheques amounted to a substantial sum. I was also receiving benefits. As I looked around me at professionally trained immigrants driving taxi cabs or stacking shelves at the grocery stores, I looked heavenwards and thanked God that I was able to use my talents in the profession I so loved – university teaching.

The recession pressed on. The years 1990 and 1991 were the most difficult in our married life. In this arduous financial time, we had to gallop, not just walk, along the new paths destiny had carved for us. In the process all our traditional religious anchors were being shaken by uncertain tides. By 1993, the economy was beginning to recover, but it would take more time for Earl's business to regain its market share. He was now sixty years old and still struggling. There were times when I was tempted to dispute his earlier decisions about the business in India. But with Earl reminding me that there was more to life than pure monetary gain, I found a way to heal my angry thoughts.

Earl survived the recession because of the steadfastness of his endurance, the judicious nature of his decision-making, coupled with his strong work ethic. Despite the vicissitudes of the recession, he remained focused on his long-term goals rather than on short-term panaceas.

Anjali, our eldest, was now poised to enter university. Earl informed her with sadness that she would have to fend for herself. My heart ached for him as I followed the conversation. Here was a man who, all through his adult years in India, had lived a life of luxury. A principled man, he had refused to capitalize on family discord, preferring instead to be the force of reconciliation, at the cost of tremendous monetary losses to himself.

However, he had raised an equally magnanimous, gifted, intelligent and capable daughter in Anjali. Looking at her father's unhappy demeanour, she replied, "Don't worry, Daddy. All that I need is board, lodging and transportation. I will manage the rest." Earl helped her purchase a used car and paid for its insurance, gas and maintenance. Anjali held down several part-time jobs during her school year and worked full-time in the summers. She would emerge from her undergraduate studies having supported herself financially and a grade point average that would get her into medical school. She is now a cardiologist with a full patient roster in one of Toronto's hospitals. Her younger sister and her brothers would also finance their own education, each emerging as a powerhouse of success and achievement. I was proud of my children's success and often recalled my conversation with Gita on the day she came home from school all those years prior. I had told her that she would face triumph and tribulation but would learn how to deal with the latter. I was pleased to see that each of my children had learned to triumph over any difficulty they may have faced to reach wholeheartedly for their dreams and grab on with all their might. Gita and Samuel are both successful engineers, while Daniel is a cardiologist.

The mid-nineties saw the Canadian economy rebound, and Earl's company took part in the upswing. During the next four years, we invested in home renovations and landscaping. Earl bought himself a luxury car. In 1997, we were able to splurge on our twenty-fifth wedding anniversary. But here, too, the generosity of our children was manifest. We were truly touched, and in keeping with their desires we cut no corners. The reception was beautifully and elegantly organised. With the help of our two daughters who have an eye for sophistication and detail, our anniversary was memorable.

‡ 25TH WEDDING ANNIVERSARY (1997)

‡ CUTTING THE CAKE (1997)

With the dawn of the twenty-first century, we recognized there would be inevitable ups and downs in the business cycle. But we were blessed as a family. In the first decade, two of our children were married to wonderful spouses. There is every reason for optimism.

TRUE ABANDON BEGETS DEEPER TRUST

The precocious stare of a twelve-year-old girl gazing at her heartthrob so long ago evolved into a wondrous love story. Providence brought Earl and me together after destiny had separated us for well over two decades. We have just completed forty-six years of married life together. We have been blessed with four beautiful children and eleven grandchildren

⁜ Anjali, Daniel, Gita, Lorin, Earl, Mercy, Stephanie, and Samuel (Christmas 2006)

My husband has provided me and our children with a template of all that is noble, good and decent. Over the years, I have learned from my husband's example that true spirituality is intertwined with every aspect of human endeavour. Earl's decision to walk away from the company in India he co-founded in the interests of our family's well-being, coupled with his refusal to capitalize on the prevailing discord in his extended family, is a testament to his strength of character. He remained anchored to the Christian principle of unshakeable faith in God's goodness, and this belief allowed him to remain grounded in his love for me and for our four children. "That is all I want," he said simply.

In our adopted land of Canada, Earl would set the course and, at the same time, steer our family ship towards a destination unknown to him. But faith allowed him to see beyond the immediate moment. "Our trust is deepened when we have no choice but trust," a priest-counselor in India once said to me. Together, Earl and I have been able to build a home for our children that has always been a fount

‡ Daniel, Anjali, Gita, and Sam (2006)

of hope, love and ultimately success. It was also a place of playful laughter, shared secrets and sometimes broken rules, only to be re-negotiated to a home of shared principles.

⸸ Anjali's wedding - family photo (2017)

⸸ Mercy and Earl visit Stella Maris College, Chennai, India (2019)

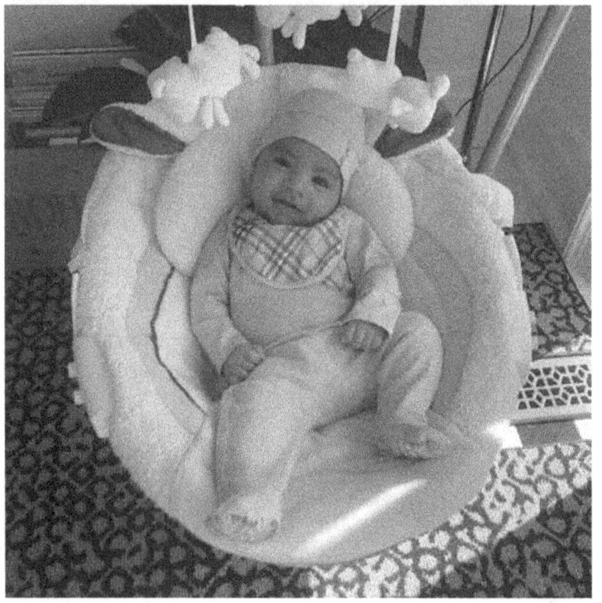

‡ Grandchildren (2021)

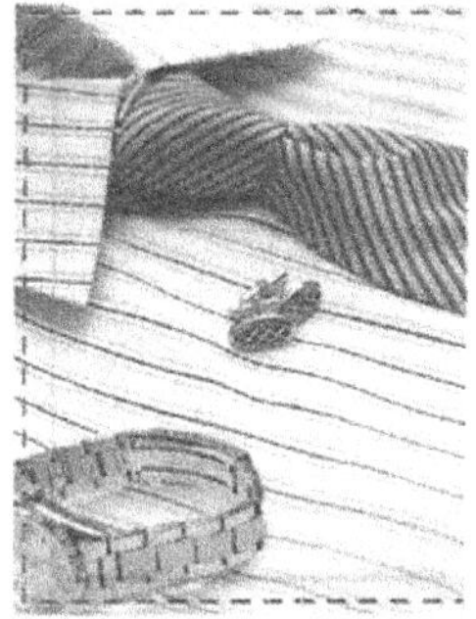

When you're special
through and through,
You deserve a wish
that's special, too.

✣ Card sent to Mercy by Mother General (Retd) Sr. Maura (2011)

Dublin – Clontarf.
7.5.'11

Dear Mercy,

My belated but none the less sincere apologies for my absence during your short stay in Ireland. It is indeed very kind of you to have left me a box of those lovely chocolates. I appreciate your great generosity + kind thoughtfulness. Through Angela, I have followed + admired your wonderful husband + family. I have seen the photos + read your book. Your life has confirmed the decision you made + which cost you + all of us much pain, was God's plan for you. Now we are all happy about it. How strange God's ways at times! But how important to follow His lead also! I saw Angela briefly yesterday. Through her I got an email address for you + wrote you a message which was returned. Then Sheila gave me your postal address + hence this effort to reach you through this scribble. Please excuse me. May you + those you love continue

to grow in the Love of God + help others to do so also. With every best wish, Maura Finn

Twelve

After five decades of unwavering commitment to his engineering and business career, Earl has sold his business and retired. His average day comprises work around our home, a one-hour power walk, shopping for groceries, prayer and the practice of daily Mass and Holy Communion. He also finds time to visit his immediate and extended family, and is always available to lend a listening ear and offer wise advice. This is the time of his life he always looked forward to: time with his God and family.

What better destiny can a man hope for? This is the reward for a man who seldom faltered, who always kept in focus the well being of others.

‡ Earl and Mercy with grandchildren Mary-Catherine and Owen (2010)

As a testament to their father's simple goodness and integrity, our children have joined the chorus. Here is their story – they write from their hearts.

ANJALI

I am a thirty-six-year-old woman and single. This distresses my mother greatly, and now even my father. It seems that at this age someone who is successful, reasonably attractive, with a decent personality should have found a husband. Many people have, at some point or another, asked me the question: "Why are you still single?" I don't like hearing this question, and even more so don't like answering it. Fortunately, most people offer their own answer: "You must be too picky." While I object by saying, "No I'm not; I'm just waiting for the right man," what I really think is: "Yes I am. I'm just waiting for the right relationship!"

You see, I was born into the most beautiful relationship between a husband and wife that I know of. My view may be biased, but it is what I know. Explaining to others what I've grown up with is difficult, as most people don't understand. Most people have not witnessed such a wonderful romance.

My parents are not perfect, but with simplicity and ease they have remained madly in love for forty-seven years. They genuinely enjoy each other's company, like spending time together alone, and do not need distractions like fine dinners, large groups of friends, or exotic vacations to keep things exciting. All they want is to be with one another. They have raised four children whom they love dearly and who dearly love them too. This is much rarer than it should be.

I've often thought about why their relationship is the beautiful thing it is. I cannot say it's because they work at it. What I see flows too easily and smoothly to be work. (That's not to say they don't have to be very patient with each other sometimes – but even that seems more natural than work.) I cannot say that it's because they've taken their vows and are steadfastly committed to them. They firmly believe in their vows, yet are with each other not because of the vows but because they want to be together. And I cannot say it's because they have a family and so are in it for the long haul. They have a loving family because they love each other so much.

What I think makes their relationship so beautiful is that my mother and father adore each other and willingly give one hundred percent of themselves to each other and to our family. This is no fifty/fifty relationship. There is no measuring stick of who gives what, and no attempt to retain one's identity. Instead, each has enabled the other to be just who they were meant to be and to flourish. I don't think that either has ever even conceived of pushing the other to grow in any particular direction. By loving each other unconditionally, they have grown together as two very independent personalities, with their very own character, who just naturally completely depend on one another.

When I wonder about how in heavens my father managed, at the age of forty, to entice a nun he hardly knew out of a convent, marry her and then have a true romance lasting into his late eighties, I think it must have been a miracle. Who could have foretold that this would be the happiness meant for him? Then I know that there could have been no other destiny for such a wholly and truly good man.

My father begins and ends with goodness. That's not to say that along the way he hasn't made mistakes. He has faced many imperfect circumstances and he is not perfect, but he is perfectly good. This has set the tone of his life and has been the barometer by which all his choices and decisions have ultimately been made. He has been blessed with real love and genuine happiness. Miracles do happen and no one deserves them more than my father.

So the real conundrum is not why I'm single, but rather how do I find the kind of relationship that I've grown up with? I'm not nearly as good as my father and not half as deserving of such a miracle. However, I am very lucky. Having been born into this family is nothing but blessings and luck. A father who is such a loving and exemplary person, and a mother who is so devoted and maternally generous, are true blessings.

I don't understand why I was bestowed with these – it's just my luck. Perhaps this luck is something I've inherited from my mother. Who would have thought that a nun in a convent, having taken her final vows, would have a man she hardly knew, but whom she dreamed of, propose to her and then have a true romance lasting into her eighties? That's just luck. And I'm hoping for the same lucky miracle.

I may not always make the right choices or the best decisions, but I know how to recognize a perfectly good man and a perfect relationship. I've lived with both for thirty-six years and will know it when I see it. How can I help but be picky when my parents each picked their perfect soul mate?

Update 2018: I am an almost forty-five-year-old woman and married with a baby. Last year my father finally was able to walk me down the aisle and my mother watched her prayers being answered. My perfectly good husband and I have a perfectly beautiful baby, who was born on my mother's birthday. My son will soon celebrate his first birthday with her. I have experienced my own miracle. I was able to recognize a perfectly good man and we have a relationship that is perfect for us. That's just the kind of thing that happens in this beautiful, prayerful family.

GITA

My earliest memory of Daddy is in the morning light of Bombay. He has just returned from his run. He is in the living room of our flat, on the floor wearing shorts and no shirt. He raises his legs into the air and performs a yoga head stand, holding it for several minutes with his eyes closed. I am awestruck. When he is finished, he stands up, his white teeth gleaming, his brown skin shining with sweat, his body limp with relaxed fatigue. He is the embodiment of physical strength, a paternal wonder. He turns to me and says, "...my dolly munchkin."

My earliest memory of Mummy is watching her by the window in that same flat. Wearing a long kaftan, she is arranging purple asters recently bought from the door-to-door flower woman. The vase being used is permanently screwed into the dining table by my father, a very practical man, to ensure that it doesn't fall and break. She is heavily pregnant and instructing one of the servants. Thick black hair surrounds her glowing face. There is something about her arms, breasts and tummy that make me feel comforted and loved – I feel happiest when I am in close proximity to her.

My childhood in India is a collection of images like these. Endless flashes of carefree running, laughing and plotting. Everything was a big deal. Learning to jump off a small corner building in the complex where we lived; experimenting with the latest death-defying shortcut across rooftops to the stores across the street; sneaking into a neighbour's yard to steal prize berries; hiding from the wicked witch who lived close by but kept away from everyone.

There was power in numbers, and we were four – a cluster with gravitational pull. All the kids in the building were our friends, and we ruled the property. There was never "nothing to do," or a sense of being bored. Every day was a chance for new adventures, and we lived fully.

I was a special child with exceptional musical and intellectual gifts. I don't recall ever doubting myself. I was always first and being first came easily to me. There was no subject I couldn't master. I loved to jabber, entertain, tell and write stories – and my Nana, who lived with us, was usually a prime victim. I was likely the most extroverted in my family, a schemer who possessed a remarkable ability to assess social dynamics.

I exhibited a talent for music early in life, and even tried composing when I was six or seven. But my real talent was singing. I had a deep, lyrical voice, a gift from my father. I won every singing competition I was entered in, save one, when I lost to a boy with a voice like a girl. I was stunned, but sure the judges had made a mistake and that I would redeem myself the following year. But it was not to be. We left for Canada a few months later, to start a new life.

Coming to Canada changed me. Moving to a new country holds such great possibilities for adult immigrants. But no one really thinks about the sheer excitement and fantasy children create around their soon-to-be new life. We were going to a land where everything was beautiful: homes, clothes, toys and people. Just as in Bombay, we would have a ton of foreign friends and life would be perfect.

I clearly remember my first day at school. Daddy had bought us fashionable clothes before we left India, and I painstakingly planned my outfit. I wore dark blue trousers and a light blue blouse with lace around the neck. The four of us went to school together. When I saw the Canadian school kids for the first time, I had an immediate sense of being apart from them. My instincts were dead on.

For a long time thereafter, I desperately struggled with exclusion and loneliness – a "Paki" whom no one could relate to. I was always a child whose pain manifested physically. I became sickly thin and drawn. I had frequent high fevers and vomiting, usually after class trips where I spent the day alone on the bus, at lunch, and trailing behind the group trying not to stick out as the one without a partner. No rejection since has ever come close to what I felt in that part of my life.

Things were hard at home also. Mummy was struggling to find a job and Daddy was always in India. But one thing remained. When things were really bad, Mummy would hold me in her arms, against her warm breast, and cry with me. I would feel safe again and somehow find the courage to face the next day. Things would get better, she promised. And they did. But I was damaged goods. The confident, fearless child was gone, replaced with a girl who felt less smart and not so very talented. I had stopped singing altogether.

But there was still power in numbers, and we held each other up. Our home was an island of safety and security where all the problems of the world could be discussed at length and solved together. Everyone got a chance to tell their story at night, after prayers, on the floor of Mummy and Daddy's room. We were a team – our own harshest critics and fiercest allies. Buffy was the ever-maternal sister, who loved to lecture and reprimand. She was the leader of our family, giving completely of herself to each and everyone, but what she said went. And if anyone tried to harm her family, she would unleash a wrath that would flatten him or her like a tidal wave.

Sam was quiet and easygoing; however, a few words and a glare from him was all it took to know exactly where he stood. Yet under his tough exterior was the soft gentleness and comforting affection of a lamb. Dan was a piece of work! His laser-like focus on achieving his latest goal exhausted everyone around him. We all had to pitch in to manage him, with Buffy usually getting the worst of it. He was either going to be massively successful or a criminal. Oh... and he made us laugh!

Mummy sat on the floor with us. She mediated and was the centre of all discussions. We teased and taunted her when she just didn't "get it," but she laughed at herself, and entertained our arrogance. Daddy sat on the chair in the room, the picture of dignity. He focused on teaching about God's love for each of us, and never gave simple or popular answers. He very often said, "...do you know how much your Daddy loves you?" There were no secrets here and nothing we couldn't discuss. In the glaring light of deep trust and love, we grew into men and women, strong, confident, and grateful for the gift of being born into this family.

The gravitational pull of our unity brought us endless friends and a home that was the centre of social activity in our community. Leaving to start my own home was a very difficult thing. The night before my wedding, I sat on the sofa in my parents' home and wept. Not because of the usual wedding jitters; I knew the life before me would be wonderful. I was consumed by a deep sadness for leaving behind my childhood and a joy for a life lived in that home. A life to be loved forever.

SAMUEL

As the third of four children and elder of two boys, my earliest memories take me back to my family's first years in Canada, some which included very trying times, but these very times were ones of deep faith and optimism for my parents.

During our very first days after emigrating from India to Canada, my father was in search of a temporary home. He rented a three-bedroom townhouse and moved our family of six there for two years, while he would travel back and forth between Canada and India to settle up his business matters.

To get ourselves started in our new community, our activities included searching the Classifieds for used or disposed of furniture, receiving hand-me-down clothes from anyone we were remotely related to, and my mother spending week after week running for her driver's test, only to learn that she would have to wait yet for another opportunity to obtain her license.

Life for each of us was nothing short of a challenge. As a young Indian immigrant boy, it would be an unusual day if I didn't hear a racial comment from a schoolmate. Like my siblings, "fitting in" and having friends was something I wanted, but felt impossible to come by. At times, it felt that being alone or secluded was better than being around classmates, because being around them could bring about an opportunity for being tormented once again.

I recall my mother jumping, as she would describe it, "from pillar to post" from York University to Humber College or to Seneca College, back and forth, sometimes all three campuses in the same day, always persevering, with the hopes of not only keeping the family ship afloat, but also perhaps landing a tenured position with one of the schools. For more than a decade, as an Indian woman in her mid-fifties, she would never rest.

It was the norm in our home that my father was at the factory six days a week. On countless occasions, his Mondays would start at 5:00 a.m. He would always make it a point to take Sundays off, as it was a day of rest and religious reflection. But the pressures of his business would drag him and keep him at work for much too long. Typical weeks during the mid-nineties, when most at his age would have been fully retired, frequently kept him at work more than 80 hours. Like my mother, he was determined to keep things running, at times taking on work he knew would be money-losing, but still better than losing out on future opportunities.

I recall countless challenges my parents have gone through in my life, too many to note in this passage. What I do know is that both my parents have been ever-persevering. A man and woman, each near the age of fifty, left India with their four young children all under the age of ten, to start a new life across the world in hopes of a better future. In spite of all their hardships, they have been forever optimistic and eternally faithful. I am ever so thankful to them for being such exemplary role models for these guiding principles, which will always be with me, no matter where life takes me.

DANIEL

Thinking back to my high school days, I recall our family going through some difficult times. It was the early 1990s and the economy was suffering a terrible recession. Dad's machine shop was struggling to stay afloat, while mom was driving "from pillar to post," as she used to say, earning a meagre salary teaching at various community colleges. She was driving a rundown Chevette and his Cavalier station wagon was also on its last legs.

My parents couldn't afford to buy us fancy clothes or the newest gadgets, but on one Sunday afternoon they decided that they were going to splurge on us. Roland Joffe's *City of Joy* was playing in the movie theatres. It was a story of a disillusioned American doctor who found salvation in the streets of Calcutta. Mom was teeming with excitement because it would be an afternoon where the family could escape back home to India, and forget about the hardships drowning us.

We all awoke that Sunday morning to have a bountiful breakfast of fried eggs, toast and bacon. We stuffed our faces and went to Mass. I remember eagerly waiting for the priest to finish his sermon signaling that the end was near. Finally, the Mass was over and we rushed back home to get ready for the movie. We all sat patiently in the family room, waiting for my dad, as usual. He walked into the room with a look of sorrow washing over him. We didn't even have forty dollars that day to watch the matinee. Instantly, we were back in Canada struggling to survive.

The next day, we all awoke for school – Gita sleeping in as usual until Mom would throw a fit. I run downstairs and see my mother in her night robe frantically making our breakfasts and sandwiches for lunch. She made me the usual – fried eggs and toast – and set my brown paper bag lunch on the counter with my name on it. She made the best sandwiches of tuna, egg salad or cold cuts. They were always delicious, except for that time when she combined the tuna, egg salad, and cold cuts with a bit of Spam and broccoli into one sandwich. I think she was trying to empty out the fridge – it was dreadful, and clearly I still haven't got over it.

School went on as usual that day, and the sadness of missing the *City of Joy* was now a distant memory. I walked home from school, kicked off my shoes, and was ready to spend the next hour watching *Gilligan's Island* followed by *Family Ties*. As soon as I turned on the TV, Mom walked in saying, "my son, your father wants you at the factory." A sinking feeling came over me.

This is the way I remember it. Suddenly, I'm filled with anger, rage and selfishness, and I start complaining relentlessly, insisting that I won't go to work. My mom pleads with me, her eyes filled with tears, and finally she hands over the telephone with my father on the line. He simply says, "my son, your father needs you." The argument is over. I sulk up to my room and put on my factory clothes. We get into the Chevette, and she drives me to the shop with worry strewn over her face as she whispers her prayers. I sit in silent misery. Finally, we arrive and I see my father standing in the doorway. He looks at me with his tired eyes, wipes his brow and kisses my forehead saying, "come, my son."

I go to the change room, put on my work boots and start

working on the boring mill. Even with all my resistance, I enjoyed the challenge of working at my dad's shop. We made custom-made parts and each job was unique. My father walks over to the machine, reviews the drawing with me, and leaves me to it. It's a relatively simple piece, but must be finished urgently and delivered tomorrow. I work diligently for the next few hours, and it's now nearing 7:00 p.m.

I start getting worried that I still have to go home and do my homework, so I start rushing through the work. Suddenly, I break a tap inside the work piece! I turn off the machine and stand there staring at the broken tool, realizing the impending doom that is about to ensue. After a few minutes, I work up the courage and walk over to my dad's office, open the door and say, "Daddy, I broke a tap."

He remains silent, but I can see that he's grinding his teeth and his lower lip is beginning to quiver. The silence is broken by a thunder of British profanity as he storms over to the machine. He looks at the broken tap and says, "my son, you'll finish off your father," and walks back to his office. After a few minutes, I follow and find him kneeling at his desk with his eyes closed, saying a prayer. I scurry back into the shop and wait for him patiently. A few minutes later, he returns, kisses me on the forehead and says, "don't worry, my son, we'll fix it."

The years passed and somehow all of our problems were eventually fixed. Our family was showered with countless blessings, making these early hardships a distant memory. Through it all, my parents always had an unshakable faith that somehow grew stronger even in the darkest times. With all they've given us throughout our lives – the lessons of hard work, determination and their unending love – it is their faith that will always stay with me.

MERCY ANSELM – IN CONCLUSION

Despite the abandonment of my religious vows of poverty, chastity and obedience, I learned early on in my married life that the sacrament of matrimony is also a call to sanctity. Our marital union testifies to our need for human love. Our bodies are innately designed to enter into communion with one another and, in the process, to beget new life.

"When you hold him in your arms, remember he is God's gift of love to you." These words of the Reverend Father Samuel Ryan still resonate with each new day I look into the eyes of Earl, my beloved husband.

‡ Earl and Mercy (Forever)

God is love and he who abides in love,
abides in God and God in him.

1 JN 4:16

Nobel Prizes have been awarded in Economics for "Matching Theory". Faith was the key to the perfect match of Mercy and Earl. All the other blessings followed. A heart-warming human story of the role of religion and faith in the trajectory of a family which included the trials associated with immigrating to a new country.

– Thomas Barbiero ,Ph.D

Professor of Economics, Ryerson University, Toronto, ON

A young nun on the verge of final vows encounters a man she met at a pivotal moment years before. In this powerful memoir, Anselm takes us from her sheltered childhood in colonial India to her settled retirement with her husband in Canada today. At each step she shows how, through God's merciful aid two lives can be woven together despite the most daunting of odds.

– Mark Lovewell

Former Editor, Literary Review of Canada

I enjoyed this story of deep faith and love that begins in youth in India. It is filled with the drive for true complementary love. Warm breezes, kindness, faithfulness and determination fill the pages as life winds through Anglo-India from the 1930's to the '80's before the family's immigration to Canada. Experience family life in the minority Christian and Catholic communities of India; then witness how that strength and character can transfer its spirit to Canada and bring goodness to all. An interesting, well written book.

– Cora Dusk

Retired University Administrator

Vows - A Roman Catholic Nun's Journey of Love was a riveting read. Traversing history continents and cultures, the book is a paean to the ineffable unity of faith in God and faith on earth. Mercy Anselm undertakes a remarkable journey from her life in the convent upholding her religious vows as a nun to extending those vows to love and Marry Earl and weaving a family with him. Throughout, Mercy exudes a seamless grace and faith in God. Anselm experiences God's eternal presence in the richness of human love. In writing this book, Mercy draws the reader into the mystery of the overlapping circles of God's love and human bonds, and blessings over all. Mercy's children's reflections stand as testaments to these truths.

– Ivy George
Professor of Sociology
Gordon College, Massachusetts, USA

A beautiful love story that begins in India and grows in depth and strength as they emigrate to Canada. Only through their life time of strong determination and commitment to each other, to their values and to their spirituality, that is their constant anchor, do they receive the Blessings of a Life well lived.

– Suzann Sutherland
Retired Social Worke

A compelling page-turner with a timeless love story: a testament to the presence of God in our lives.

– Cathy Sbrolla
Retired Educator

Vows - A Roman Catholic Nun's Journey of Love is a beautiful recounting of how God "always gets his man ... or woman" as the case may be. Laced with insight into the Lord's indomitable will, but also meted out with His sense of humor, if we choose to see it. Love does conquer all, whether we love as religious, or as lay ministers, both holy vocations, which ever our Loving Lord chooses for us. An awe-inspiring read and a source of hope and trust in the Lord's working in our lives.

– Barbara Nytko, MSc.

Former CEO, Copernicus Lodge and

Former Director, St. Joseph's Health Centre Board of Directors

A truly moving and heart-warming story of two people totally committed to doing God's will through all the twists and turns of life. Mercy is a gifted writer - it was hard to put the book down

– Grace Milligan

Office Manager

Milton Keynes UK
Ingram Content Group UK Ltd.
UKHW051205260324
440132UK00013B/1585

9 781773 707266